INTRODUCING GENETICALLY MODIFIED ORGANISMS – GMO's

The History, Research and the TRUTH You're Not Being Told

Food Conspiracy - Volume 1 (Third Edition)

by Mark Plummer (B.Sc./PGCE)

www.viddapublishing.com

**This edition published by
VIDDA Publishing Ltd in 2018. www.viddapublishing.com
Copyright © VIDDA Publishing Ltd 2018**

Cover design by John Hodges.

__For Helen__

Without Her Love And Support

This Writing Would Not Have Happened

"How can the public, governments and regulatory agencies really evaluate the efficiency of technologies like GMO's when commercial interests continue to distort the narrative and hide behind slick public relation messages that are intended to mislead and misinform, while at the same time they co-opt politicians, trade policies, scientists and research?"

Colin Todhunter - Independent Writer/Analyst - from the book 'Green Revolution to GMO's, Living in the Shadow of Global Agri-business'

Table of Content

Abbreviations Used In This Book

PP – Precautionary Principle

HGT – Horizontal Gene Transfer

GMO – Genetically Modified Organism

GM – Genetically Modified

GE – Genetic Engineering

GOI – Gene of Interest

MYA – millions of years ago (ya)

SE – Substantial equivalence

The abbreviations **GMO, GM, GE** and the word **transgenic** are used interchangeably.

The words **Trait** and **Characteristic** are also interchangeable.

The acronym **DNA** and the phrase **genetic code** are also identical.

Similarly, the words **hereditary** and **inherited** all refer to the **genetic information** held on molecules of **DNA.**

Introduction: What to Expect and How To Read This Book

This Book will attempt to provide an objective overview of what genetic engineering (GE) in agriculture and animal husbandry really means. I hope to present a sense of where the science and technology behind GMO's and the drivers behind them comes from and how they are applied. Genetics, GE or GM is a highly complex issue. It connects with science, ethics, politics, international law, human rights, faith and religion as well as social and environmental justice. There is no middle ground with the issue. You either support Genetically Modified Organisms (GMO's) in agriculture, or you don't. To paraphrase Yoda from Star Wars there is no "maybe" or "let's see what happens" there is "support" or there is "not support". The same is true of nuclear power, perpetual war, fracking and climate change, these are red line issues. An individual either accepts a necessity of GMO's in agriculture or they do not. A person supports the rights of indigenous peoples or they don't. You get the point. Either way, it is essential to get some grasp of the principle techniques involved. I have tried to strike a balance between imparting critical knowledge against putting people off by "overdoing" the science, history and politics. It is not necessary to have a detailed understanding of a given technique or be able to argue their respective virtues; this is the domain of those who work as geneticists. You do need to know the nuts and bolts of how GE is conducted. The early chapters contain various YouTube links of the type I have used in the class room. The intent is not to patronise or insult anyone but to advance the necessary biological knowledge. Getting to grips with Genetically Modified (GM) foods requires a basic understanding of how GE is carried out. This book represents only an imperceptible scratch on a very large surface area. There is plenty more research occurring globally in life science and biotechnology laboratories which you, I and everyone else alive today, or in the future, will likely never hear about. This book is an **overview**. It is impossible for **all** the issues raised here to be discussed in forensic detail. So, the text uses real examples as well as hyperlinks and references aplenty by way of compromise and empowerment. As with all non-fiction writing the onus is on the reader to follow up and explore the subject as they see fit. The reader should view the book as a springboard with which to explore subject further. GMO's are **not** an abstract concept or the domain of a science fiction movie. They are real, already here, an irreversible policy and if they really do become the norm, i dread to think as to the future consequences. This writing is at times likely to make you feel uncomfortable, ill at ease or even flat out frightened. This is not my intention, but if you do begin to experience **that** feeling in the pit of your belly, you're eliciting the correct and humane response. The sensible reaction to a policy which is an exceptionally bad idea on **all** counts, a stance I have had since the mid 1990's. With good reason, in 2018, I see absolutely no reason to change my mind. I hope this book will provide a foundation make your **own** mind up on the issue. I will, however, **clearly** state my own position. GMO's in food, agriculture, intensive farming and animal husbandry are not a solution to our current food security problems. GMO's are part of the problem and will only succeed in making matters infinitely worse. Irrespective of other factors, the objectives of the agencies involved in GMO's are highly questionable to say the least. The **only** beneficiaries of the entire enterprise are the transnational corporations and the biotechnology and life science (both defined in chapter three) firms connected to them. This construct is often called "big-agriculture" and is introduced in chapter six. If we are to ever live in a genuinely sustainable world, "big-agriculture" along with other institutions pre-fixed by the word "big" need to be consigned to the dustbin of human history. GMO's have been in our food for about 20 years. They are a product of "big-agriculture" and so ought to be equally untenable. Furthermore, when we know real long-term and sustainable alternatives exist, the stated need for them invites even more questions. GM foods are everything about maximising profits for the biotechnology firms which pursue them along with the agribusiness firms which created and business interests which continue to fund them. In other words, GM foods are last about sustainability, diversity, productivity, or health and nutrition. They are first about profits and astronomical profits too, as well as the control and influence such financial clout brings. I hope the reader adopts a principled position of opposition, but the choice is yours to make and **not** mine to impose.

This book begins with an overview of the history involved with the subject in hand. The middle sections concern how the industry operates and what its objectives are for global agriculture in the future. The last chapter presents GMO's in a frame which stretches back into geologic time. The most relevant period begins at about 12,000 ya. If the reader wishes to they can start their reading with chapter eight, in fact, you may begin your reading at any point. There are plenty of sign posts such as, (see chapter five) or "this point is revisited in....." It is not necessary to read this book sequentially, feel free to navigate as you see fit through the text. Chapter 1 to 4 explain the "how" and "what" of FMO's in agriculture. The "why" is the subject of furious and often vitriolic debate but really comes down (as these things often do) to power, control and money. Chapter 5 will introduce the flavr-savr tomato. The last three chapters will hopefully provide some perspective on the wider economic, scientific and philosophical issues which are intrinsic to a full understanding of GMO's in agriculture. The GM food industry has circumvented the edicts good objective, evidence based science. The industry and its supporters always attempt to rubbish and discredit any science, the scientists or anyone else who challenge its assertions. At its core, this book concludes, aside from generating profits for the industry GMO's serve **no** purpose at all. Furthermore, GMO's represent a technology which has been foisted upon **all** of us based on a pack of **lies**. The same is true of fracking, nuclear power and pretty much any other issue the reader can think of. The middle chapters present a case whereby the whole issue is driven by transnational corporations. These institutions have everything to gain from the uptake of GMO's and plenty to lose should their endeavour fail. The lies themselves are promulgated by the proponents of the technology and an establishment which is in bed with the industry. If I'm being strong here, I ask you to think if the people in charge **and** the politicians who serve them ever tell the truth about anything, exactly, they don't, so why listen to them around GMO's? Transgenic organisms exist for the benefit of the agribusiness oligarch, (see chapter six). They exist as an attempt to gain even more control of the global food supply. GM crops will only exacerbate the very real systemic problems of the current food distribution system. We do not, as of 2018, have the unregulated and unfettered uptake of GMO's in agriculture, but things are looking dicey. If it ever happens they **will** contribute to the global environmental meltdown which is well and truly on the cards, which could result in a total **global** environmental and economic collapse. I hope when you have finished reading, arriving at a **different** conclusion has you swimming in the long river in Egypt, fed by its equally famous tributary without a paddle.

Chapter 1: What is Genetic Engineering?

This Book properly starts with the humble pea plant. More precisely it is about the scientist and clergyman by default who dedicated every spare moment in the pursuit of studying their characteristics. In 1856 an Austrian monk, physicist and botanist Gregor Mendel (1822 - 1884) began collating and analysing the transfer of hereditary or genetic information. Without question, Gregor Mendel set the foundation for what has become a crucially important branch of modern science. He is rightly regarded as the "father" of this quintessentially modern discipline, hence the phrase "Mendelian Genetics". In 1863 after seven years of painstaking and meticulous science, he established the guiding principles of the science we call genetics. Four years previously "On the Origin of Species" by Charles Darwin had been published. Clearly, Darwin, Mendel and Alfred Russel Wallace[1] (who came to the same conclusions as and co-authored with Darwin) knew some mechanism for the transfer of characteristics from parent to offspring must be in evidence. Gregor Mendel spent seven years of his life dissecting and organising the inherited and transferred characteristics of a sample of about 13,000 pea plants out of a population of 28,000. He completed his work with no electricity, computers or mathematical algorithms to speed up the repetition. Plus Mendel was still required to fulfil his monastic duties. His work established the four cornerstones of genetics:

- Plants contain a material which determines their form and characteristics.

- Beneficial and undesirable characteristics are passed on from one generation to the next.

- A particular characteristic could be dominant or recessive.

- A particular trait could skip one or more generations.

In the 21st century, these principles would be explained in terms of genes, chromosomes, and DNA. In the 19th century, such terminology simply did not exist. Mendel published[2] his work in 1866, in a primary science report or paper called *"Experiments on Plant Hybridization"*. Until the turn of the 20th century, it was greeted with a deafening silence. Yet, knowing these four principles existed is rightly regarded as one catalyst which drove modern farming. Farmers could now make definite predictions as to the most likely traits expressed in a given cross breeding scenario. They were also able to continuously develop evermore precise cross and selective breeding techniques. From a knowledge perspective, science and the developing discipline of genetics now had a vehicle for explaining and understanding hereditary and inheritance. A simple mechanism for predicting the expression of a gene is explained by virtue of the *"three to one ratio"* and it goes something like this...

Sticking with peas, suppose a farmer is looking to produce a pea plants which are medium in height as compared to the smaller and larger pea plants he or she currently has. Suppose the farmer has plenty of large pea plants and the small pea plants are few and far between. Our pea farmer needs to embark on some pretty nifty selective breeding. He or she also needs to have some grasp of terms such as dominant and recessive. Where two different forms of the same gene occupy corresponding positions on the chromosome. 3 The structure which contains the DNA **and** genes of the organism in question. The position of the genes and their relative strength to each other control the expression of the same characteristic. The words expression or traits refer to the characteristics an organism is going to have. Geneticists use words like phenotype and genotype to explain this further. In our example, we are looking at cross-breeding Tall (T) pea plants with small (t) pea plants to produce a medium-sized (Tt) plant. An uppercase letter indicates a dominant gene a lower case letter a recessive gene. A dominant gene is stronger than a recessive gene and stronger genes are more likely to be expressed. The following statement is not strictly speaking true but it is sufficient for our purposes. Dominant and recessive genes are the same but are of a different form; hence we use the term allele 4 (allele-morphic gene) to describe them. Each pea plant in question contains both alleles. The trick is to get the right genes expressed in as many plants as possible with each growing season. In this case we are looking for as many pea plants as possible to produce the (Tt) expression. So how does it work? The best way to explain it is to list the outcomes of each meeting of pollen and ova in the plant:

- If a T pollen fertilises a t ova the result is a Tt plant.

- If a T pollen fertilises a T ova the result is a TT plant.

- If a t pollen fertilises a t ova the result is a tt plant.

- If a t pollen crosses a T ova the result is a tT plant.

There is no difference between the tT and Tt varieties. For simplicity, we are only referring to the inheritance of one desired trait, the size of the plant. In the real world, all traits are inherited but are not always expressed. With the above scenario, the tt pea plants have both recessive alleles for height and so will likely be the smallest. With the TT plant, where two dominant genes for height are expressed, likely resulting in a taller plant. The grower will be able to select those plants which express the best of a whole range of traits. From there they incorporate the desired traits into producing the medium or (Tt) sized plant. The grower now has 3 out of every four plants expressing the dominant form of the "tall gene", hence the 3:1 ratio. Common sense dictates even if the (tt) or (TT) plants do not express the characteristics we are looking for; the seed should still be kept for the future. If agriculture was organised as it should be some viable crops which do **not** demonstrate the desired trait would be allowed to grow and reproduce too. Such sensible and sane notions thread throughout permaculture and organic systems but are seen as problematic by intensive farming in general and by biotechnology in particular. After the Tt plants are established, the next stage is to keep selecting them hence the term selective breeding. A further way of showing the possible outcomes is to construct a punnet square:

Diagram One - Punnet Square for Predicting a Genetic Trait

	T	t
T	TT	Tt
t	tT	tt

From here the grower will be able to identify any plants which express the desired trait or those which may carry it. In this example, the trait is carried by plants which carry either allele or the dominant alleles for height. Over many seasons further selective breeding for the given characteristic (and others) occurs until the desired trait is expressed in sufficient numbers. Therefore, **selective breeding** is the deliberate breeding of organisms from the same species. The aim is to produce offspring with the desired range of characteristics and then ensure they are passed on to their progeny. **Cross breeding** or **hybridisation** is a slightly different proposition; it normally involves crossing pure-bred plants or animals with individuals of a different variety or species. As with selective breeding the intent is to produce offspring which express beneficial traits, but often from both lineages. Both techniques have been recognised for millennia as an effective mechanism by which to maintain diversity. In many cross breeding scenarios the progeny is sterile. So it is impossible to create a new species of plant or animal. In biology a pre-requisite of the term species is the ability of the organism to mate and reproduce fertile offspring, a progeny which can also reproduce. For a new species to evolve the offspring must be able to reproduce. To do so it will need food, a habitat and a secure environment in which to grow. Even when organisms of a different species are cross-bred they must be from the same genus for the hybridisation to be biologically viable. Genus describes organisms in the same species in possession of a similar form. Taxonomists are biologists who classify organisms according to their features and character. From these characteristics they develop the scientific name for a species. Two Latin words are used to demonstrate the uniqueness of a given species. Genus is the first and the second tells us the species. In other words we have a generic name and a specific name. For example:

- Modern Human beings are classified as Homo sapiens.

- The now extinct Handy human, one form of the genus Homo is Homo habilis.

- One species of albatross is the Laysan albatross Phoebastria immutabilis

- Another species is the black-footed albatross Phoebastria nigripes

- One species of frog is the Gopher Frog Rana capito

- Another species of frog is the Bull Frog Rana catesbeiana

In selective breeding, the pollen grains of a plant which contains the desired characteristic are transferred to the flowers of a different variety, a plant within the same species. When this happens, the beneficial characteristic will only appear in a few plants of the next generation. In turn, these plants are selected for the next season. Eventually, the desired characteristic allows a new variety of crop plant to be grown. Selective and cross-breeding has been occurring over the last ten millennia and has produced the different varieties we see around us today. Without doubt cross-breeding and the search for evermore beneficial traits is absolutely essential to our current and future food security. We need to look no further than wheat to have the point exemplified.

All conventional crops, (cultivars) are dependent on fertilisers for their growth and wheat is no different. The years after

WW2 marked the advent of the green revolution.[5] For wheat, a clear and present problem was more than apparent. In fact, for this staple food crop, the worst of all possible worlds was occurring. Wheat varieties from the US were high yielding, but due to the mass of the grain in its bushels, the plants would collapse before the grain was ready for harvest. To make matters worse this was occurring despite the application of fertilisers. Yields remained low, despite the extra costs in chemical fertilisers with no increase in productivity_[6]. Clearly a new cultivar was needed, one which was shorter but more productive than the current variety. In other words, a similar objective to our hypothetical pea farmers, outlined above. The wheat had to remain standing long enough for the grain to ripen. Coordinated by individuals such as Norman Borlaug [7], (1914 – 2009) green revolution auspices, breeders and scientists sought to overcome such obstacles. For wheat the search involved the pursuit of a gene for wheat dwarfness. By 1952 some 20,000 different varieties had been cross-bred but success was still proving elusive. This all changed in 1953 with the work of a team headed by an American wheat breeder called Orville Vogel [8], (1908-1991). History is not without a sense of irony. The answer for the wheat conundrum came from Japan. By 1953 Vogel's team had some success in cross breeding dwarf Japanese winter wheat with tall American varieties of winter wheat. Perhaps if the spoilt children who run things learned how to behave properly, the answer could have been found earlier. It could also have happened without the horror, carnage, and destruction of the avoidable Secondglobal conflict. When Norman Borlaug heard of this success he obtained the best of Orville Vogel's plants. They were cross-bred with the best of the Mexican varieties he had at his disposal. Within one season a new wheat variety was well on the way to becoming established. A shorter, stockier but still high yielding plant variety was developing. All kinds of crosses and re-crosses were carried out, in much the same way as Gregor Mendel had carried out in the 19th century. By 1961 a new wheat variety called Norin 10 was introduced in Mexico and wheat yields doubled from an average of roughly 4,500 kg to 9,000kg per hectare. Two of the varieties produced in the 1950's and early 1960's were used to catalyse the Green Revolution in India and Pakistan. There is much more to the story and one must remove the rose-tinted glasses, especially when questions concerning water use, pesticides, land ownership and biodiversity are presented. Nevertheless, the above story represents the textbook example of effective cross-breeding of different varieties of the same species.

It must be clearly stressed; **no** GM whatsoever occurred in the development of the Norin 10 wheat. In fact, no GE of any kind occurred at any point in the development of any crop during the green revolution. Why? Well, prior to the discovery of the **structure** of DNA (outlined in chapter two) GM was impossible. Think about it, how can you engineer something when you don't know what the structure to be engineered is or how it is organised? In other words I wish to inculcate in the strongest possible terms, GE is as similar to cross and selective breeding as the Earth is to Pluto. A GMO is **any** plant or animal which has had DNA from another organism (irrespective of the species involved) inserted into its genome (DNA). If we are considering genes from within a genus or species, the combination of genes is supremely unlikely. When genes from different species are used, as they often are in the creation of GMO's, the combination is, by definition, flat out impossible when compared to cross or selective breeding. Looking at the species examples above, one would expect a hypothetical mating and subsequent progeny from two species of hominid, such as between Homo sapiens and Homo habilis or Homo neanderthalensis. We would not expect a mating between a salamander and a toad to produce any progeny. Without going into the nuances of evolutionary theory and the biology of reproduction a genetic barrier is in place. As stated previously chromosomes are the structures in the cell nucleus which carry DNA. The male and female gametes (sex cells) of two different species have different numbers of chromosomes. Also different species have different numbers of chromosomes in the nucleus. If the number of chromosomes in the gametes is different, the exchange of genetic material which occurs during fertilisation does not happen. At the moment of fertilisation, a structure called a zygote [9] forms. It is produced when the gametes of male and female organisms of the same species or genus fuse together. All the inherited information an organism will ever possess is coded for at this instant. It is the sequence of complementary base pairs, the nucleotides, which determines the expression of characteristics. The zygote is a single cell made up of half each of male and female chromosomes. If the number of chromosomes does not match then fertilisation is impossible and a zygote is not formed. Plant and animal GE circumvents this position. It directly transfers hereditary information (DNA) between organisms of different species and often from different biological kingdoms (see chapter two). Sections of DNA from one or more species are spliced with great precision into the DNA of another. The aim, Irrespective of the species involved, is to create a novel (new) organism, which expresses pre-determined traits. The supporters of GMO's laud the various techniques they employ under a heading called precision agriculture.[10]

There are exceptions to the genetic rules which allow a zygote to form. Perhaps the most familiar example is the offspring of a male donkey, (a jack), and a female horse, (a mare). A mating between these two animals produces a mule. The jack has 62 chromosomes in the nucleus and the mare has 64. The mule ends up in the middle with 62 chromosomes in the nucleus, but it cannot reproduce. Yet, there are documented cases of mules and other hybrid animals being able to reproduce, but the instances are exceptionally rare. If the rules can be broken, extra weight must surely be given to the real possibility of unforeseen genetic consequences concerning the release of GMO's into the natural world. Aside from the creation of hybrid and sterile animals the number of chromosomes in each of the gametes has to match. If a proponent of genetically modified (GM) foods tells you any different then they are lying or are plain wrong. Plus, cross breeding, selective breeding and hybridisation of animals has been occurring since the end of the last ice age (see chapter eight). Human beings have been manipulating the expression of genes (but not the genes themselves) of both crop plants and livestock animals for approximately 12 millennia. In this frame the plant or animals with desirable characteristics have been chosen for selective or cross breeding based on their biological characacteristics. Yet, this is not GM or precision agriculture. So, at this early stage we can debunk one of the many systemic lies told by those who wish to benefit from GMO's in farming. First, GM has only been in existence since the 1970's. Second, GMO's have only existed on a large scale since the mid-1990's. So we can without equivocation state "the GE of organisms is a novel technology and as such we have **NOT** been carrying out GE, manipulating genes or creating new organisms for thousands of years". Plus, by any

22

reasonable and objective benchmark, the technology and its application is untested. We are talking of real human made organisms which have only been in existence since the early 1980's. Hence, GM cannot in anyway be equivalent to the kind of cross and / or selective breeding techniques outlined above. In selective cross-breeding the genes from the DNA of each plant combine randomly, as they are supposed to in nature; the genes also come from the same species or genus. The objective of GM (in fitting with the definition of biotechnology shown in chapter two) is to express desireable genetic traits. The term beneficial is almost always framed in terms of what suits big agri-business (see chapter six). This almost always results in detrimental impact for the rest of us and the natural world. For example, plants can be engineered to produce their own insect poisons (see chapter four), this is supposed to mean fewer insecticides are needed as the crop grows. **One** big problem connected with these plants is the evolution of resistance to the pesticide itself. A secondly, the over application of herbicides and pesticides in general has facilitated the growth of plants which are resistant to the poisons being sprayed on them. These plants are called super-weeds (chapters two and seven). These two problems and plenty more on top did **not** exist prior to the introduction of the transgenic cotton. The collective agency behind GMO's is telling the world hybridisation and cross breeding is inferior to GE. With reference to hybridisation or cross breeding, the supporters use vacuous phrases such as "manipulation" instead of engineering. They are trying to equate the two positions. I have seen it with my own two eyes, from the supposedly objective pillars of science itself and from "A" level (grade 13) course books on the subject. The more the phrase gene manipulation turns up in biology text books, the more successfully will the waters be muddied. It often takes many years for the beneficial traits in selective or cross-breeding to be expressed. According to supporters this is not good enough, not efficient and does not produce the necessary yields. None of those assertions stand up to real scrutiny. It is also a nonsensical and oxymoronic position, which misses the point entirely; cross breeding is about maximising diversity and yield within a species. In the interests of diversity a balance has to be struck between predictable and unpredictable results. Under intensive, profit-driven agriculture selective breeding is about finding one or two beneficial traits and discarding the plants which do not. Thus new varieties which may be beneficial in the future are lost. Such behaviour is directly comparable to the activities of the big pharmaceutical companies who are known to discard research which does not deliver a precise set of objectives. Under such a construct the only important factor is the bottom line; otherwise, results which do not apply today would be kept until they had some utility, no matter the time scale involved. On average it takes 15 years to develop a new crop variety. The level of expertise and dedication required is impossible to quantify, but if you imagine the amount of work Gregor Mendel took on, you'll get the idea. Only under capitalism and one of its bedfellows, GM foods, is the expertise, knowledge and potential future benefit tied up in longer time scales seen as a problem. The GM food and all connected enterprises, view farming and agriculture as a planet-wide cash cow, all it wants is to control it and extract profit from it. For this reason alone GMO's represent the complete antithesis of sustainable agriculture. One festering sore which cuts right to the quick of the whole issue is the control of seeds. While the GM food industry likes to present a benign face [11] to the wider world it has actually prosecuted farmers for daring to save seeds [12] for the next growing season. There you go straight from the horse's mouth, not only does the GM industry prosecute for breach of contract but it is also proud of its position. Now, I'm no expert on growing crops but I'll bet farmers would prefer to keep seed for the next year. I know we will be when we start our food self-sufficiency drive. Keeping seeds is a practice intrinsic to the future of sustainable agriculture. It has been occurring as a matter of common sense since the first seeds were sown during the Neolithic revolution (See chapter eight). On a related point, you may have heard the phrase terminator technology. [13] The practice of developing plants which produce seeds which are infertile, thus making seed saving pointless. The industry claims it has never [14] deliberately created sterile GMO's for profit. This simply is not true, and there is a tonne of literature on the subject, which backs this up. Chapter seven also details the existence of terminator genes in corn, salmon and mosquitos. This particular thread of opposition to GM crops taps into notions of trust, of who you believe and why. On all counts, the objectives and organisations involved in GMO's are **not** trustworthy and genetic contamination of non-GM crops is an ever present danger.

Mutation, Inheritance and Disorder

To really understand terms such as GE, GMO, transgenic and GMO we have to be clear on our understanding of the term mutation [15] and the impact it has on DNA and living organisms. At its absolute simplest a genetic mutation is any change to the genome (DNA) of an organism. The order or sequence of nucleotides [16], bases or base pairs (see below and chapter two) in a molecule of DNA is changed. A mutation can occur during fertilisation, mitosis (asexual) or meiosis (sexual) reproduction in the gametes. A key locus of mutation is the point at which DNA replicates itself during the cell cycle (the life cycle of a cell). Overall, mutations are generally dangerous and/or life-threatening for the organism concerned. There are various biological processes which stop the expression of such characteristics, but "mistakes" do occur. Gene therapy is a positive application of GE and seeks to rectify the "errors" which cause the expression of "defective" genes. Genetic diseases in human beings are caused by mutations and almost always have some "negative" impact on the person. The terms in quotations are accepted biological phrases and should imply **only** there is a fault with the gene and not the individual. To suggest otherwise will position you on the slipway which leads to the abyss of eugenics and so should be avoided at all costs, assuming you value your humanity!

One example of a common genetic disease is Cystic Fibrosis (CF). The condition affects individuals whose DNA produces a defective transport protein [17]. As the name suggests these are molecules [18] which carry substances through the various systems of the body allowing essential processes to occur. A second form transports electrically charged particles [19] (ions) within the cell and / or to its immediate environment. In CF the DNA mutation produces a defective from of a transport protein called Cystic Fibrosis Transmembrane Regulator (CFTR). The CFTR protein normally pumps negatively charged chloride [20] ions out of our cells. If a person has CF the pump does not exist and the reason is down to the absence of **one** gene. The gene which codes for the CFTR protein is found on chromosome 719 and is composed of about 250,000 complementary base pairs (see below). The base pairs are molecules which make up DNA. A person who has cystic fibrosis is missing only three base pairs on the chromosome. The defective CFTR protein does **not** allow for the transport of chloride ions **out** of living cells. The result is a build-up of thick mucus in the lungs and membranes in the body. The person needs varying degrees of percussion therapy [21] to shift the build-up, sufferers are often prone to secondary infections. The mucus is a fertile breeding ground for various forms of bacteria. The defective gene can be passed on from one generation to the next. Hence CF is an example of a genetic mutation which causes an inherited disease [22]. It is these sorts of diseases which gene therapy seeks to eradicate. You would have to have something wrong with you to oppose the notion and basic objectives of those involved. The technology and science being eviscerated throughout this book is an entirely different proposition.

We now have knowledge (albeit incomplete) of the structure of DNA and how it codes for protein manufacture. Genetic engineers can selectively change the organisation of any segment of DNA in a given plant or animal genome. [23] A genome is loosely defined as the entirety of the DNA which makes up the chromosomes of a given species. Geneticists are also able to move genes between different organisms. They are able to alter the genome of any organisms they wish, with whatever genes they wish. For GMO's in agriculture, GE represents a deliberate and precise change to the DNA of any living organism. The genome of a particular organism is altered by a direct change to the sequence of nucleotides or bases which compose its DNA. In selective cross breeding, the grower chooses which plants (or animals) to cross and the results are at least in theory varied, there is always the element of chance. And if there is an element of chance there is always the possibility of beneficial mutations and improved prospects for biodiversity. The pro-GM lobby wants you to believe this reality is somehow undesirable, it isn't. GE of plants and animals permits a specific and rapid transfer of genetic material between different genomes. The industry and its supporters always proclaim GMO's increase yields, reduce pesticide use and promote biodiversity as well as sustainability. As stated above these claims just do not stand up, especially when compared to organic and permaculture systems. A further problem is the ever present reality of genetic migration by means of horizontal gene transfer (HGT) and cross pollination. Gene transfer and cross pollination of engineered DNA, do **not** exist with non-GM forms of agriculture and animal husbandry, surely enough on its own to oppose GMO's in agriculture.

In the realm of GM foods, the engineering tends to be applied to plants. Worryingly, the technology to engineer animal livestock DNA absolutely exists. Worse, genetic material from plants and animals is spliced together as a matter of routine. For instance, an ornamental animal called the glo-fish [24] has the dubious honour of being one of the first transgenic animals. Originally used in medical research and for pollution monitoring, the first glo-fish were made from the genes of three separate organisms. The fish itself is a GM form of a species called Zebra Danios, a freshwater tropical fish. The glow comes from the genes of two different organisms. First, a gene which codes for a red fluorescent protein from an anemone [25] species called Discoma sp. Second a green fluorescent protein from the genome of a jellyfish called Aequorea Victoria. [26] This is a relatively benign example as compared to growing GM crops or farming GM animals (see chapter six) on a commercial basis. In the EU and as of late

2017 no GE animals are used directly in agriculture and no applications for GM animals in agriculture have been made. However, most animals reared across the EU are eating GM animal feed. Speaking of feed eating animals we can now connect with a breed of cattle called the Belgian blue [27]. In the 19th century shorthorn cattle were transported from Britain to Belgium. The reasons for doing so were to improve milk and meat yields. However, by the mid 1920's the focus moved to solely improving meat yield. By the 1950's after decades of selective breeding the Belgian blue breed was born. Belgian blue calves start to produce the extra muscle when they are about a month old. The "double muscling" process carries on as the animal grows and leads to an increase in bulk of up to 80%. The extra bulk is produced because the gene which codes for the manufacture of a protein called myostatin [28] is switched off. Myostatin functions by regulating muscle growth, without the protein muscle growth is pretty much uninhibited. In other words a genetic mutation as a result of selective breeding is allowed to be inherited and passed on. The cows themselves are very docile, grow and reproduce very quickly and produce high quantities of milk to boot, perfect for the meat and dairy industries. Speaking personally, after putting this section together, this nugget of information is a straw breaking the camel's back moment, intensively produced red meat and I are done. This chain of events is **not** GE, it **is** selective breeding and profit driven animal husbandry. The next example does concern a GM animal. The gene which switches **off** the myostatin has been integrated into the genome of rainbow trout. The result is a transgenic fish which is up to 15% larger [29] than its non-transgenic counterpart. Apparently, this will benefit us all as consumers because such developments will provide a ready source of cheap farmed fish. The GE trout produce more flesh per unit of feed, which is supposed to benefit the aquaculture industry. We are supposed to ignore two fundamental issues which cut straight to the heart of opposition to GM crops and animals. First, it fails to address why there has been such a catastrophic decline in freshwater fish species all over the world. It seems the industry is only interested in preserving GE animals it can profit from. Secondly, it absolutely ignores the very real potential for the fish to escape into what is left of the wild and pass on the engineered gene to other animals. It doesn't stop with fish! In keeping with the operations of this thoroughly repugnant industry, the protagonists, have for several years, been carrying out genetic experiments on our nearest evolutionary neighbours, the primates.

Selective or crossbreeding this most definitely is not. We have not been manipulating genes in this manner for thousands of years either. It is more like decades at most. Mutation is an entirely natural phenomenon, with clear evolutionary benefits. GM, along with intensive and monocultured methods, is not a "natural" way to produce food or rear animals. I am not in possession of a GMO crystal ball and neither is the industry. The long term consequences of GMO's living in the natural world are absolutely unpredictable. Any genetic consequences are also going to be irreversible. We alos likely have no way of dealing with them either, certainly as of April 2018, surely enough for any rational person to say "no and **full** stop". Plus, I have yet to see any of the supposed benefits stand up to any detailed scrutiny. The unpredictability of the movement of genetic information (DNA) and its ability to mutate in the environment are both factors the proponents of GM food would rather not discuss. In fact, they are more than likely to laugh at you, pour scorn on your whole premise for opposition and wash it all down with a good dose of superior vitriol and vilification. In nature a mutation is generally a random event. Plus, during the making of DNA (outlined in chapter two) mechanisms exist to correct mistakes. Mutation can occur spontaneously and on a long enough time line the Belgian blue mutation could have happened without the interference of human beings. Some mutations are beneficial, for instance in human beings our ability to see the world based on three primary colours (red blue and green) or trichromatic vision, would not be possible without mutated genes. Other examples include the incidence of HIV resistance. Although very rare some people will not contract the virus. Their target cells have different receptors as compared to those who do become infected. Genetic mutation can be induced and **any** substance or form of energy which does this is called a mutagen. The obvious examples include excessive exposure to radiation and UV rays. Carcinogenesis caused by pollution and known carcinogens are also mutations as is exposure to poisons, pesticides and pollution across the board. The Western diet and the processed food which makes it up represent a hot bed of exposure to carcinogens (substances which cause cancer) and mutagenic substances. Again there are plenty of examples of beneficial induced mutation in medicine. However, using mutation to cure disease or repair damaged DNA is **not** the same as deliberately altering the genetic make-up of plant or animal cells to make GMO's. In the 1940's plant breeders realised they could control the frequency of mutations by applying mutagens to crop plants of their choosing. The mutagen will change the genome (i.e. its sequence of nucleotides) of the plant, but no GE takes place. Mutagenesis is wholly unregulated and in broad terms can be criticised on the same grounds as GE and the modern agribusiness

31

construct which spawned it. According to the UN Food and Agriculture Organisation (FAO), approximately 2,700 plant foods derived from mutagenic techniques have been developed and released into the environment. Mutagenesis was used extensively in the 1970's, but has largely been, but not completely superseded by GM. However, the "did you know that?" question remains. I don't mind admitting I didn't until 3.50pm on the 20th of August 2015. And as I update two plus years later I am equally as annoyed!

With a few exceptions, [31] DNA is identical and present in the nucleus of every cell of every living organism on Earth. Genetic engineers are routinely able to remove one or more genes (the GOI) from any organism and place into a specific point (i.e. chromosome) of another organism. This form of GM is known as recombinant DNA technology [32] (rDNA), the genes are cut or copied and then pasted from one set of chromosomes to another. The first product of rDNA technology was the synthetic insulin developed in 1978. [33] In 1988 the first enzyme produced from rDNA techniques was chymosin [34]. Previously, chymosin which is essential for cheese production was sourced from the stomach lining of slaughtered cows. In the GE of plants (not necessarily by rDNA), the genome of the plant is changed directly. Once the desirable trait is identified it can be inserted into the genome of another organism. Once the gene is spliced the new engineered organism is transgenic, GM, GE or a GMO, from here it takes about a decade for the crop to become viable. Developing such a plant is an expensive business and the agencies involved are very keen to see a return on their investment. It is far too simplistic to answer the question "what is all this GM food malarkey all about then?" with the short and succinct reply "money". Yet the simple truth is, it is and you will be provided with a massive corpus of exemplified knowledge to support this position.

The fundamental point of this chapter, indeed a key point of the writing, is GE, by human beings, did **not** exist in any form on the planet prior to 1973. The first transgenic crop did not exist until a decade later and the crops themselves have only been cultivated since the mid 1990's. Creating GMO's involves the direct transfer of genes from one organism into the genome of another, ensuring a particular trait is expressed in the transgenic organism. Whether transgenic or not it takes years to establish the viability of any crop, likely longer for animals. For all intents and purposes, GM foods cannot be considered tried and tested as compared to any foodstuff which existed prior to 1983. The reason is simple, there was no such organism as a transgenic plant or animal on this planet before 35 then. The supporters of GM foods would rather not acknowledge this fact. We have **not** been manipulating genes via recombinant DNA or other techniques since we started growing food for ourselves.

Before the 1970's human beings had **never** inserted the genes of one organism across the species barrier (mentioned in chapter four) into the DNA of another. Chapter seven will impart this happens in nature but over timescales measured in hundreds or thousands of years, or longer. It is also very common in the community of microbes which call planet Earth home. Yet, this does not give carte blanche to biotechnology, life science or its backers to do the same as and when they see fit, with no consultation regard or transparency, in genetic combinations of their choosing. For now, we are leaving issues of ethics and animal welfare aside. The bottom line is crystal clear; GM of food stuffs and all other agricultural practices are entirely different propositions and need to be treated as such. The industry just does not see things in those terms. One reason why there is so much global resistance to GM foods and the agency which produces them. We have no idea as to the long term consequences of adopting GMO's wholesale. In the future, there could be horrific consequences or there could be none at all, we simply do not know. Most of us have seen Jurassic Park and I think Jeff Goldblum's [36] character is absolutely spot on especially when he says words to the effect of *"we scientists spend plenty of time thinking about the fact that we can do something, not enough of us seem to stop and ask if we should"*

Chapter 2: Genes, DNA biotechnology and other words...

Biology is the scientific study of life. Its bedfellow ecology studies how different organisms interact with each other and the habitats which support them. Intertwined throughout the complexity of life around us is the molecule we know as Deoxyribonucleic Acid (DNA [1]). Every organism on the planet uses the same DNA to construct itself. DNA codes for the same proteins which allow essential biological processes to occur as they should. For example, aerobic respiration [2] which occurs inside the mitochondria [3] of human cells also occurs inside the cells of other mammals. A multicellular organism is technically any organism which is made up of two or more cells. Really we mean complex organisms such as crop plants, insects, fish, dogs, whales and of course human beings. Generally speaking, the more related multicellular organisms are to each other, the closer are their anatomies. For instance, the arthropods [4] are arguably the most successful organisms on the planet. They are known to make up a minimum of one million individual species. Other estimates [5] put the number somewhere between five and ten million species. Either way, most of these species are insects, meaning the phylum [6] (family) is on the brink of catastrophic decline, [7] if not absolute collapse. For instance, what is left of the tropical rainforests is one crucial habitat for the arthropods. They are also crucial for the survival of all other life on this Earth too. These habitats could well be completely removed from the surface of the Earth by about 2050. However, given the rate of deforestation (as but one example) in Indonesia, the Pacific Islands and the forthcoming Congo carve up; this date may well have to be revised closer toward today. By today, I mean the day you read the previous sentence. The rainforest could, of course, be completely gone when you read it. If that happens, there probably is no way you will be reading it, as we likely won't be here. Despite such rapacious destruction, the arthropods are still distributed all over the biosphere; their range literally encompasses the deepest hydrothermal vents to the peaks of the highest mountains. The remainder of the sea bed is absolutely set to be turned into wasteland too, if the deep sea mining corporations get their way. One of the largest arthropods is the Japanese Spider Crab [8] and the smallest are unicellular insects. One extinct species of arthropod is the trilobite. Their primary ecological niche was lost during the Late Ordovician [9] Mass Extinction (LOME) event of 440mya. The arthropods have been around for literally hundreds of millions of years. Clearly this reflects their evolutionary success and biodiversity. However, the basic characteristics of all arthropods are identical. They are all invertebrates with a body broken down into a series of segments, which may have a unique and distinctive pattern. They all have an exoskeleton composed of chitin [10] (a tough strong polymer material), proteins and in some cases calcium carbonate. The variety within the arthropod phyla is in part driven by the DNA, present within the nucleus of every cell which contains it. The diversity is also driven by the time they have been on the Earth and the number of different habits their adaptability. Many of the target organisms for the insecticides manufactured by businesses connected to (or part of) "big agriculture" (see chapter six) are arthropods. They have proved resilient and absolutely adaptive despite the application of tens of millions of tonnes of different classes of insecticide. The use of pesticides provided the impetus for the great Rachel Carson to write her seminal book "The Silent Spring". A book which really ought to be compulsory reading for every person on the planet. The use of chemicals to conduct unrestricted biological and chemical warfare on the biosphere is but one strand of the arguments against GM crops. The negative impacts of insecticides and other poisons on the environment and human health are clear and present. The arguments against synthetic pesticides form one of the many powerful and growing voices in support of alternatives to GMO's in particular and intensive agriculture in general.

Ok, so by now you are asking "This is all well and good, but what does this have to do with GMO's?" Well, a key driver of the agricultural success we as a species have enjoyed for the last 10-12,000 years is our manipulation of bacteria and microorganisms. Over this time we have also sought to remove pest organisms, whether they are plant or animal, and / or the microbes they carry from our food supply. If the arthropods are the most successful animals then by the same criteria the bacteria are the most numerous and self-sustaining form of life on the planet. There are many tens of thousands of individual microbial species [11] on the Earth, likely there are equivalent numbers awaiting discovery. Or there would be if our once thriving world was not systematically being turned into desert. In their entirety bacteria are part of the Eubacteria kingdom of organisms. In the classification of life, living organisms are classified into five kingdoms. [12] Human beings belong to the animal kingdom and trees belong in the plant kingdom. Microbes [13] are found in the Monera, Fungi and Protista kingdoms. In very broad strokes the term microbe includes:

- Bacteria

- Algae

- The Protozoa [14] (single celled organisms with a nucleus)

- The Archaea [15] (single celled organisms without a nucleus)

- Viruses

Without microbes, life would not have evolved on the Earth, at least as we understand it. The microbes are highly adaptable and can reproduce at phenomenal rates. These two attributes mean they can survive in the most inhospitable and most benign environments on the planet. If this evolutionary strength can be harnessed then the adaptability and reproductive rate of a given microbe can be harnessed for the benefit of our own species. Microbes have shaped the course of evolution and as such are absolutely essential to our continued survival on the planet. It is no comfort when you have a "lergy", but aside from the relatively tiny number of pathogenic [16] species, bacteria are essential to our survival and have garnered huge benefits to humanity. The use of biotechnology dates back into antiquity. For example some 8000 ya the ancient Sumerians and Babylonians discovered the ability of yeast to convert sugar into alcohol and produce beer. Unsurprisingly, fermenting grapes to produce wine rapidly followed suit. Similarly, some 6000 ya the ancient Egyptians and Chinese employed yeast in bread making and yoghurt making. In the 21st century, the results and benefits of biotechnology [17] are everywhere. Humanity has been employing biotechnology for thousands of years. We use it in applications ranging from food production and preservation to medicine. It seems obvious to gain some appreciation of what the word really means. Put simply, biotechnology is concerned with using or modifying molecular and biological processes to achieve a given set of aims. For instance, the production of insulin, enzymes in washing powder and the isolation of penicillin represent clear positive uses of biotechnology. It is also concerned with the treating of inherited genetic disorders and the largely horrific biological consequences they cause. The word biotechnology was first coined in 1919 by a Hungarian engineer called Karl Ereky. [18] He used the word to mean "any product produced from raw materials with the aid of living organisms". Biotechnology represents a clear set of benefits to our way of life and the future potential is undeniably huge, particularly in medical research.

The picture is much less clear-cut in the area of food and nutrition. The overall frame of the GMO discourse ought to consider, as an absolute minimum, the arguments presented thus far in this text and reiterated in this article by LiveStrong.com (http://bit.ly/2kt8Jvc). [19] Unfortunately, and like so much in the modern world, the industry and its supporters are not even prepared to discuss it, unless it is solely in scientific terms. Speaking personally, one insulting and aggravating attitude from supporters of GM foods is the notion we opponents are:

- Intrinsically anti-science.

- Ill-informed and hysterical in our opposition.

- Ignorant of science itself

- Turning the clock backwards

- Standing in the way of progress

- Too emotional for a reasonable scientific debate

- Misunderstanding the technology.

Controversies such as GM foods definitely have a scientific and technical foundation. If there is one argument from GMO supporters which is really going to test my temperament and ability to communicate properly, it is the suggestion I'm anti-science. I am **not** anti-science because I see no value in or need for GM crops or animals. On the contrary, to those who support GMO's I charge you with being "anti-science", with being against the best interests of humanity and of behaving with an attitude which is most kindly described as arrogantly superior. I care **not** a jot if the science says GMO's are safe. I reject the whole construct and the "establishment" reasoning for supporting them. I **do** care when billions of meals containing GMO's are being eaten all over the world. This reality is **not** a cause for celebration or acceptance, as supporters of GMO's seem to imply, it is quite the opposite. I **do** care with every fibre of my being when most processed food eaten in the world contains GMO's or their derivatives (see chapter four). It makes me sick to my back teeth when this reality is presented as a reason for accepting GMO's. I **do** care and very much so, that I wasn't asked **and** when given a genuinely fair choice, I would choose **not** to eat them. Given the massive opposition which exists to GMO's there are millions of people, if not more all over the word who feel the same way. Those who drive GMO's truly think we should accept our lot and carry on regardless of the consequences for ourselves or the environment. For those people who support GMO's who state they are "exasperated" or "frustrated" with such opposition, tough. We are not going anywhere and in the name of humanity you will be opposed while there is still breath in our collective bodies. You do **not** speak for me or millions of others and you have **no** right to act on our behalf. Along with so many other arguments, the GMO controversy has been created by the existence of the issue in the first place. As with nuclear issues, war, climate change and environmental destruction in general, GMO's themselves cause the problem, **not** the opposition to them. As far as i can work out this is a reality which supporters are not psychologically equipped to acknowledge let alone deal with. Opponents such as yours truly oppose GMO's for good solid reasons based on:

- Objective science.

- History, politics, sociology and psychology.

- Total commitment to human rights, intertwined with social and environmental justice.

- A principled ability to put people, planet and community before profit.

- Opposition to conflict, war and dictatorship.

- An understanding of corporate and environmental crime.

- An understanding of patent law, bio-piracy, [20] i.e. theft, (see chapter six).

- Knowledge of the alternative practices, i.e. permaculture [21] and organic [22] systems.

- A connection to the Earth itself, along with the people and cultures upon it.

- An ability to act with basic humanity and display cognitive and holistic thought.

In my experience, supporters of GMO's do not demonstrate any of these qualities. If you are informed on such issues and have a global perspective on them, you can make evidence-based connections, you will be able to deposit the supporting GMO position into a bin marked "condescending and wrong", sub-headed by "science-centric arrogance". Related to biotechnology is the equally complex discipline of biochemistry, [23] the study of the chemistry of biological processes which occur within living organisms. These chemical reactions are the result of interactions between the four main classes of biological molecules:

- Nucleic Acids [24] (DNA and RNA).

- Carbohydrates.

- Proteins.

- Lipids (fats and oils).

A biochemist will research the function, reactivity and structure of specific classes of and / or individual biological molecules. Biochemistry is a fiendishly complex scientific discipline and its practitioners know more about it than I ever will. This does **not** mean the biochemists and geneticists employed in the pursuit of GMO's are correct in the development and application of the plants and animals they are engineering. A further locus of objection to GMO's concerns the need for the technology in the first place. Once you start looking into this issue and all those connected therein, it becomes obvious the so called advantages and benefits just do not stand up. If you put, people, planet, community and sustainability above all other concerns. Furthermore, the secrecy and doublespeak associated with GM foods is a concern we are supposed to ignore. We are supposed to accept without question what we are told by those who have most to gain from our acceptance. For example, one staple claim of the biotechnology industry is GM crops require fewer insecticides; such claims are now in almost total disrepute [25]. Using herbicides and GE of plants to produce their own pesticides has resulted in the target organisms evolving resistance to some of the most toxic substances in existence. A sensible policy would be to reconsider how we deal with pest organisms, a strategy the organic and permacultured farming has pursued. Big agriculture is seriously advocating a next generation [26] of pesticides to deal with a super-weed (resistant plant) problem of its own making. Super-weeds are revisited throughout this book. One of Monsanto's bright ideas is to spray 2-4 Dioxin, the substance the people of South East Asia know and love as agent-orange [27], which according to the manufacturers is "safe at current usage levels", well OK then; I'm done here and off to the pub! Before I go, perhaps I ought to make **one** glaringly obvious point even more so. If agent orange and other poisons are safe to use at recommended levels, then surely the levels used in Vietnam, Laos and Cambodia where anything but. A clear double standard and flat out lie presents itself here. Explaining, why, grudgingly during the Vietnam War the manufacturers [28] (Dow chemical and Monsanto) were obliged to stop supplying the US military with Agent Orange. What is not well understood is the dioxin in the herbicide was a contaminant. The US government Dow and Monsanto knew all along it was one of the most toxic substances hitherto made. Despite this knowledge the dioxin was not removed from the herbicide mix. Operation Ranch hand systematically defoliated and poisoned huge areas of Southern Vietnam. The cost to the Vietnamese environment, the people and to US and other service personnel has been as incalculable as it has been absolutely devastating. After all how can you put a financial price on life and the environment? Well, you can't. Only the warped twisted and inhumane mentality of the capitalist system presents such view points as legitimate. Sadly the same cessation of production did not apply to the manufacture, (courtesy of The Dow Chemical Company) and supply of napalm [29] and other grotesquely obscene weapons. Similarly the British army used Agent Orange during its 1950's dirty war in Malaya. To my mind we are talking of chemical warfare, environmental crime and crimes against humanity. So I say off to the International Criminal Court in The Hague [30] with the lot of them. By a stunning coincidence the agencies involved in making Agent Orange and other poisons are all instrumental in the drive for the world to embrace GMO's. If you are supporting GM crops you are letting such crimes slide, which is on your conscience, not mine.

GE became possible only after the structure of the DNA molecule was revealed. To be sure scientists had known since the time of Gregor Mendel "something must be going on" they just didn't know what or how. After the discovery, the new discipline of molecular biology [31] came into being. This relatively new branch of science is concerned with the structure and function of the molecules of life. By the 1970's molecular biologists were able to isolate, identify, clone and otherwise manipulate (i.e. engineer) individual genes. Once altered these engineered genes could then be inserted (recombined) into the genes of other organisms. A catalytic

44

moment in the history of biotechnology occurred on 11th July 1977. A biotech company called Genetech synthesized somatostatin. A hormone produced mainly by the digestive and nervous systems. Somatostatin functions by suppressing the secretion of specific hormones including growth hormone and insulin. Genetech itself is credited as being the first biotechnology company and was founded by a venture capitalist called Herb Boyer (Born 10/07/36). The first insulin from GE was manufactured in 1982 after approval from the US FDA. Similarly in 1981 Genetech produced the first human growth hormone from modified E.coli. In 1983, the laboratories of Washington University in the state of Missouri became home to the first GE plant. The GMO in question was a tobacco [32] plant engineered to be anti-biotic resistant. By 1985 the US patent office ruled GM crops and traits the express can be patented. In 1985 the very first GM crops to undergo field trials were planted in the US and France. The crop was a variety of tobacco which was engineered to be resistant to glyphosate, [33] which is mentioned in chapter three. The technique employed uses the workhorse of plant based GE, a bacterium called Agrobacterium tumefaciens, also outlined in chapter three. This development has set the foundation for all plant based GE and the rest as the saying goes is history. Except it isn't I prefer to say consequence instead of history. The first field trials were in 1985 and in 1994 the first commercial GM crop the flavr-savr tomato was developed (see chapter 5). These nuggets of information provide us with more examples of how we have **not** been conducting GM for millennia. The GM food industry is quite happy for you to believe we have, after all, if it has been going on for so long, it can't be bad can it? They want you to believe GMO's represent an extension of the selective and cross-breeding outlined in chapter one. They also want us to see the scientific and technical aspects as being for the greater good, well it isn't. Please permit me to reiterate without sounding too boorish, human beings have not been conducting GE or precision agriculture for millennia. Aside from any other points, science only established the structure of DNA in 1953. This absolutely crucial point requires a very brief foray into the history of the discovery of the molecule itself.

Discovering the Structure of DNA

Gregor Mendel absolutely established the existence of some mechanism for the inheritance of biological information. Yet, knowing something is there does not mean you understand what it does. As the 1950's began biologists, knew DNA existed, but had yet to ascertain how the DNA molecule was organised. Clearly, essential for understanding how inherited information is transferred. I mean to say, you wouldn't start building a scaffold if you didn't know how the standards (vertical poles), the ledgers (horizontal poles) or the transoms (the points which hold it all together) fit together would you? Similarly, how can you engineer a molecule if you don't know how it is constructed or how its components fit together? Exactly, you can't. No one is saying our knowledge of genetics was non-existent before the structure of DNA was established. The opposite is true; science picked up on Mendelian genetics in the early 1900's. From there it is safe to say it has never looked back, but the actual structure of DNA remained something of an enigma until 1953. In other words science was able to make predictions concerning likely genetic outcomes, but did not know how the standards, ledgers or transoms of

DNA fit together. In 1950 DNA was generally accepted to be the molecular vehicle which carried genetic information, i.e. genes. It just had not been established "beyond all reasonable doubt", the scientific phrase for proof! A Swiss chemist by the name of Friedrich Miescher first identified DNA in 1869. In 1919 a Russian chemist Phoebus Levene [34] suggested a polynucleotide structure for the DNA molecule. A poly nucleotide is a molecule made of many nucleotides [35] chemically bonded together. In 1946 science established the ability DNA has to transfer between organisms in a process called horizontal gene transfer (HGT [36]). The exact mechanisms by which it occurs are not fully understood **and** science certainly new DNA was not a passive molecule. Amongst other abilities DNA can transfer [37] between micro-organisms irrespective of the species or environmental circumstances. This is a further reality which the GM industry doesn't, (well didn't until very recently) want anyone to acknowledge, let alone discuss. This notion of HGT and its relationship to GMO's, science, politics and communication is revisited in chapter seven. The duplicity of the industry and the scientists, who drive it, represents another strand of opposition to GMO's.

In 1952, at Cambridge University James Watson (an American biologist) and Frances Crick (A British biophysicist) began investigating the structure of nucleic acids. They were looking to uncover the structure of DNA and then how hereditary works. Watson and Crick did **not** discover DNA, they discovered its structure and they have the credit for it too, whether it is deserved or not, is still being debated in the 21st century. The X-Ray diffraction [38] work of Rosalind Franklin (a British physical chemist) and Maurice Wilkins (A New Zealand born physicist) is often overlooked. Their work in the same area contributed greatly to the final discovery. Which is why Franklin and Wilkins were also awarded the Nobel Prize for the structural discovery. Both Watson and Crick began to study the images produced by Wilkins and Franklin. How they obtained the images is a somewhat murky business, but we won't go there. Well, not in this book at any rate! By this time scientists thought nucleic acids were likely to be the substances which made up the DNA molecule; the objective here was to establish their arrangement. The images and data produced by Franklin and Wilkins were used by the men at Cambridge to create a viable 3D structure of DNA. After some considerable time re-arranging prospective DNA models Watson and Crick came upon the double helix [39] shape we recognise today.[40] A structure which enables DNA to replicate and transfer genetic information from one generation to the next. Irrespective of who deserves the laurels, the **structural** discovery revolutionised biology. It allowed for the inception of a new science called molecular biology, which studies the workings of living organisms at a molecular and cellular level. In terms of medical research and the prediction of gene expression molecular biology has garnered huge benefits. As the secrets of the genetic basis of hereditary began to be revealed, it became clear different organisms could be related to each other according to their genetic make-up (their genome). The discovery of DNA allowed the central dogma [41] of molecular biology to be constructed.[42] The dogma states, DNA dictates the sequence of ribonucleic acid [43](RNA), for our purposes a single strand of DNA. In turn the RNA determines the sequence of individual amino acids [44] which make up proteins.[45] The dogma also eliminates any possibility of a reverse flow of genetic information. As of 2018 the dogma [46] may not be as clear cut as was previously thought. In one sentence research at the frontiers of science is documenting cases where genes do flow in the reverse direction. Which surely is another reason to say "hang on a minute" when it comes to GMO's

What is DNA?

The base uracil is **not** mentioned in this section. Now we can begin to explain the meaning of keywords and phrases. DNA [47] contains the genetic information which is passed on to the next generation of cells and therefore living organisms. DNA is an example of a nucleic acid (found in the nucleus of living cells). As one of the molecules of life, it is composed of a precise arrangement of atoms of carbon, hydrogen, phosphorous and nitrogen. They never contain sulphur which is one way to distinguished them from proteins. DNA is made up of four nitrogen bases, called adenine (A), cytosine (C), guanosine (G) and thymine (T). Attached to each base are sugar and phosphate molecules. Each nucleotide is the building block (monomer) which chemically bonds to other nucleotides, forming a polymer chain of nucleotides. DNA is composed of two polymer strands of nucleotides (RNA) which are chemically bonded to each other. Attached to each nucleotide (any one of the four bases) is a sugar and phosphate group, which alternate along the chain of nucleotides. The sugar is a substance called deoxyribose [48], which contains a ring of five carbon atoms and one oxygen atom. The phosphate group [49] is made up of one phosphorous atom chemically bonded to another four oxygen atoms. Each strand of the helix [50] is held together by very strong covalent bonds [51] (chemical bonding between non-metals) between the phosphate groups and the sugar. Each of the bases (A, C, G, and T) is attached to the sugar molecules which project inwards toward each other. It is helpful to see the structure of DNA as a scaffold. Each of the bases (nucleotides) and attached sugar and phosphate groups is a transom. Connecting each transom to its neighbour and running vertically throughout the molecule on both sides of the helix is a standard. Connecting the bases with each other are the steps across the scaffold, or the steps across the ladder you might use to climb up it. A structure called a hydrogen bond [52] connects the bases to each other. So it is helpful to see the hydrogen bonds as the ledgers. Hydrogen is the smallest element in the periodic table; it is also the building block of the entire universe. Its importance cannot be understated. In hydrogen bonding, hydrogen is electrostatically attached to larger atoms such as nitrogen and oxygen. In DNA there are three hydrogen bonds between the nucleotides G and C and two hydrogen bonds between the nucleotides A and T. Each molecule of DNA is found inside the nucleus. It is densely packed onto a structure we call a chromosome. These structures are form as a result of bonding between the DNA molecule itself and specialist proteins; in turn, each chromosome is covered with a layer of water molecules. Each of the base pairs interlocks with its opposite via the hydrogen bonds thus forming a step or standard on the DNA ladder. However, the bases only bond to each other if they are compatible. DNA is organised such that G **only** bonds with C and A **only** bonds with T (or vice versa). The bases are said to match or complement each other. This gives scientists the term complementary base pair [53] to explain the structure of DNA. The notion is crucial as it allows prediction with total confidence as to which base is on the opposite end of the step on the ladder. For example, suppose we have one strand of

DNA composed of the nucleotides (the transoms) GGTACAT, then the other strand must be CCATGTA, with hydrogen bonds (the ledgers) holding the DNA molecule in place. (See diagram two). The ordering of individual nucleotides results in a sequence of DNA. The order of nucleotides determines which proteins are going to be made. It also determines where they will be expressed. DNA is a linear chain of the four base pairs. The whole structure contains the genetic information which enables all known life to function. A helpful comparison is to consider the way in which the 26 letters of the alphabet are ordered. The letters are used to make the words, sentences, paragraphs and chapters which make up all the books you read and the language(s) you speak.

Diagram Two - A Simple Representation of DNA

Nucleotide G.........C Nucleotide (A transom)

G.........C

T.........A

A.........T

C.........G

A.........T

T.........A

.... Hydrogen Bond (a ledger)

[Running vertically through both sides of the molecule is the standard. This provides additional structure for the molecule. The standard enables the chromosome to form.]

A molecule of DNA can be millions of complementary base pairs in length. The nucleus of each cell in a given organism contains a definite number of pairs of chromosomes [54], collectively composing its genome. For instance, human beings have 23 pairs of chromosomes whilst the genome of an aardvark is encoded on 20 pairs of chromosomes. The human genome consists of approximately 3.5 billion base pairs spread across the 23 sets (46 individual) of chromosomes. If it were possible to lay each genome from each cell out it would stretch to about 2-3 metres. There are roughly 10 trillion cells with a nucleus in an adult human being. If the genome from each of these cells were laid out end to end, the distance covered would be just shy of a billion (10^9) miles. Furthermore, the storage capacity of DNA is staggeringly huge; one microgram/micron (1/1000th) of a gram can in theory store the equivalent information found in one million compact discs (10^6 X 700MB).

A sequence of DNA which codes for a specific characteristic, such as eye or hair colour is called a gene [55]. However, just to confuse matters we must understand not all DNA is made of genes; in fact, most of the DNA molecule is not actually used for making (synthesising) new proteins. In human beings, less than 5% of the genome is known to code for the manufacture of new molecules. This point brings us to another assertion put forward by the pro-GM food lobby, which demonstrates it's sheer and systemic insolence. DNA which does **not** code for new proteins and appears to exist only to replicate itself is termed junk [56] DNA. The supporters of GM foods would have us believe because (as far as is understood) junk DNA does not code for the manufacture of proteins, there is no danger in inserting engineered DNA into the junk DNA of other organisms. I believe such a position demonstrates supreme arrogance and foolhardiness of the worst kind. Just because we have yet to ascertain a function for strands of DNA does not mean there isn't one. In any case, it now appears the notion of junk DNA is itself due for retirement but don't expect the biotechnology industry to acknowledge this reality.

DNA is the molecule which codes for the manufacture (synthesis) of protein molecules. On each DNA molecule, the precise sequence of nucleotides corresponds to the ordering and assembly of individual amino acids which are the building blocks of proteins. Thus all of these elements can be brought together to define a gene as a biological code for a specific instruction, normally the code for a specific protein. These instructions are determined by the order of complementary base pairs. Proteins themselves are composed of amino acids. The order in which the amino acids will be assembled into a protein is determined by the order of nucleotides in the DNA molecule. From this perspective it is helpful to break DNA down into sections called codons [57]. A codon is a set of three complimentary base pairs and each codon codes for one amino acid. Each set of three base pairs (6 nucleotides) codes for one of the twenty amino acids. The genetic code (DNA) allows an organism to translate the information held on its chromosomes into the proteins needed for its survival. In its entirety DNA is composed of four different nucleotides and the proteins they code for are made from the same twenty amino acids. The contents of living animal cells [58] are protected from their external environment by a structure called the cell membrane. Plants also have a structure called the cell wall. The contents of each cell are suspended in a water solution called the cytoplasm. It is in the cytoplasm where all of the biochemical reactions which make the whole organism function occur. Most of these reactions happen in specialist structures called organelles. Chapter one mentions the mitochondria; these are the organelles where respiration occurs. In plants the site of photosynthesis (PHS) is an organelle called the chloroplasts. The sites of protein manufacture (synthesis) in all living cells across the biosphere are the organelles known as the ribosomes. [59] Here, genetic information is transported from the nucleus in the form of a single strand of DNA, i.e. a strand of RNA. The strand of RNA is a template and is converted to DNA through the base pair rules mentioned above. The DNA is used to convert genetic information via amino acids into functioning proteins. Each protein molecule is constructed one amino acid at a time based on the arrangement of nucleotides in DNA.

A gene is more than a collection of organised nucleotides. Its structure determines the characteristic or trait it produces (expresses) in the organism. In other words, we must inquire as to the characteristic expressed by a particular gene. At their most basic level genes code for the manufacture of the specialist cells which go on to form organs which allow organisms to function. Furthermore, genes carry the instructions which allow all **inherited** traits to be carried to the next generation of organism. Finally, DNA codes for the manufacture of proteins, therefore, a definition of the word "gene" must also include genes as conveyers of protein synthesis (manufacture). DNA via genes provides the biological information which codes for the building of all biological molecules. A given sequence of DNA will code for a specific protein, in scientific parlance the gene is said to be expressed.

These are the codes which GE in all its forms seeks to alter. For our purposes, GE or GM is any process by which DNA is transported from one organism and spliced into the DNA of another organism. The resultant GMO is normally a cash crop plant such as corn, soy or canola. The aim is to produce a novel plant which expresses characteristics it didn't have before it was engineered. We are not talking about a few mad long haired scientists but of a multi-billion dollar a year industry which is inextricably linked to the agencies which compose big agriculture (see chapter six). The technology has been imposed on all of us without any consideration of the long-term impacts on both human health [60] and the environment. The GM industry and the biotech firms have been insidiously clever in targeting the world's staple food crops without even giving us the choice to avoid eating them. Subsequent chapters will impart the industry opposes mandatory labelling. It has also lobbied successfully meaning food products labelled as GM free are not always so. Without being alarmist it is absolutely true GM technology represents a clear-cut grab for control of the world's food supply. But enough! All of these assertions – and more – will be backed up, referenced and discussed in the kind of detail the proponents of GM foods would rather we all ignored. Carrying on with walking before we start running, the next chapter will explain what is meant by GE.

Chapter 3: The Principles of Plant Genetic Engineering

One question to pose toward those who support GMO's is as simple as it is incisive and it goes a little like this. *"I don't want to eat food contaminated with GMO's, their derivatives or metabolites. Isn't that my right as a human being and any children I may be responsible for?"* You can expect an incredulous and blank look from those who cannot cope with such questions. They will revert to saying things like *"but we have been growing GM crops for twenty years and billions of meals have been served and no ill health effects have been reported"* Furthermore, the movers and shakers whom are driving GMO's choose to ignore or deflect the external issues to "the science" intertwined within their activities. They see nothing sacrosanct about the term "species" or DNA itself; if they did they would not be moving genes between different genomes would they? Clearly, if you see DNA as a biological mechanism which exists only to transfer specific proteins coded for by specific genes, there is no problem. Especially when set against the huge profits to be made from doing so. As far as biotechnology and life sciences are concerned living organisms across the biosphere become nothing more than vehicles for carrying DNA. Clearly, the expertise, knowledge, finance, technology and science tied up in GMO's and intensive agriculture is desperately needed in permaculture and organic systems. If such a shift does **not** occur, the reader is invited to have a look at the horrific, avoidable and absolutely criminal famines in Yemen, South Sudan and the Horn of Africa as examples of what is on the cards closer to home. At its simplest life science is concerned with the science of living organisms. It connects with pharmaceuticals, nutrition, medicine, physiology, food processing and manufacture, medical technology and biotechnology. Life science is also concerned with the organisation of the institutions which work in these areas. Sadly, in all of these areas the pursuit of profit has absolutely subsumed any other objectives, such as the prolongation of life, respect for the environment, sustainability and human need. The language contained in meaningless corporate babble and double speak such as this drivel,[1] for me sums it up entirely. As an industry, biotechnology [2] is part of life sciences.[3] It is concerned with the deliberate alteration of living organisms, the cells, the organs and the processes carried out by them and within them. It is usually concerned with generating substances which can be used as fuel, food or medicines. It is related to the microbiology mentioned in chapter two and draws upon existing knowledge of chemistry, physics and biology in pursuit of its aims. This writing is concerned with the facet of life science and biotechnology connected with the use of GMO's in intensive agriculture, factory farming and food processing. In this frame GMO's are developed with the express purpose of making profits for the industry which drives them. As such DNA and living organisms are wide open and legitimate targets for the food, plant and animal geneticists employed by the industry. Hence, another fundamental question is to ask *"how is plant and animal genetic engineering carried out?"* During my first year at university way back in the deep dark mists of time, well, late 1989, I remember writing a similar sentence in an essay on the Neolithic revolution. The lecturers comment was priceless, he wrote the following. *"A remarkable piece of work I didn't know plants and animals could interbreed today and I'm sure*

Neolithic hominids didn't know how to do it either". I would love to hear what he has to say on the subject now. For simplicities sake I have omitted the role of marker and promoter genes.

In the world of GMO's the first task is to ascertain which traits or characteristics are to be expressed. Such traits include:

- Herbicide tolerance, the plant has been engineered to be resistant to a particular weed killer such as glyphosate (trade name roundup [4] which is readily available [5]). All other plants except the engineered plant are killed. At the time of writing glyphosate is the highest selling herbicide on the planet and has at best questionable [6] health credentials. [7]

- Resistance to viral diseases and other agents in the crop plant itself.

- Resistance to antibiotics.

- Insect resistance, the crop plant is engineered to produce its own pesticides such as an engineered form of a natural pesticide called Bacillus thuringiensis [8] (Bt).

The gene which codes for the expression of the desired traits is called the gene of interest or GOI [9]. Often more than one gene is required. The GOI is usually taken from the genome of a living organism. For example, suppose the objective is to produce a soybean which produces precursor fatty acids. When they are eaten the human body is able to convert these molecules into the omega 3 form–which has proven to be so beneficial to our metabolism. I have **not** picked this example out of the air; it **is** actually happening **and** being presented as an avenue for improving our health. Monsanto [10] have developed a pulse (MON 87769) called the stearidonic acid (SDA [11]) soybean_which produces the precursor fatty acids. Furthermore the company is exceptionally proud_[12] of their wholly unnecessary bean. I think it's fair to ask the reader again *"did you know about this?"* I didn't, and I also didn't know Monsanto [13] wants this form of GM soya on your dinner plate as quickly as they can get it there. The quicker this happens the quicker they can start to rake in the dollars. After all there is no other reason for a strategic partnership between two or more different profit driven enterprises is there? The SDA bean has been approved for use in the US since June 2013. The Canadian government is another cheerleader for GMO's, unsurprisingly; they too have no problem with the SDA soybean. Other pro-GMO governments are guaranteed to follow suit. As for those which adopt a case by case approach to GMO approval, I argue come to terms with what you are up against. The MON 87769 variety and others will by hook or crook find their way into the human food chain unless the whole sordid business is stopped. Now I don't know about you, but speaking personally and given a real choice, I would prefer to ingest my essential fish oils from fish and not beans. Funnily enough I also subscribe to another outlandish idea, shouldn't I/we/you have a choice as to what I eat. Wouldn't it be great if the Monsanto's of this world took it upon themselves as a minimum courtesy, to ask if we wanted their GMO's in the first place. **One** glaringly obvious reason why this has **not** occurred is because they know people don't want it. Or they realise enough people will be suspicious and untrusting enough to query what is being done and why. The other point missing from their narrative is achingly obvious. If you are following a healthy balanced diet, you can ingest your omega 3 and all other nutrients your metabolism needs without ingesting supplements or novel products like the SDA bean. Plus the real reasons for nutrient deficiencies [14] in the food we eat are seldom discussed. A point levied with equal ferocity at the processed food industry. Perhaps if the food we eat was grown naturally and planned under the auspices of permaculture and organic systems we would be providing genuinely nutritious food for everyone on the planet. Agriculture would be more productive than it currently is plus pesticide and fertiliser use would at **worst** be significantly reduced. Any pesticides used would **not** be anything like as toxic as produced by the chemical companies, the conglomerates which also benefit from GMO's. Permaculture and organic systems promote biodiversity and ecological connections between people, their communities and the natural world itself. Big agriculture outlined in chapter six and the drivers behind GMO's do not. In other words, we do not have a farming system which is anything like fit for purpose; it certainly does not serve the interests of us the peoples of this world. If the institutions which control global food production were striving toward genuine food security and sustainability, GMO's in agriculture would **not** even be an option.

Genes of Interest in the SDA MON 87769 Soy Bean

An obvious question to ask here is *"where the genes to manufacture the fatty acids came from?"* A quick perusal of the sources involved in promoting the SDA bean shows they have not answered this question. At best this is being economical with the truth; I prefer to call it lying through their back teeth. In the SDA soybean, the genes which code for the precursor fatty acids are coded for from two unrelated species and are inserted (by GE) into a third unrelated species. The genes in this example code for the manufacture of two specific enzymes [15] coded for by specific genes. Enzymes are proteins and biological catalysts. They function by reducing the amount of energy needed to kick start a biochemical reaction. In the MON 87769 SDA soybean, the enzymes accelerate the rate of reactions which produce the precursor fatty acids. The first enzyme is derived from the genome of a flower called primula juliae [16], a species of primrose. The second enzyme comes from a species of mould called neurospora crassa, [17] known in everyday language as red bread mould. This particular microbe has been used in genetics since the early 1940's.

Before genetic engineers can insert the GOI it has to be extracted from the source organism. This happens irrespective of what it is or what biological kingdom it belongs to. The GOI can be sourced from any organism anywhere on the planet. Then it is inserted into the DNA of what becomes the transgenic or GMO. The objective is to ensure the GOI is expressed in the transgenic plant or animal. In fitting with the definition of biotechnology, we have a clear example of DNA being relegated to a corpus of protein producing molecules which exists **only** for our benefit. Once extracted the next stage is to transfer the GOI into the genome of the organism to be engineered. The genetic engineer is looking for a specific gene which codes for the manufacture (synthesis) of a particular protein or codes for a particular trait. In the SDA soy bean example, each GOI codes for enzymes which allow the plant to produce beans which contain the precursor oils for omega 3 synthesis (manufacture), the synthesis happens in the human body. Hmmm can I have access to affordable, locally produced and fresh food whch already has all the necessary nutrients? Just a though is all! There are several mechanisms for insertion of the GOI at the disposal of the genetic engineers involved. A common technique is to employ a structure known as a plasmid, [18] or circular section [19] of DNA. Eventually, the plasmid and the extracted DNA are combined and then transferred into the genome of the plant. At this stage, the genome is set to produce a plant which is a GM or transgenic organism. A soil bacterium called Agrobacterium tumefaciens [20] is commonly used as the vehicle [21] (or vector) by which the desired traits are transferred.

In the soil, a.tumefaciens is a pathogenic [22] microbe. A pathogen is any microbe [23] which causes disease or metabolic harm to an organism it comes into contact with or when it is ingested by them. A. tumefaciens has an affinity for two leaved or dicotyledonous plants.[24] Almost all engineered plants are of the dicot or two leaved form. If a. tumefaciens gets inside a host plant it will cause damage to its normal metabolism and/or physiology. In nature, the point of egress, or entry, for the bacterium is the juncture of the root and stem. The microbe only gains entry if damage to the juncture has occurred. Once inside the plant the microbe rapidly ingratiates itself into the cells of the now host plant. From here on the pathology of the microbe is analogous to human forms of cancer. The bacteria inserts its own DNA into the chromosomes of the host plant, (acting as a virus) infecting and "tricking" it into over producing auxin [25] and cytokine [26] plant growth hormones. A hormone is any chemical produced by an organism which changes its metabolism or physiology by chemical means. In human beings and other mammals, hormones work under the control of the endocrine [27] system. A.tumefaciens also converts plant amino acids into sources of carbon and nitrogen which it needs to carry out its own metabolism. The end result is a multitude of cells which can have more than one nucleus which clump together in a structure called a crown gall; [28] we would recognise it as a tumour. The gall [29] has no external protection and so is directly exposed to the environment. This makes the infected plant very vulnerable to secondary attack. The resulting incurable biological consequence of infection is called crown gall disease [30]. The only way to stop infection is to prevent damage to the plants themselves.

In plant GE the genes which initiate the above pathology are removed. Once this has happened the next task in the transfer stage is to open up the plasmid. This is achieved by the action of specialist biological molecules called restriction enzymes.[31] These function by opening up the plasmid DNA at specific sites on the nucleotide chain. Along the stretch of plasmid DNA, one side of the DNA helix is opened up, which exposes a row of individual nucleotides; these nucleotides are called sticky ends. [32] Then the same restriction enzymes are used on the chromosomes of the extracted cells of the source organism, i.e. those which contain the GOI. Thus, in SDA soybeans the restriction enzymes would be used on the cells of the mould and primrose flower. The genes which code for the desired enzymes would then be matched to the exposed sticky ends in the plasmid. Each sticky end is obliged by the rules of genetics (complimentary base pairing) to complement its opposite number. Thus for the hydrogen bonding discussed in chapter two to occur without mutation Guanine **and** Cytosine and Adenine **and** Thymine must chemically bond to each other forming the rungs (ledgers) of the DNA ladder or scaffold. The complementary bonding is made possible by the action of an enzyme called DNA ligase [33]. Hence the process of joining two strands of nucleic acid together to form DNA is called DNA ligation [34].

Diagram Three - DNA Recombination

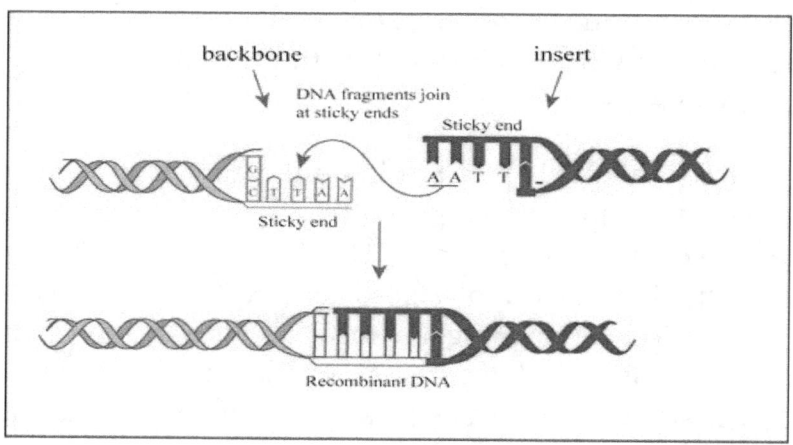

When GMO's are created, DNA ligation ensures the nucleotides on the GOI compliment exactly those of the plasmid. Success ensures the plasmid contains the DNA which codes for the desired characteristic.

The GOI has been inserted by DNA recombination into the plasmid. The objective is to produce a vector (transport) mechanism for the trait coded by the GOI. The GOI is taken from the genome of the source organism and then inserted into the plasmid. Only those plasmids which have successfully taken up the GOI are allowed to multiply. These plasmids are then inserted into the genome of what becomes the transgenic organism. The integration of plasmid and GOI DNA is not an efficient process. It has a success rate of roughly 1%. However, as with many natural processes, it's all about trade-offs and optimisation. If the bacterium is enjoying favourable conditions, where nutrients are present and there is a source of heat, then rates of reproduction are very high. In a very short time very large amounts of the "new gene" can be made and the protein it codes for put to fulfilling its purpose.

Recombining DNA is **not** an intrinsically bad scientific technique, quite the opposite. Just ask anybody who requires insulin to treat their diabetes, or the scientists involved in gene therapy. In the large scale manufacture of insulin the gene which codes for its production is inserted into the plasmid. The plasmid is then inserted into E.coli bacteria, which then produces the insulin in huge quantities. Furthermore, if I were writing about gene therapy and its utility in treating the Cystic Fibrosis outlined in chapter two, or indeed other genetic diseases I would be singing its virtues from the roof tops to **all** who would listen. However, we are not discussing gene therapy in medicine; we are discussing GMO's under the control of profit driven transnational corporations and here we reach a fork in the road. At this juncture GE becomes a little more insidious and frightening. In insulin the engineered E.coli is stored in giant fermenting vats (bioreactors) and huge amounts of insulin are syphoned off. The reality is orders of magnitude more complex, but there are the nuts and bolts of the entire exercise. In this type of GM the bacteria is not inserted into the genome of another organism. The E.coli has been engineered to produce insulin under very tightly controlled and favourable conditions to the microbe. The production of insulin represents a closed or isolated system,[35] whilst GE in agriculture, represents an open [36] system. A closed system is one in which there is no interaction between different components of the system and the outside world. Components inside the system are completely sealed from the outside world. Taking a simple example, a flask which keeps a drink hot is a closed system; well it tries to be, eventually all the heat will leave. However, the analogy is fair it is not possible to have a system which is completely closed to heat. A person who needs insulin to treat their diabetes is not passing their treatment on to anyone else or the external environment. Aside from any other considerations, what would be the point? An open system is one where the components of the system do interact with the outside world. Sticking with our hot drink, once you pour the drink into a cup, it immediately loses heat to the surroundings. With GE the whole point is to create organisms which exist and live in the real world. If you think about it, GMO's represents bio-engineering and the application of biotechnology occurring in the biggest open system of all, the planet itself. And this reality brings us to another perfectly reasonable reason to **oppose** GM crops. The engineered genes **will** at some stage interact with existing DNA in the natural world. And the more individual GMO's released into the environment, the more interactions there will be. On a long enough time line genetic consequences are inevitable. It is highly likely; if not flat out certain these consequences will be absolutely irreversible.

OK back to piggy backing on the SDA soybean to explain GM. The next stage is called transformation. 37 The aim is to get the GOI inserted into the genome of the plant to be engineered. Clearly, plants are well organised multi-cellular organisms; they are made of hundreds of millions of individual cells. One cannot insert the engineered GOI on a cell by cell basis, so what happens? In the laboratory cell cultures are grown, these provide the cells to which the engineered genes will be added. These cells are undifferentiated, 38 meaning they have not developed into specialist cells. Plus the genes which trigger

66

differentiation [39] into specific cell types are switched off. The culture of cells is known as a callus, not be confused with hard toughened skin! The engineered DNA is then transferred cell by cell to the chromosomes of the callus cells. Not all of the cells will accept the engineered DNA. The procedure itself is exceptionally delicate meaning some of the callus cells will be "killed" in the process. Any surviving callus cells which incorporate the engineered DNA are transgenic. The cells are then allowed to grow in a nutrient rich media which facilitates the growth of the cells into plantlets. The plantlets are allowed to take root and kept under strictly controlled laboratory conditions. It is entirely possible for a plant to be generated from a single transgenic cell. Any plants which grow successfully will have the engineered trait in every cell which has a nucleus. This is exactly how DNA functions; it passes genetic information through different generations. And it does so by being present in every cell which has a nucleus.

The plants themselves are matured in the laboratory and any seeds produced are collected. Various tests are carried out to ensure :

- The seeds carry the engineered trait.

- The plant behaves as expected

- The plant yields seeds which produce plants which express the engineered trait.

In our example the second or third generation soy bean seeds would be tested for the expression of the SDA genes. Testing can take many months or years to complete. Once testing is complete the plants are ready for field trials and here things become even more worrying. GM plants are being grown in the real world, in real soil, in real fields, in a real environment. This was the state of play in the late spring and summer of 2003. Back then, the UK government headed by Tony Blair [40] tried to introduce wide scale field trials across the UK. They hoped whilst we were all distracted by the conflict in Afghanistan and Iraq, we wouldn't notice. Thankfully, they were wrong! Due to massive, organised and coordinated opposition, of which I am proud to this day to be a part of, this particular endeavour, was stopped. Sadly, there were and still are plenty of opt out clauses, meaning EU countries can go for GMO's if a government wants to. With the far right making gains in Eastern Germany, Austria, France and the Czech Republic, the GMO spectre is unfortunately rising again. Aside from any other concerns "the business case" is more likely to over-ride other points of view. The prospect of GM crops has anything but disappeared. The UK elite have always embraced GM crops. In a post Brexit Britain they are clearly going to have another go at implementing them. Furthermore, if you thought the SDA example outlined above is somehow unique then unfortunately you need to think again. A UK based research company called Rothamsted Research [41] has employed equivalent techniques to produce omega 3 oils from oil seed rape right here in the UK. For obvious reasons rape seed really ought to be canola. Once again the likes of Rothemsted Research tell you very little about what they do or how they do it. There is plenty of the usual vacuous guff and vague platitudes about why but not much else. Most important the trial sites themselves are often at secret and sometimes guarded locations. This represents the power of direct action, the implication the drivers behind GMO's know what they are doing is wrong **and** people will act against them. In 2008 [42] the locations for trial sites for canola were only released after pressure from NGO's such as friends of the Earth. This is set against another reality, in 2004 [43] about sixty different trial sites were set up for corn,[44] canola and sugar beet, again in industry demanded secrecy. As of 2012 there were some two thousand trial sites for various GM crops across the European Union. Likely, there are more now in late 2017 and early 2018. None of this has been officially declared, we have not been consulted in any meaningful sense and there has been no objective assessment concerning the utility, environmental impact or need for the whole enterprise. So, it seems only fair to ask, "what are they hiding"? Plus, if all of this is for our benefit, "why the secrecy and disinformation"?

As usual, the stated reasons for the need for GMO's do not stand up to detailed and objective analysis. For instance, the food security argument is as spurious over the years 2015-17 as it was in 2003. It states GM crops are going to deliver the goods which they don't. GMO's are just a clear extension of the big agriculture construct outlined in chapter six, reason enough to oppose them. We have organic and permaculture systems which have proven time and time again to deliver more food acre for acre than both mono-cultured and GM varieties. They know this to be true as much as I do and as much as the organic / permaculture sector does too. The whole enterprise is riddled with deceit and lies (as is everything else) and this is only one part of it. The question for you, the reader is "who are you going to believe and why?"

Overall the developing a GMO can be broken down into a series of steps:

- Determine and isolate the gene or genes (the GOI) we are looking to be expressed in the transgenic plant.

69

- Insert the gene into the vector (plasmid) from a bacterial or viral species of microbe.

- The modified bacterial cells are recombined with plant cells from the species to be engineered. The modified bacterial DNA is inserted at a precise point on the chromosome.

- Selection of the modified plant cells which have taken up the new characteristic. Most cells will not have taken up the genes carried by the plasmid. A marker [45] gene is used to indicate those cells which have. The cells which have not taken up the inserted gene are destroyed.

- The modified cells and/or plant parts are placed into a cultured environment in which they will thrive and reproduce rapidly.

- From the point of view of the company which produces it **and** once the transgenic plants have grown, the plant is tested. The GOI must be expressed and must function as required. It should not have any undesired or negative traits.

- Plants which perform well under testing are then subject to field trials in different environments and this determines whether or not the plant will perform as expected in the real world.

- Assuming the plant passes these tests, the variety is earmarked for full commercial growing.

Finally, there is supposed to be safety assessments but as we are operating under the wholly inappropriate banner of substantial equivalence (SE) these assessments fall well short of what is required. The equivalence paradigm would have us believe GM food is no different from other food stuffs and so the two are identical. It also misses the key **and** clear point, the technology itself and its application in the real world is the problem. Along with so much which has gone wrong in our world, the problems are caused by the way things are done and the degree of acceptance thereof. The above text is an overview of the essential nuts and bolts of what happens in the plant GM laboratory. The next chapter summarises some of how the industry communicates its position.

Chapter 4: Misconceptions And Flat Out Lies - What Are GMO's And Where Did They Come From?

Arguably, GMO's represent the most complex and interconnected issue of our times. The subject touches on every facet of our lives and how we see our relationship with the Earth upon which we live. It is intertwined with notions of politics, history, economics, sociology, philosophy, human rights, democracy, sustainability, environmental awareness, social and environmental justice, equality, ethics, religion, morality, corporate power, and science. Other global issues such as climate change and nuclear weapons operate in the same areas, but they are significantly less complex to deal with and certainly easier to explain. All of the huge system inflicted problems humanity faces are as important and interconnected as each other. Yet, as an issue GMO's is orders of magnitude more complex and is further down the list of priorities than it should be. Thus illustrating one reason why this writing came into existence. One area GMO's is **not** about, is spending hundreds of billions of currency units on creating the kind of monsters which feature so regularly in the horror and sci-fi movies I love so much. Still, I will eat my hat if there are not agencies such as the "umbrella corporation [1]" from Resident Evil at work in this world today. However, this is not the core business of the drivers behind GMO's it's not even on their radar. The industry is concerned with one over-riding goal and it is far more evil than any scary monster or alien invasion. The objective is profit and profit at all costs, even the future food security of the whole planet. Those who seek to benefit from GMO's in agriculture are never going to tell the basic truth about the technology they support. GM seeds are developed solely to generate profits in a market which exists only to serve itself. There is no other reason for their existence; everything else is distortion, bribery, lies and the consummate and necessary amounts of smoke and mirrors. We are **not** talking about the kind of experiments presented in David Cronenberg's wonderful interpretation of The Fly [2]. We **are** concerned with the transfer of genes between genomes **and** how the resultant transgenic organism interacts with the environment around it. For example, in 1991 [3] a biotechnology company called DNA plant technologies engineered tomatoes and strawberries to express frost resistance. This was achieved by using the anti-freeze genes from various species of arctic dwelling fish. The process created engineered tomatoes and strawberries which express resistance to frost. The company was merged with a bigger concern in 1994 and wound up in 1996.[4] The engineered fruits were never grown commercially and chapter five goes some way to explaining why. To supporters of GMO's such developments and creations are not problematic,[5] indeed, from their perspective they are to be welcomed. For them it is more an issue of communication and **not** the GE and its application. From these perspectives we are not supposed to feel anything, we are supposed to merely accept what is being done as completely normal and absolutely essential. Supporters of GMO's seriously believe they have the moral high ground **and** concerns expressed are merely myths or unscientific bunkum to be discredited. Now, for sure, one has to get these things right, which definitely includes the science. However, this does not mean questions, concerns or opposition are unfounded, irrelevant or anti-science. Also raising such questions is not about "scaring consumers [5]", asking questions is about finding out what really goes on in the industry. And surely asking questions, testing results and assessing alternatives in context is the foundation of good science and policy direction. Apparently this is not the case in the world of GMO's. Plus, supporters of GMO's genuinely believe (or they are lying) there is nothing "yucky" or "icky" or indeed "unsafe" about engineering genes in this way. I say there is on all counts, but I am a rational, emotionally intelligent human being. I'm also **not** blinded and seduced by the science, or more likely the dollar signs. I would also like to point out, I am not a consumer; I am a human being, just like the other seven billion or so people on this planet.

Is It A Profit Driven, Genetic Free For All?

As of 2018, the only GE animal I know of approved for human beings is the aqua-bounty salmon mentioned in chapter seven. A big reason for it is down to the trenchant and principled opposition to the technology demonstrated by those who see this issue in the widest possible terms. Such holistic resistance is in stark contrast to the science-centric position demonstrated by those who support the technology and its application. Were it not for the awareness, consideration and courage of those who resist, GMO's would be a much bigger [6] feature in the human food chain, than they currently are. So, I say three cheers for the activists! Other examples of this type of GM include:

- Genes from golden orb spiders [7] have been inserted [8] into the genome of farm goats so they produce milk which contains the silk normally produced by the spider. The milk is then evaporated and the silk extracted. Ethics? What ethics?

- In the early 1990's, genes from venomous scorpions [9] were inserted into cabbage plants so the crop produces its own pesticide. [10] The potential impact of an invasive poison on indigenous species of insect was ignored or underplayed. This and other developments are directly comparable to the Bt cotton, mentioned throughout this book.

- Although not directly connected to agriculture, in 2010 Japanese researchers engineered [11] mice which chirp like birds.

- In 1999 geneticists [12] at the University of Edinburgh developed potatoes which glow in the dark when they need watering. The fluorescence comes from different species of jelly fish. Wheat [13] has been engineered in a similar way.

- In 2013 pigs, rabbits and sheep were engineered to glow with the genes for fluorescence taken once again from jellyfish.[14]

- A brand of Ice cream approved for sale in the US contains yeast based variant of arctic fish genes which code for antifreeze proteins. Similar [15] moves have been made in the UK and EU.

- In 2001 it was reported GM corn could be engineered to act as a spermicidal contraceptive. [16]

- Various staple food crops have been engineered [17] to contain human genes and express for the production of particular enzymes and other proteins.

The bullet points above came about from two hours of independent follow up. They represent a quark sized component of a universal whole. They are also relatively benign examples; I truly do dread to think what is occurring behind closed doors. The primary reason for all of it is to generate profit for the industry. The ideological justification for these engineering experiments is clear once you start looking. The list of possible combinations is for all intents and purposes limitless. The only constraint is the number of possible combinations allowed for by DNA, which is practically infinite. Referring back to chapter one, I fail to see how the examples mentioned here and GMO's in agriculture, can be equated to cross breeding, selective breeding or hybridisation. The same goes for GM plants which have been engineered to produce nutrients, including the golden rice mentioned below and the enhanced bananas mentioned in chapter seven. The reader is advised, nay implored, to investigate this area of the subject as a matter of utmost urgency. Such techniques are not the same as those already mentioned and can in no way be compared to permaculture or organic systems. The drivers behind GMO's know this. The real reason for their position is insidiously frightening. They see absolutely nothing sacred or sacrosanct about profiting from the genetic code itself. In contrast, one strand of opposition to GMO's is the opposite position. So **yes** I argue in the strongest possible terms GMO's do represent a profit driven genetic free for all.

Genes and the Species Barrier

As sentient organisms human beings also ought to elicit some sort of "hang on a second" response when presented with the kind of examples presented in this book. In scientific terms we are talking of a "yuck" or the "wisdom of disgust" response.[18] Apparantly, such considerations do not enter into the collective consciousness of the industry or its supporters. Those who support GM foods see DNA as no more than a biological blue print, which contains specific genes which allow particular traits to be expressed. This perspective reduces the wonders of the natural world and it's rapidly diminishing biodiversity down to a collection of molecular machines. Here sections of DNA can be transferred as required with no thought given to the consequences. Individual genes are not separate entities; they are an integral part of a whole organism. Genes also intermingle through living organisms and with the environment which surrounds amd supports them. No individual gene functions in isolation from the others. Genes operate through complex, interdependent networks which are not fully understood. By networks I mean the biological processes which ensure genetic traits are expressed where they should, when they should and as they should. Concurrently, if the environment with which genes interact and / or the genome itself is altered, it is likely genetic expression itself will also be affected. There are clear and present genetic similarities between different organisms across the natural world, and no one is saying otherwise. This reality does not mean DNA is some sort of scientific toy for us to play with as we see fit. It means DNA is a core driver of evolution, inheritance and variation. GMO's are global in their application, meaning any consequences are going to be global too. Once GMO's are released any consequences are almost

77

certain to be irreversible. The real tragedy is we already have clear and present alternatives to GMO's, which repeatedly out perform both monocultured and transgenic crops. Organic and permaculture systems also have none of the issues intrinsic to this branch of biotechnology. Alone this ought to ensure subservience to the Precautionary Principle (PP), which runs throughout this book. The PP means if an activity has the potential (however remote) to harm the environment or human health then precautionary measures ought to be taken, even if no actual harm or damage has occurred. For GMO's the burden of proof should **fall** absolutely on those proposing them and **not** on those opposing them. Once novel engineered genes are established in the biosphere, there is no removing them or counteracting any negative consequences. Such thinking represents merely **one** reason why GM foods ought to be filed under the heading PP. It goes without saying, those who support GMO's disagree.[19]

In biological and evolutionary terms, new species arise over long periods of time under conditions of geographic isolation from other organisms. A given environment is going to be different from another, so when new adaptations arise a given organism is able to survive as compared to those which do not adapt. The genes for the adaptations are expressed and those organisms are able to take advantage of the habitat in question. Geographic separation is in part responsible for the rich biodiversity which used to thrive on the Earth. This process can take millions of years and is called speciation. Inserting genes from different genomes into the genome of what becomes the transgenic organism ought to instinctively raise concerns and questions. For instance, the species barrier comes about as a natural buttress which stops pathogens, mutations and genetic defects from jumping from one species to another. Microbes of all kinds are highly adept at swapping [20] DNA and RNA amongst themselves. In 2018 we know genetic interaction between multi-cellular organisms is more common than was thought in the 20th century. This is the HGT or bacterial conjugation mentioned in chapter one. We already know microbes including pathogens are well adapted to the biology of the host organisms they target. They have specific receptors, antigens, [21] RNA and other biological molecules which enable them to carry out their life cycle and / or pathology when they come into contact with target organisms. Life on Earth has evolved constructs like the species barrier for good reason. At its absolute simplest the barrier is a defence mechanism. It takes time for a microbe to evolve to a point where it can infect one species or members of different animal kingdoms. Two infamous examples immediately spring to mind, first, is the morphing [22] of BSE into CJD. Second, the various forms of influenza which are known to infect birds, human beings and swine represent adaptations which enable pathogens to migrate [23] through the web of life. In agricultural GMO's degraded forms of pathogenic microbes are used as vectors. The vectors are used to transfer DNA across the species barrier. Again, such activity is not supposed to be problematic and such realities are downplayed. Explaining why genetic material from different species is routinely used to express pre-determined traits in GMO's. The drivers will always seek to project concerns about their activities onto those who raise them, the opposite of the PP. In the PP the proponents of a given technology or process are required to demonstrate its safety and utility. For GMO's it should also happen with direct comparison to the alternatives, **including** monoculture, which already exist. The drivers behind GMO's will continually seek to fudge (read lie about) the crystal clear differences between GE and the selective and cross breeding techniques outlined thus far. This quote [24] from the University of Nebraska demonstrates exactly the type of fudging, superiority and self-importance I am seeking to impart.

"Plant breeding is an important tool but has limitations. First, breeding can only be done between two plants that can sexually mate with each other. This limits the new traits that can be added to those that already exist in that species"

What? Four billion years of evolution not good enough for you?

The purposely engineered traits are supposed to garner advantages over conventional or mono-cultured crops. Certainly, as far as the industry is concerned GMO's most definitely out-perform agriculture and animal husbandry carried out by means of permacultured and organic systems. These systems represent how food crops ought to be grown and how livestock ought to be reared. From the industries perspective, the reasoning is, intensive large scale farming methods are more productive and sustainable than small scale production methods. Big agriculture (see chapter six) also maintains mono-cultured and engineered crops use less pesticides, promote biodiversity and do not significantly affect soil quality. These assertions simply do not stand up to detailed analysis. [25] Still, it is not all sunshine and lollipops in the organic / permaculture sector [26] and what works in one region may not work in another. However, this is one of the many strengths of the entire philosophy; it is about working with nature and not against it. Permaculture is certainly **not** concerned with bending or changing the natural world to suit our ends, especially, if those ends are solely profit driven. A global agriculture based on organic / permaculture systems is not going to happen overnight. Such a transition has to form part of an overall shift in the way things are done. Organic food and permaculture systems are not a magic bullet to fix everything; they should form part of an overall strategy. A strategy built around sustainable agriculture at a local, regional, national and ultimately international level. One fact is clear, it is the economy of scale which produces the yield in conventional and transgenic crop systems. It is **not** the productivity [27] per unit of land, which makes big agriculture economically, i.e. financially viable. To me it is very simple; I have yet to meet a small holder who has anything good to say about GMOs in agriculture. I'll put it succinctly, over the years I have asked perhaps two dozen growers and small holders (whose ranks i am about to join) what they think of GMO's. Not **one** has expressed support for GMO's, and I mean **not** one, either in the UK or in mainland Europe. So, if you believe there is no case for GE plants or animals you are not alone. I am not an expert on "farming" but I know who I stand with and I know what kind of future I want and GMO's do **not** figure in it. The reasons for this position tap right into notions of:

- Genuinely good citizenship.

- Environmental sustainability.

- Adopting a systemic approach to complex issues, many of which are of the systems own making.

- Social justice, corporate crime and accountability.

- The meaning of objective science and its role in our future.

- Genuine food security for all peoples.

- Genetic pollution of the natural world.

The best response I had from a local producer was "*well, clearly, it's a load of rotten bollocks isn't it*". You, the reader have no reason to believe the exchange; after all, I can't reference the conversation, can I? It did happen, I did ask the question and that answer was forthcoming, with no prompting from either! At the end of the day, it comes down to how **you** want **your** food produced **and** who **you** want in control of agriculture. Do you want **your** hard earned going to independent and local producers? Or do **you** want it going into the coffers of big business? As an individual who is embarking in the direction of food and energy self-sufficiency, I know what **my** answer is. The bottom line and crucial question, the reader needs to ask is "*who do I believe, who do I stand with and why?*" So, do I stand with "*well, it's a load of rotten bollocks*", or not?

Substantial Equivalence and Setting the Scene for GMO's

Speaking of bollocks, which also means nonsense, those who support GMO's promulgate yet another lie. They impart GMO's are identical to the foods which already exist. In 1992 the US FDA began the approval for GM crops because "*are not inherently dangerous*" [28] to human health or the environment. To arrive at this conclusion with **no** evidence, you understand, industry and the FDA concocted a notion called substantial equivalence (SE).[29] The idea was brokered in 1993 by the Organisation for Economic Cooperation and Development

(OECD) with specific reference to GMO's. It doesn't get any clearer; SE demonstrates "the food is as safe as its traditional counterpart" [30]. This is a strategy which reverses and short-circuits the PP and objective peer reviewed science. It places responsibility for proving harm or negative impact onto those who oppose GMOs. It attempts to reverse discourse, by framing concerns as the problem and **not** the technology or its application in the real world. The paradigm means if the industry can show a GM food is "substantially equivalent" to a non-GM food, then both ought to be seen in the same light. Those involved in GM crops can eliminate the need for any special regulatory approval with respect to health, nutrition and the environment. At best things are somewhat shonky in these areas regardless, and yet, GMO's have been given a regulatory green light from the outset. From the beginning the industry, supportive politicians and its financial backers, have shown no interest whatsoever in even acknowledging any concerns or outright fears the opponents to GMO's in agriculture have. Due to industry pressure including seriously dark legal shenanigans, GMO's are **not** subject to the same kind of testing regimes which perhaps, new pesticides, new drugs, industrial chemicals or food additives might be. It means GMO's can be exempt from toxicology and environmental impact assessment. At time of writing GM foods are subject to the **same** regulatory [31] frameworks (such as they are) as non-GM foods. Plus it means if any negative impacts present themselves the industry is able to say "*not me guv, there is no difference between a GM and non-GM food, so your health issue must be caused by something else*". The same attitude goes for any environmental impact. The same goes for any cross pollination, the same goes when the lies disguised as promises made to farmers and growers turn to

83

dust. The industry is taking a position whereby the kind of examples mentioned in this writing, along with all the others they have made and those in the pipe line are the same as those which already exist, "rotten bollocks" indeed! Additionally, SE itself is at best scientifically spurious and goes against basic common sense. You don't need a degree in "science" to understand the next sentence. A cabbage which contains scorpion genes is **not** in any way equivalent to one which doesn't. And neither is rice which has been engineered to produce vitamin A as compared to rice which has not. Neither are bananas which have had genes from another variety of banana inserted into their genome (see chapter seven). Yet, this is the **exact** position the global agency driving GMO's want you, me and everyone else on the planet to have. We are also supposed to be happy and excited about the prospect too. Think about this notion of no inherent danger, well permacultured and organic systems have no inherent danger either, so why not upscale those?

In 1993 as substantial equivalence became legitimised, the UK conservative government headed by John Major published a white paper called "realising our potential" [32]. As far as GMO's are concerned the document takes an identical stance as the US FDA. So it came to pass, through the development of a new technology, bankrolled to the tune of many hundreds of millions of currency units, with full regulatory approval, that in 1996 [33] the first commercial GM soy bean crop was grown in the United States. This crop was a form of soy bean engineered to be resistant to the glyphosate herbicide mention previously. Over the years 1996 to 2002 the global acreage of GM crops increased from 1.7 million hectares to just shy of 60 million hectares. It was concentrated in four countries:

- The US grew 39 million hectares - 66% of the total.

- Argentina grew 13.5 million hectares – 22.5% of the total

- Canada grew 3.5 million hectares - 5.84% of the total

- China grew 2.1 million hectares – 3.5% of the total

By 2007 the global total of GM soya grown along with other staple foods represented about [34] 9% of all crops grown. In 2013 the percentage of GM soya grown in the US was about 90%. [35] The total global percentage in hectares was about 180 million,[36] representing about 12% [37] of the global total [38]. As of 2016, the global total of GM crops grown was about 185 million hectares. Almost half (46%) of this total is grown in 7 countries in the industrialised [39] world. In turn, most of this comes from the US and Canada. The remaining 54% is grown in 19 countries (mainly Brazil and Argentina) all found in the global south. As of late 2017, about 90% of the GM crops in the world are grown in the Americas. Soya is the main crop grown in the US, Brazil and Canada. In Latin and South America corn is a close second. China is the next biggest producer, accounting for about 4% of the total. All the GM crops grown on planet Earth can be found in just ten countries with the US, Brazil and Canada accounting for the lions share. And it is the corporate interests linked to these countries which are driving the whole enterprise. It is **not** a global demand being met, it is an artificial market created for the benefit of those who have funded and developed the technology. In the face of opposition, the GM food industry and its backers are financially benefitting from a **yearly** compound increase of about 6% in the acreage turned over to transgenic crops.

Where Are GMO's Found?

Put simply, the entire enterprise is dominated by only 10 seed companies [40] and chemical manufacturers. Some like Monsanto, DuPont and Bayer are seriously large transnational corporations with a nasty history of crimes against humanity and crimes against the environment. To these organisations GE is just another income stream. These companies fund the research which creates the GMO's, they develop the pesticides,[41] they develop the marketing strategy, the legal framework but **most** important they **lie** to the world and its peoples. A clear connection exists between the biased and skewed science, the crops themselves and the herbicides as well as all other concerns which runs straight into the dark heart of the whole artificial construct. The four single largest GM crops grown are soybeans, corn, cotton and canola. These four crops are merely the opening gambit, the industry is seeking to engineer every plant and animal it seeks to make a profit from. Pretty much every agricultural plant and livestock animal is in the cross hairs of the biotechnology industry. If they are allowed to get away with it (which they will unless it is stopped) every mouthful of every meal you and your children eat for their lifetimes will contain food made with GMO's. To this day soya and GMO's in their entirety are big business and by big I mean global. As of 2016 the seed business turned over some 100 billion USD by 2022 it could well increase to 113 billion USD. Things are already catastrophic; we cannot even buy vegetarian pies from the local supermarket which do **not** contain palm oil, canola or a whole host of additives with **no** demonstrable links to GM crops or to big agriculture (see chapter six). GM Cotton has been mentioned as one of the mainstays of GE in agriculture. This crop was the first **non-food** GM variety to be grown, it too arrived in 1996. Cotton is clearly not a food crop and the issues pertaining to Bt cotton represent only the tip of that particular nefarious iceberg. As a non-food crop there will be even fewer safeguards as to how it is grown, distributed and regulated. And even less consideration given to the environmental crime, impact [42] on the soil and human rights abuses, including child slave labour [43] contained therein. Since 1996 the industry has continually rubbished, dismissed and ridiculed these concerns. All they keep repeating is the false benefit to small holders. I say allow the small holders to take control of the entire mechanism themselves, but there would be **no** profit for big business if agriculture were organised on those terms?

Put simply if you eat meat, fish or dairy products, any form of processed food or any staple crop or vegetable, wear cotton which is not certified organic / GM free, you are eating or wearing GMO's. I'm not preaching or berating here, this is how it is! Our household until very recently (late 2017) did eat meat and fish. We have now removed both from our diet. This may change if we can get locally sourced meat and if we can catch our own fish. With the advent of fish meal derived from GM crops more than on the horizon another conduit for GMO's into the human food chain is presenting itself. We live in a food desert so avoiding processed food, (vegan, and vegetarian or not) is almost impossible, so yes we do eat GMO's almost every day and prop up the industry I am eviscerating here. I am also wearing cotton clothing which has almost certainly been engineered the Bt way, **one** reason why I buy second hand clothes whenever I can. I could go on for ever, truly, the only way to avoid eating GMO's is to stop producing them and ban them out right. As things stand this is just not on the cards, I mean the whole subject is barely mentioned in mainstream discourse. The current state of affairs is not looking good. In the United States you can expect to find GMO's and / or GM produced ingredients in at least 80% [44] of all processed foods. As stated above the percentage of acreage devoted to GM crops is steadily increasing. This means we can expect a consummate increase in their presence in all foods. As far as the UK is concerned, Brexit will almost certainly involve a push to open the door even further.[45] A huge percentage of the GM crops grown today is earmarked for animal feed [46] and is not subject to the same degree of scrutiny as food for direct human consumption. For any processed foodstuff take a look at the ingredients, if the product contains soy, corn or any derivatives thereof, it is going to contain GM ingredients. The industry and its supporters will present these realities as a demand for their product, ever **more** staple foods [48] are prime targets for GM. At this point another kicker rears its ugly head. Even with a certified GM free food you cannot be absolutely be sure it is GM free. Under EU law manufacturers are able to say a food is GM free if it contains 0.9% or less GMO's. In other parts of the world the delimiting number can be up to **10%**. As the UK blunders into Brexit, we can expect our limit to head upward too, if the industry gets its way and if Brexit is allowed to continue as it is. Aside from all other considerations every person of every creed, culture, religion (or not) and race, is entitled to know whatthey are eating. Labelling represents a basic human right to make an informed choice about what you feed yourself and family. It also represents a connection to the food you eat and where it really comes from. The industry and its supporters in the biotechnology industry do not agree. They oppose [49] mandatory labelling, some even oppose voluntary labelling and in some cases the scientific press has come out against any form of labelling. In all cases the drivers behind GMO's have attempted to sue [50] or otherwise rollback laws which impede the implementation of their technology. The industry position has nothing to do with confusing the people it sees as consumers. It has everything to do with pulling every dirty trick they can think of, to ride roughshod over any opposition [51] to GMO's. Labelling is also opposed [52] because the industry then cannot control where you're hard earned ends up. They also **know,** given a straight and fair choice, people will always opt for non-GM alternatives. In a sensibly run world this would mean food produced as it should be, through organic and permaculture systems. Notions which represent the exact opposite [53] of everything GMO's stand for. On top of this, I'm willing to bet hitherto the reader had no idea of the extent to which GMO's are intertwined with agriculture, food production and processing in general.[54] We now have a ridiculous position whereby we are confronted with the products of a technology which nobody asked for, has a dubious and dishonest history, is irreversible in terms of impacts on health and the environment, is regulatorily challenged and overall does not stand up to any real analysis or objective assessment. By itself, this should make you disgusted and furious enough to understand the flat out frustration behind songs as amazing as this belter from New Model Army [55]. Angry, your teeth should be itching, you should be livid; you should be spitting for and baying for blood!

The proponents for GMO's are continually regurgitate the myth and downright lie that GE in agriculture is merely the next step onwards from processes which began some 10-12,000 ya. Truly, the crops grown and animals reared today have little in common with those of just a few hundred ya, but this is not the result of GE. Humanity has been manipulating beneficial traits within a given species or family of animal for millennia. In cross and selective breeding genes from different species would be incompatible and so genetically speaking the organism is not viable. Putting it succinctly, if the combination of genes does not work then the organism does not survive. In evolution, various biological safeguards exist to stop the transfer of genes between different species. The science behind GM foods enables the industry itself to circumvent such safeguards and we are supposed to be OK with this activity. Outside of the microbial world geneticists had never knowingly and precisely combined genes from different species. And even then science only knew something was going on with microbes by observation. For the agencies which do not see the difference between GE and selective or cross breeding, the former merely accelerates naturally evolved processes. This position ignores the instant rate of change to the organism's genome. A precise genetic alteration may have supreme significance or it may have none at all, or a position between the two extremes may present itself. The truth is we simply don't know. Perhaps, many rapid genetic changes to the crops we grow to feed ourselves could in themselves create a GM foods or genetic cocktail effect [56] (see chapter seven) in the natural world. Whereby, exposure to a variety of different GM foods could cause effects which may not happen with exposure to a single variety. Such a possibility is directly comparable to the cocktail effect [57] known to exist for exposure to industrial chemicals. Furthermore, the agencies which are touting GM foods are the same agencies which created the chemicals [58] implicated in the hypothesised cocktail effect. Yet, we just don't know with any certainty what the future long term consequences of unfettered GM foods could be. In the interest of basic common sense and knowledge of the alternatives, you have to at least ask if the risk [58] is worth it. I say it isn't.[59]

A similar line of reasoning permeates through the thought process of those who support nuclear power. They will say radioactivity is an entirely natural phenomenon as well as a useful scientific tool, which is completely correct. Yet it never ceases to amaze me how much supporters of nuclear power downplay the very real risks of employing it. They do not bat an eyelid at the environmental impact [60] of uranium mining even when it is near or in areas of outstanding natural beauty.[61]They care not a jot if the land the mines are situated on belongs to indigenous people. Disasters such as Chernobyl and Fukushima are conveniently ignored or downplayed too. As far as the reactors themselves are concerned nuclear supporters ignore the reality of accelerated nuclear reactions in the reactor core. As with GMO's they ignore that radioactive elements including plutonium only exist in the concentrations they do because of the process itself. In the world of GMO's the only reason opposition exists is because of the technology and its application. In a nuclear free world we would not even be discussing nuclear issues because these elements would be where they belong. They would be in the uranium ore still steadily decaying away into other elements. Plus, we would not have to worry about the dozens of dangerous radioactive elements produced by the nuclear reactions themselves. Exactly the same holds true for GMO's in agriculture. They are both an equivalently dangerous and self-inflicted disaster of the capitalist systems own making. Supporters of nuclear power also choose to ignore the irrational subsidy [62] the nuclear industry enjoys. Just as they ignore the huge subsidies big agriculture (see chapter six) enjoys **and** the huge amounts of cash tied up in GMO's. This is our money and financial resources which has been stolen from our collective pockets. In this frame it is cash which should be spent on developing real, healthy and sustainably grown food, i.e. agriculture based on organic and permaculture systems. Furthermore, nuclear power is well known nuclear to generate the material needed for nuclear weapons [63]. Here in the UK we also have the insanity of what is even being suggested at Hinckley Point, in the South West of England. A nuclear white elephant, which will tie this country into various problems which I cannot go into here, are other issues supporters of nuclear power tend to ignore.

Returning to GMO's! Over the two decades from 1985 to 2015 the number of GM licenses granted has steadily increased. At time of writing no new licenses have been granted in the EU since 1998 [64], likely this will change as 2020 approaches. It **cannot** be understated; the onus will be on the peoples of the world to take control of this issue. It is the only way we are to have any hope of stopping this for good. To my mind failure (in combination with climate change, perpetual global war and nuclear proliferation) is simply to horrific an alternative to contemplate. As an absolute minimum any future which embraces GMO's is doomed to failure and total collapse. GMO's in agriculture represent a future I want absolutely nothing to do with. If climate, war, food and nuclear issues are not resolved and we embrace GMO's I can honestly say, I am glad I don't have children. In this context the question is obvious, *"do you want GM crops or not?"* Speaking personally, I want to live in a world free from GM foods and where as much effort as possible is directed toward undoing the damage already done. You, the reader, your friends, your family and members of the community you live in, can be assured in very near future you are going to be forced to make a decision and then answer the question. Along with every other question hitherto raised, I reiterate there is no reversal option, the central dogma of molecular biology holds true at a genetic level as much as it does with the environment. Since the end of 20th century, the adoption of GM crops has increased but is facing resistance—[65] all over the world. Additionally, as more people wake up to the reality of what GMO's **really** mean, such resistance can only continue.

Without a doubt, increased public awareness is directly correlated with increased resistance and as such, it is little wonder Africa_and Asia-are next in line. Given the events in Zimbabwe in late 2017, I fully expect the circling vultures to try it on there too. The Philippine Islands is a major front in the fight to stop further encroachment on the part of the GM food and seed companies. The authorities in those Islands have listened to reason and have as of 2015 rejected [66] new crop trials. This rejection appears to include the golden rice engineered to produce vitamin A. As things stand the Islands are left with existing GM crops namely a variety of Bt cotton, the main non-food GMO grown in Asia. Sadly, as of early 2016 [67,] it seems the Philippine authorities have to some extent caved in to corporate pressure. Given the nature of the current regime, I guess I should not be surprised. I hope the resistance to the technology continues and I hope the experience can be transplanted to any European activity. The uptake of GM crops appears to correlate with regimes with dubious records in the rights and justice department, another factor supporters of GMO's tend to ignore, deny or dismiss. On top of this, thousands more patent applications are in the pipeline. Plants are being engineered to produce everything from folate to

93

prescription drugs and vaccines. Overall, government institutions are in bed with the GM industry and this liaison will have devastating consequences for all of us unless the relationship is curtailed.

Resistance to GM crops occurs because they offer **no** clear cut benefit and the rhetoric does **not** match the reality on the ground. A bit like the waffle around cuts and austerity spouted forth by the establishment political parties here in the UK. They **all** say they will work for our best interests but all carry on as before, certainly in the cuts department at any rate. As with GMO's it is somehow the fault of people like yours truly for pointing the dichotomy out. The whole GMO notion also elicits a natural response in the pit of the belly to anyone who joins up all the issues intrinsic to the technology and how it is applied. Resistance also occurs because the alternatives consistently outperform the GM and monoculture counterpart. Alternatives also have **none** of the systemic issues directly connected to GE in agriculture. As 2020 approaches, the questions around GMO's will continue. The rhetoric is not matching the reality on the ground. They are **not** delivering on their promises **and** their long term environmental impact has yet to be considered. As usual the drive for profit above **all** else, includes the systems which support life on Earth and the fabric of life itself is the prime and only objective. Other factors have been relegated to the position of cost free (at least for the GM food industry) externally. Since the 1990's there have been thousands of patent applications to the US patent office and many thousands more with equivalent offices around the world. Thus we are presented with a principle argument against GMO's and the construct which applies them. In short how can it be right for any agency to place a monetary value on any organism, or its characteristics, GM or otherwise? Patents are one massive revenue stream for the life science and biotechnology industries. The practice of granting patents also called bio-piracy (see chapter six) has inflicted terrible financial hardship, and disrupted farming practices which have been established and successful for hundreds if not thousands of years. The corporate ownership of both seeds and the herbicides which enable them to grow into plants represents a clear grab for control of the global food supply. If you think I am being alarmist or am somehow making this up then you definitely need to keep reading. The next chapter will provide an overview of what happened when the first commercially grown GM crop, for human consumption became available and will explain exactly what is meant by the term GMO in a real world context. So here it is the flavr-savr tomato.

Chapter 5: The Flavr-Savr Tomato

The tomato fruit has a lineage stretching back some 1300 years. The earliest recorded evidence of human cultivation lies with the Aztec civilisations of central and Latin America. The centres of productivity were what are now Peru, Ecuador, Chile and Bolivia. Likely, other cultures were cultivating tomatoes [1] well before the rise of the Roman Empire. One strand of evidence ends with the indigenous peoples of what is now Mexico. The truth is we simply don't know where the first tomato crops were grown. The European conquistadors discovered the tomato as they were engaging in their orgy of rape, religious genocide, pillage, torture, enslavement, and desecration which annihilated all indigenous cultures in Central and South America. As an example of historic bio-piracy (see chapter 6), tomatoes were stolen from the Americas and first cultivated in Southern Europe in 1540. By the 18th century tomatoes were well established in the Mediterranean regions of Europe, particularly in Spain. The plant belongs to the solanaceae [2] (nightshade) plant family which also includes potatoes, aubergine and sweet peppers. The tomato fruit itself is a rich source [3] of various vitamins and minerals. Tomatoes are also rich in an anti-oxidant and a carotenoid compound called lycopene [4]. The compound is able to neutralise the free radical compounds which are implicated in a variety of cancers. Overall, tomatoes are good stuff, surely another reason to leave them well alone. As this chapter will impart the life science and biotechnology industries disagree. The tomato fruit is one of humanities most important staple food crops. As of 2016 global production of tomatoes is between 130 [5] and 160 million tonnes. About two thirds of this figure comes from four regions, the EU, India, the US and

China. Spain is the largest single producer of fresh tomatoes, so I will not be surprised to see a push for GM tomatoes there. The global tomato business is massive; the monetary value is measured in dozens of billions of dollars. The GM industry would like a slice, likely all of, that particular pie. Under the insanity of the current food distribution system the majority of these tomatoes accumulate thousands of food miles [6]. The tomatoes are transported between multiple destinations. They are ferried between, producer, distributor and retailer. Often the same consignment is moved several times before it reaches its final destination. Equivalent figures apply for pretty much every mass produced food you can think of. Only locally sourced foods which most of us cannot afford or access do not accumulate food miles in this manner. The flavr-savr tomato has a dubious honour. It was the first GM foodstuff to be developed for marketing direct to the human food chain. It came into being in 1994, at around the time the first GM soya crops were being trialled in the US. So what is it and where did it come from?

What Is The Flavr-Savr Tomato?

When fruits ripen they undergo radical changes in their biochemistry. We see these as a deepening of colour and experience them as improvements in taste. From a general nutritional perspective ripe fruits contain more nutrients than those which are not. When tomatoes ripen a hydrocarbon gas called ethylene [7] (C_2H_4 ethene) begins to accumulate inside the tomato. A hydrocarbon is any compound which contains only atoms of hydrogen and carbon. As a hydrocarbon ethene is produced in combustion reactions and as a product of catalytic cracking in crude oil refining. As a chemical it belongs to a family of organic compounds called the alkenes, [8] of which it is the simplest. In fruits such as tomatoes, apples or pears ethylene functions as a ripening_[9] hormone. From the fruits perspective ripening represents profound changes in physiology by chemical means. The most obvious sign of ripening is the colour change. In tomatoes the characteristic change in colour from green to deep red is caused by the accumulation of lycopene. Mass produced tomatoes are picked before they begin to ripen, at the mature green or breaker point in their growth. Supermarket [10] fresh tomatoes have been ripened artificially by blowing a stream of ethene gas over them. At a temperature of 20°C the tomatoes are treated with the gas for 12 to 18 hours. Tomatoes directed for canning or pureeing are allowed to start maturing. They are then treated with an ethylene containing compound such as ethephon [11] or ethrel [12]. Both of these compounds also act as pesticides. The tomatoes are handled in this way because they simply would not survive if transported and distributed already ripened. The same is true in general terms for fruits overall. If you are looking to understand why so many ostensibly ripe tomatoes taste like cardboard, then this reality presents one reason. So instead of taking stock as to how tomatoes and other crops are grown, and reorganising in a sustainable direction, GE is touted as the answer to a problem of the systems own making. No change there then!

The objective behind developing the flavr-savr (AKA CGN - 89564-2) tomato was to develop a GM food stuff which could be picked after it had ripened and be transported without bruising or spoiling. The notion of intertwining food production, distribution and final destination was completely absent from the collective thinking of those behind the novel tomato. The entire corpus of official reasoning pertaining to GM tomatoes is framed in industry terms. It is all about maintaining profits and keeping costs down, and not about sustainability, biodiversity or food security. The flavr-savr tomato was developed by a biotechnology firm called Calgene, which was based in California and a subsidiary of (drum roll please); yup you've got it, the Monsanto Chemical Company. The catalyst for the work which led to the GM tomato was the workings of an enzyme called polygalacturonase (PG), which breaks down the pectin (a polysaccharide [13]) in the cell walls of the tomato fruit. The cell wall is a structure found in plant cells, algae, fungi and bacteria. It provides cohesion, structure and support to the organism in question. Pectin is a structural molecule and is made in the cell in a structure called the Golgi apparatus.[14] Once made; pectin is transported to the cell wall and then secreted into the cells which make it up. During ripening PG breaks down the pectin and the less PG produced in the tomato, the slower is the breakdown of pectin, meaning cell walls take longer to break down. In other words the less PG, the longer the tomato stays harder for. The PG enzyme contributes to the ripening process by making the tomato softer. On the other side of the coin as the tomato ripens it becomes more prone to infection by fungi. At this point the flavr-savr tomato comes into the proceedings. An anti-PG enzyme inhibits the activity of the naturally present PG form, without interfering with the ripening process. The pectin takes longer to breakdown and the cell wall stays cohesive for longer than it otherwise would have. So the flavr-savr tomato was engineered to remain solid and ripe for as long as possible. Another enzyme called Aminoglyocoside 3-Phosphotransgerase [15] II, inserted into the genome worked as an anti-biotic. In commercial settings most tomatoes are picked whilst they are still un-ripened and when no PG enzyme is detected inside the tomato. The anti-PG enzyme is still used and patented by Monsanto today, in the production of canola and cotton. It functions in a similar manner as applied to the flavr-savr tomato. Whether the gene which codes for the enzyme comes from the tomato plant, I have yet to determine.

The geneticists at Calgene were seeking to inhibit the accumulation of PG by inserting an antisense [16] gene, (the GOI) into the genome of the tomato. These genes function by silencing the expression of a particular gene. They can be seen as the opposite of a given gene which cancels out its expression. So the antisense gene in the flavr-savr tomato worked against the expression of the PG enzyme. The anti-sense gene was developed from those which code for the expression of the PG enzyme itself. It works against the natural expression of the PG enzyme. Calgene began developing the flavr-savr tomato in 1984. About two years after substantial equivalence became official FDA policy. In 1992 the flavr-savr tomato was deemed both safe to eat **and** to have no adverse impact on the environment. The reader can be assured the individuals who came to the conclusion did not have the necessary credentials to conclude it. The time scale ought to give some indication of the expertise and finance necessary to develop a GE crop. It costs the biotechnology industry an average of $136 million [17] to develop each trait in each new GMO it creates. Even under the banner of substantial equivalence, it takes an average of 3-5 years to get a GMO through the regulatory process. In contrast the certification process for organic food (food grown as it should be) costs peanuts in comparison. The organic certification process also depends on the crop or animal in question. We are talking hundreds or thousands of currency units. The certification process is not generally subsidised and so the cost is front loaded to the grower, which can only act as a deterrent. Looking at the sums of money involved with GMO's, it seems beyond obvious that a core driver behind it all is the need for a return on the investment. Imagine for a second if the organic / permaculture sector enjoyed a fraction of the cash tied up with GMO's. Imagine what could be done! Sadly, we do not live in such a world; we have the opposite state of affairs. For example, the UK government [18] announced in late November 2017, billions of pounds are to be ploughed into biotechnology, pharmaceuticals, robotics and artificial intelligence. This is UK taxpayer's money which should be, for example, ploughed into genuinely sustainable agriculture and meaningful solutions to climate change.[19] I would also argue the British elite have stolen enough from the population under the banner of austerity. It misses the point, but the billions mentioned here really ought to come from that pile of stolen cash. Still it goes to show what people who support and profit from GMO's are in bed with, so it's not all bad. If you're looking you can see it for what it is, pure and unbridled theft. In the early 1990's, the GM lobby needed the flavr-savr tomato to deliver the financial goods. Thankfully it didn't. If it had the transgenic tomato would have catalysed equivalent activity in other foodstuffs. And today in 2018 GMO's would be much more established than they currently are. As a minimum Calgene were looking forward to a share of the US tomato market, worth between three and five billion US dollars. Growing tens of millions of tomatoes every year represents a huge amount of turnover, which of course makes the fruit a staple food. The tomato was also selected because it can be engineered relatively easily as compared to other fruits. These are the global realities of big agriculture (see chapter six). They coalesce into the real reason for GM tomatoes in particular and GMO's in general. The industry seeks to profit from agriculture which already exists **and** wants to take control of production, into the bargain. This is occurring on a global scale and all other considerations are an exercise in lies and distraction.

The whole point of the flavr-savr tomato was to control the expression of the gene which codes for the PG enzyme. The objective was to engineer a delayed ripening trait in the tomato, which stays fresher in its ripened state for longer. As it travels through the labyrinth of channels which compose the modern food distribution network, the tomato would not ripen, let alone spoil. Non-GM tomatoes are picked before ripening begins and then ripened artificially, with the ethene gas, presumably, when they are at or close to their final destination. If the softening effect of ripening could be halted without interfering with the ripening process then the best of both worlds could present itself. The industry and growers would have a tomato which could be grown and ripened on the vine and then be picked before transportation. The tomatoes could then be distributed as if they were green but with no softening as they ripened. The flavr-savr tomato [20] was developed using the recombinant DNA a.tumefacians technique outlined in chapter three. In the language of the GM food industry Calgene sought to develop "a delayed ripening tomato" which would:

- Have a much longer shelf life.

- Spend growing and ripening before being picked.

- Remain solid for a longer time as it ripened.

- Be less prone to bruising and damage.

- Produce thicker juice or as the industry puts it "have better processing properties".

- Result in tastier tomatoes because they have been growing for longer.

- Produce a tomato with a longer transportation life even after ripening.

The plasmid was the a.tumefacians bacterium which was inserted into the genome of a species of tomato called *Lycopersicon esculentum*. [21] The tomato was engineered to express the anti-PG gene and also had genes from a species of E.coli called K12 inserted into its genome. This form of E.coli is normally found in the human colon.[22] I'm not saying real human E.coli bacteria were inserted into the flavr-savr tomato, even in 2018 that is illegal. However, as I said in chapter four, the industry sees nothing sacrosanct about the genetic code, it doesn't care where the genes come from or to what purpose they are set to. And despite industry protestations to the contrary the flavr-savr tomato did have terminator genes inserted into its genome. A sentence which is directly quoted from their own literature imparts *"the terminator sequences were from the tml gene and the transcript 7 gene from the octopine-type 1 plasmid pT1A6 from a.tumefacians"*. None of this is supposed to matter; the flavr-savr tomato was grown for five seasons over the years 1988 until 1992. From the industries perspective, the plants remained genetically stable, meaning no unforeseen traits expressed themselves. And no HGT or other forms of genetic migration or interaction occurred. As chapter eight explains humanity has been growing food for about ten thousand years. Five years is nothing like enough time to assess the genetic stability or environmental suitability for a GMO. This is where the HGT and cystic fibrosis mentioned in chapter two comes into play. Supporters of GMO's absolutely down-play the real risk inherent to the organisms they create. Each GMO has the same genome, but each is a separate entity and there are millions of individual GMO's in existence at any given time. Cystic fibrosis is caused by one mutation, a mutation which has devastating consequences for the individual affected. All it takes is one mutation from one organism to be passed on or find a way to be passed on via the processes discovered by Gregor Mendel (see chapter one). Again as Jeff Goldblum categorically states in Jurassic Park, "life will find a way". Such an eventuality may well be remote, then again it may not, but it does not even exist in other forms of agriculture. The laws of probability are clear, on a long enough timeline; something somewhere will eventually go wrong. GMO's represent an irreversible technology and when something goes wrong, one cannot turn the clock back. This alone is enough for this writer to oppose it and embrace the PP, mentioned throughout this book, especially when it is set against organic and permaculture systems. The drivers behind GMO's see things in opposite terms. On the back of the results obtained from the field trials, the flavr-savr tomato gained approval for human consumption. If the flavr-savr tomato had worked, further GMO's produced and marketed by Calgene and others would have been in the offing. It would have meant, for instance GM papaya, GM cotton and the SDA soy bean mentioned in chapter three would now be the norm **and** it would have happened without FDA approval. Once one variety of a given plant has been approved, any others which carry the **same** gene or are engineered by the same company do **not** need approval. Such is the insidiousness of substantial equivalence. Thankfully, things did not pan out as they expected. The tomato was a complete failure and plenty of investors in GE lost tonnes of money, which is always good to hear!

What happened with the Flavr-Savr Tomato?

In October 1992 the GM tomato plant was approved by the US department of Agriculture [23] (USDA). According to them, the PG antisense flavr-savr tomato is not a plant-pest risk **and** the flavr-savr *"tomato is as safe as other commonly consumed tomatoes"*. Alternatively, the flavr-savr tomato is "substantially equivalent" to all other tomatoes. In the eyes of the GM industry and its supporters, the transgenic tomato requires no additional regulation. Furthermore, Calgene itself asked [24] (read lobbied) the US FDA to approve its GM tomato. Calgene and their backers pushed the FDA to declare the flavr-savr tomato as safe for human consumption. The FDA acquiesced to this demand, as far as the industry and the regulatory authorities are concerned, the position is clear. The flavr-savr tomato and by association other GM crops are perfectly safe and that is final. In this oxymoronic paradigm, GMO's require no more regulation than their non-GM counterpart. They require no special risk or environmental assessment before they are released into the real world. The already proven workable alternative (read organic and permaculture systems) were as usual not even considered. Even food additives undergo a modicum of testing before they become part of your diet. Not so then with GMO's and not so now either. Even before the first GMO's were trialed or even engineered, the proponents of GM technology have always adopted the same cavalier attitude to any form of criticism, no matter the evidence presented or other objections to the contrary.

As of 2017 there is no statutory testing regime for GMO's in the food we eat anywhere on the planet. The proponents of GM foods want us to think this is perfectly acceptable too. Leaving aside any of the concerns and points raised hitherto in this writing, at a basic human level, surely such a position violates common sense. A scientist called Belinda Martineau [25] who was a fervent supporter of the whole GM endeavour and one of those involved in creating the flavr-savr tomato sums it up perfectly. *"Calgene's tomato should not serve as a safety standard for this new industry, no single genetically engineered product should"*. She goes on to impart, in the true spirit of objective science and the PP, [26] *"simply proclaiming these foods are safe where there is no scientific evidence to the contrary, is not the same as saying extensive tests have been conducted"*. Overall, when I look at GMO's and the way it is communicated, I argue and proclaim the supporters and drivers behind it are anti-scientific. Any proposition, in the scientific arena which is **not** thoroughly assessed, **not** tested and then **measured** against objective criteria **and** compared to alternatives, is **not** by any benchmark scientific, how can it be? It's like me saying the sky is going to be green tomorrow, and expecting you to agree with me, even though it has never happened before and the only evidence for it happening is my peer-reviewed say so. No research on the long term health and safety impacts or safety of the flavr-savr tomato has, as far as I know, ever been carried out. In 1993, before the first flavr-savr tomatoes were even harvested a lawsuit against the FDA was successful. It compelled the administration to release tens of thousands, (44,000 [27] to be precise) of pages, concerning the approval of the novel tomato. Scientists in the employ of the FDA but not connected to either biotechnology or their political paymasters, warned repeatedly about the health risks of GMO's in general and the flavr-savr tomato in particular. All of these considerations were as usual ignored. So you can imagine where the environment lay on the industries list of priorities. Even as the FDA granted approval for the transgenic tomato, some of its scientists were imparting eating it could cause lesions (the precursor to cancer) in the human alimentary canal. Clearly such concerns were at best marginalised and the flavr-savr tomato got the go ahead. After 10 years of research and development by Calgene the first seeds were sown in California on May 21st 1994. About two years after the initial approval was granted. So after its approval and distribution to retailers, what actually happened and did it work?

Well, the answer to the second part of the question is a resounding no. However, the lessons from the whole story are of critical importance for the current lay of the land. The whole project was a disaster in the making from the outset. First the engineering itself didn't work. The tomatoes ripened as they were supposed to, but they softened in the same way as non-GM tomatoes do, defeating the object of the whole exercise. The transgenic tomatoes were too soft to transport and started to rot. Following on from here and despite all of the manoeuvrings designed to make the flavr-savr tomato more affordable than those which already existed, the GM tomato failed to make a profit. From a commercial perspective the new tomato was an unmitigated disaster. The parent company effectively bank rolled the whole enterprise. As such, Monsanto who owned Calgene, acted like the corporate vulture it is, and picked whatever carrion it could from the debacle. Monsanto did not take any responsibility, it never does, and neither do any of the other companies involved in GM foods. As far as Monsanto are concerned the whole collapse was Calgene's fault and they acted accordingly. As the whole fiasco played out Calgene found itself on the receiving end of some very costly lawsuits issued by its paymaster. Right at this point, just when the tomato was ready, a double whammy made things even more untenable. First, Flavr-savr production costs began a journey to the outer reaches of the ionosphere. Second, the commodity price of tomatoes collapsed. Thus, in 1997 Monsanto [28] began the ruthless damage limitation characteristic of any commercial entity. Once any capitalist organisation begins to see a particular investment is not going to pay off; it starts to pull the plug on the whole deal. Just as Union Carbide did a runner from Bhopal, Monsanto bought out Calgene under the auspices of breach of contract, citing patent infringement. A position, which anybody who has had any dealings with the GM, life science or biotechnology industries knows all about. As far as Calgene and any other life science or biotechnology enterprise is concerned, I have no sympathy, none at all; this is what happens when you get into bed with the beast. Exactly the same holds true with the madness and criminality intertwined with the self-inflicted and unfolding disaster, AKA known as Brexit. You voted for it, I didn't, I have no love for the EU, but Brexit is even worse, and Brexit voters millions of people told you so, and it's **not** our fault you didn't listen. Similarly, it will be continually recapitulated GMO's in agriculture is about money, astronomically huge piles of filthy lucre. Agencies such as, Monsanto, Syngenta, Dow Chemical and the DuPont chemical company are as their titles make clear chemical companies. All they care about is profit, to them agriculture is just another market and they want to control as much of it as they can. The actors driving yet another system inflicted and ensuing global catastrophe will say and do anything they can to maximise the return on their investment, whether the product is tenable or not. And it is here another kicker comes to the fore. After its failure, in the US the flavr-savr tomato was crossbred by traditional means with much tastier existing varieties. People, then had the option of buying a watered down GM version of the flavr-savr tomato, at a premium rate of course, now guess where the extra cash went? Exactly, back to the industry, truly, a shocking but not surprising display of hypocrisy!

So, from biotechnologies perspective, first and foremost, the tomato did not generate the anticipated financial return. This fact demonstrates exactly the priorities of the whole GM enterprise. The industry literature even repeats and continually reiterates this fact. However, instead of accepting this reality it blames "the organic sector" and "environmental groups" for fear mongering and misleading you as consumers. This shows absolutely what they think of the likes of yours truly, but they are also saying you don't know how to think for yourself. They also see you as a cash cow to exploit, you're a consumer, you are not a person or sentient being, you are a commodity, don't ever forget your place. They are also saying they know best and give us another chance and we'll get it right, whilst at the same time discrediting all other options. They are also saying they are right and the likes of this writer and the hundreds of millions of people in the same ball park and scientists who speak out are wrong. Again the question "who do you believe and why?" becomes supremely relevant. If my assertions are wrong then I am also wrong with the next scenario. Suppose, hypothetically, we have a GM crop which works **and** delivers on its promises Suppose this crop **did** produce high yields, **did** result in less pesticide use, **did** improve biodiversity, **did** use less water, **did** improve the soil, but did **not** deliver a high enough bottom line. Are we really to believe the industry would keep it going? If this were so, the industry would be investing in organic and permaculture agriculture. So, call me Mr Cynical if you must, but I do **not** think biotechnology would keep such a crop going. They haven't paid any attention to systems which already exist, so why should they now? Also, no other strand of capitalism considers these terms, so why should the GM, life science or biotechnology industries? Any individual who thinks the GM food industry would **not** behave in this manner needs to take a deep and objective look at how human activity is organised. In the mid 1990's as now, non-GM varieties of tomato, paste and other derivatives are available. And the consummate demand was clear and present too.

As to what actually happened, the flavr-savr tomato was sold from a mere 2,500 food outlets across California and the US Midwest. The tomatoes themselves could only stay fresh for about ten days longer than the non-GM counterparts. Almost immediately systemic problems presented themselves and from the perspective of a person buying food the flavr-savr tomato:

- Cost about twice the price of the next cheapest variety.

- Showed no discernible difference in taste.

- In some cases failed the taste test as compared to other tomatoes.

- Was still prone to bruising, softening and rotting – just like tomatoes are supposed to be!

All four points would put any sensible person off from choosing the GM tomato. Point four demonstrates even on its own terms, the tomato itself did not live up to expectations. Overall, we have a clear cut inauspicious start for a nascent profit driven industry. Unsurprisingly, sales plummeted, and when 1995 drew to a close the flavr-savr tomato was withdrawn. As of 2015 there is no GM tomato available anywhere in the Western world. However, as of 2017 this could well change [29]. The lessons from the fiasco outlined above have apparently not been learned. The industry is gearing up to release a flavr-savr tomato two. One example [30] is the engineering of tomato plants to produce more of a compound called resveratrol, [31] which is found in grapes, berries and peanuts. It belongs to a family of chemicals called flavonoids. These are believed to be powerful anti-oxidants, anti-inflammatories and boost the immune system. Another compound called genistein [32] is thought to be an anti-oxidant and may or may not have beneficial health [33] qualities. As stated above tomatoes are relatively easy to engineer, grow quickly and produce lots of fruit per plant too. So the industry wants to create new varieties of tomato which can be farmed quickly and to produce synthetic nutrients and pharmaceutical drugs. The industry views these practices as a cheaper and more efficient than making synthetic copies or extracting them from existing sources. In these examples the genes of interest (see chapter three) come from a plant called Arabisopsis thaliana, a species of mustard plant, which is then inserted into the tomato plant genome. The industry has been using a.thaliana since 1987, since then the genome has been a mainstay of GE across the board. Likely, genes from a.thaliana

111

are in other GMO's too. Other genes of interest come from berries, grapes and nuts. The engineered tomato plants metabolism is engineered to produce specific molecules such as those mentioned above. Additional genes from different organisms are inserted into the genome of the tomato, again, violating the species barrier, the genetic code itself, and the common sense of any right thinking person. To quote one of the researchers involved in the project *"The tomato is a wonderful production system. If metabolic engineering is targeted to the end of fruit development, the fruit can serve as a bag in which to accumulate natural products, without impacting yield"*. I think the above quote tells you all you need to know about how the industry and its employees view the wonders of the natural world. The language these people use is in itself problematic and if I'm being kind at best it demonstrates a total lack of respect for life itself. Still it is in keeping with the definition of biotechnology presented in chapter two, so I guess I should not be surprised. And here is yet another reason to oppose the technology. It appears GE tomatoes as a matter of course are well and truly on the cards, if the industry gets its way. Overall, 25 years after the first attempt, unless it is stopped, GM tomatoes could be on to your dinner plate.

Labelling the Flavr-Savr Tomato

A further contributor to the absolute and total failure of the flavr-savr tomato failure beggar's belief! The next part of the story should make you laugh and cry in equal measure. Never forget, the drivers behind GMO's are telling you what is good to eat, they know best, they know better than nature, they have your best interests at heart and they are rubbishing organic and permaculture systems as a matter of course. **Sarcasm alert**, I simply cannot conceive as to why they are taking this position. You the reader need to realise, along with everything else they do, these people lie, cheat and steal for a living. As far as GMO's are concerned **one** bright shining lie is the industry knows what it is doing, it doesn't. Not if you put people, planet, community, sustainability as well as a future worth have first and certainly above generating profit. The whole point about the flavr-savr tomato was to produce a more viable whole fruit. It was supposed to taste nicer, be cheaper to produce, easier to distribute, and was meant to generate a profit for all concerned. It didn't and no GM crop has ever lived up to these basic expectations, never mind notions of pesticide and water use or environmental impacts in general. So in their infinite wisdom Calgene decided to engineer tomatoes more suited to processing, sieving and canning, as opposed for eating whole and fresh. Again this gives an indication as to how big agriculture operates (see chapter six). I'm sure you'll agree engineering a tomato more suited to processing and then marketing it as a fresh wholesome tomato makes perfect sense. Furthermore, the flavr-savr was developed in California but production and distribution was moved to Florida. These are two entirely different regions in the US and in terms of agriculture there are no commonalities. The tomato developed in California was wholly unsuited to the climate and soil of Florida. They also had no defence against pathogens present in a different part of the US. The flavr-savr tomato was more susceptible to disease than it otherwise might have been. Calgene was beset from the outset by levels of incompetence (read deliberate choices) which would cost any individual in a company their job. Such a move just would not happen in a permaculture or organic system.

In the interests of balance and good social science, I am bound to convey that the flavr-savr tomato was labelled as containing GM ingredients. The labelling of the flavr-savr as a GE food explains the current reticence and flat out opposition on the part of the GM food industry to label its products. The GM food industry knows there is resistance and wants to undermine it by any means necessary. This is where substantial equivalence comes from too. They knew there was going to be resistance from the outset. They targeted staple crops because of the huge profits to be made from doing so. Also, as far as they are concerned, once the GMO is in the food chain there is no point in resisting or campaigning because you can't avoid it. They want you to be thinking there is nothing to be done about it, so just don't bother and make the best of it. This is the **real** reason they are opposed to labelling, they know levels of opposition and concern are very high. They know a direct relationship between knowledge and questions exists. As awareness of what the acronym GMO really means increases, so does the opposition. One way to undermine opposition is to oppose labelling. A clear "contains GMO's" label means plenty of people would avoid buying it. Opposing labelling also means GE becomes veiled under even more secrecy, exactly what the industry wants. No labelling means you and I will be even less aware of what we are eating, where the food comes from, how the food was created and what we are financially contributing too. All of these things will impact on their bottom line, which is also why the industry opposes labelling.

Resistance to GM foods is not homogenous; it varies in intensity depending on awareness and circumstances. One could be forgiven for thinking concerns which morph into poorly answered questions, which then further evolve into resistance is a new occurrence. I am pleased to impart it is not; from the outset, questions were already being asked of transgenic organisms. For instance, concerns over the potential for GM plants to contain dangerously high levels of toxic alkaloids (tomatine and solanine) were cited with specific reference to the flavr-savr tomato. This may, or may not be the case, but the point is, the industry dismissed the concerns, and still does when any and all questions or points of view which critique its activity present themselves. Often, their reasoning is framed in terms of questions **not** being scientific or peer reviewed. An alkaloid 34 is any plant chemical which has a physiological effect on mammals. The capsaicinoids which give chillies their kick are an example of an alkaloid and caffeine is another. The psychoactive chemicals inside the opium poppy and the coca plant represent another set of powerful alkaloids. As mentioned previously, the US FDA only revealed concerns over the flavr-savr in 1993 after legal pressure from US advocacy groups. Equivalent levels of pressure are required to expose the skewed nature of much of the science which supports GMO's. None of this stopped the flavr-savr tomato being approved for sale in the UK in February 1996. The position of the British conservative party and their backers on issues as diverse as climate change, human rights, fracking, GMO's, nuclear power and weapons and animal welfare, indicates why this is so. They will vote and push for policies which fatten their collective wallets, irrespective of the cost to you and I or the environment. And it all happens in the face of any evidence to the contrary.

Although as of 2017 no new GM tomatoes have ever been sold in the EU the same is not true of tomato paste. In 1996 [35] a licensed variant of flavr-savr tomato paste was made available through the Sainsbury's and now defunct Safeway supermarket chains. The first I knew about it was a notification from Greenpeace and the only reason it made the news was because of the ensuing non-violent direct action. From the industries point of view GM tomatoes were a total disaster, by 1999 the last cans of flavr-savr paste had been sold. Once people knew it was a GM food, they stopped buying it. The industry insults your intelligence and mine by saying it was fear mongering by a few lunatic extremists, or some such squirrilistic and gerrymandering twaddle. As we have said both the flavr-savr tomato and the pastes made from it were labelled as containing GMO's. The paste derived from the GM tomato cost about 30p (50c) per 170g, whilst the normal puree cost 30p for 140g. This presents another point about the activities of the global food industry; the price is engineered to keep processed and GE food cheaper than the alternatives. Even then the GM variety only sold about 25% more than the non-GM form. The GM flavr-savr paste was positioned to be sold in larger tins next to smaller more expensive tins of non-GM paste. Inequality driven by an individuals or households possession of money will drive the how and where of spending it. The figures for unemployment, housing, poverty and homelessness, amongst other statistics back in the late 1990's did not exactly make one feel proud to be British. In 2015 [36] and early 2018 things are orders of magnitude worse. We live in a time of austerity, characterised by vicious, swinging and totally criminal policies which are systematically and deliberately killing [37] the most vulnerable people. Hundreds of thousands more are condemned [38] to subsistence by food banks. Even leaving such abuse aside, if you're on a budget and you see two prices, be honest which paste are you going to buy? In 1997 both Safeway and Sainsbury's were reporting sales of the GM tomato paste accounted for about 70% of the total, given the context, I can sarcastically wonder why.

By the end of June 1999 GM tomato paste was no longer present on supermarket shelves. The primary reason for product withdrawal was the lack of generated and expected profit. Despite the 25% price reduction and brisk sales, profits were not high enough to make the paste commercially viable. If it had been an organic tomato paste under the control of the same construct, exactly the same withdrawal and stated reasons thereof would have played out. What the industry is less keen to discuss is the impact of increased awareness as to what GMO's are and where they came from. The UK house of commons 39 acknowledges this reality. And not just with transgenic tomatoes. It goes to show, educating and empowering people really does affect profits for big business. As result of a defacto boycott on GM flavr-savr tomato paste, sales dropped. By 1998 sales of GM tomato paste along with profits were in free fall. In short no agency involved in the flavr-savr fiasco made a profit, it did not deliver even on its own terms and the whole enterprise achieved a huge great shining "*NOTHING*". If you are looking for reasons as to why biotechnology despises, rubbishes and attacks the likes of this writer, this is why, we take cash out of their collective wallet and they hate it. Returning to the relationship between science and GMO's and who is anti-science and who is not, the flavr-savr tomato represents an epic fail. In the run up to the approval given by the FDA the tomato was tested on the industries terms. The tomato clearly met their standards because approval was given. Apparently, the flavr-savr did not pass subsequent independent and more stringent safety tests. For example, in 1999 when laboratory animals were fed a diet containing the flavr-savr tomato, some of the population developed erosions (the precursor to ulcers) on the lining of their stomachs. The study authors were compelled on the basis of scientific technicalities to withdraw their findings. The pressure to do so came from scientists in the employ of biotechnology and life sciences. The results from animal experiments must be taken with a pinch of salt because they are generally not representative of the "real world" and at best should serve only as an indicator. However, the GM industry will **always** vilify any research no matter how scientific, which contradicts its own skewed findings. There is no depth to which they will not stoop to discredit and undermine any opposition to what they are doing. It cannot be made clear enough the drivers behind GMO's only consider the science and nothing else. They will attempt to draw you in to pointless debates about the research and obfuscate, obviate and ignore everything else. They are absolutely hell bent on the entire world taking up their technology. They will never ever look in the mirror and will always project outwards, they have done nothing wrong and when things do not work it's not their fault. If they did take responsibility the whole enterprise would collapse, and they know it too. Plus, they will **never** acknowledge these issues only exist because of their technology. It simply does not occur to so many scientists in the employ of this industry that they are at fault. It never occurs to them that the work they are doing is problematic, worse, some acknowledge the questions raised in this book and then carry on regardless! These issues do not exist with permaculture or organic systems, where the expertise of those employed in developing GMO's is so desperately needed. The above chain of events is not an isolated example, it is merely the first. None of this has stopped the industry, quite the opposite has occurred. Despite the failure of the flavr-savr tomato, in the US insect resistant cotton and herbicide soybeans were first grown commercially in 1996. The rest as they say is history. A history steeped in self-created controversy, disinformation, abuse of rights, violation of the code of life, environmental crime and a total disregard for any form ethics, morality or basic humanity. Remember this is an industry which employs scientists who absolutely believe they are doing the right thing. They truly believe their creations will live up to their own expectations, even in the face of total failure. Another word for this behaviour is delusion, I used it in the early 2000's to describe their attitude and I use it now, but with extra bells on. They seem incapable of taking on board the alternatives and view organic / permaculture systems as a hindrance to the progress of science and technology. The people who fund the industry are absolutely profit driven and see GMO's as just another revenue stream. Sadly far too many in the scientific establishment have bought into the nonsense. I believe in the long run this attitude will cost them and science in its widest possible sense dear. Along with those employed in weapons, armaments and the nuclear industry, the corporate science intertwined with GMO's abuses and violates the basic principles upon which science is founded. And it staggers me completely they cannot (or more likely refuse to) see it. The scientists employed by or through biotechnology and involved in creating GMO's are, in my view and experience, blinkered reactionary, scientific zealots to the point of fanaticism. All they seem able to talk about is what the science tells them to. Nothing else seems to matter, I have lost count of the times I have been told *"I'll only debate with you scientifically"*, whatever that means. They continually state extra scientific objections have no merit and should not form the basis of any critique whatsoever. They care not a jot for the abuse of regulatory framework which has facilitated the uptake of the organisms they create. They truly do not know how to think outside of the scientific box, or it's flat out denial or self-serving acceptance. They seem incapable of acting with any form of empathy, logic, consequence, connection or understanding to or with the world, cultures and people around them. They certainly continually fail to comprehend the bigger picture concerning the application of the technology they support. As far as they are concerned once the research has been peer reviewed and published, the debate is over. For them, those of us who oppose are the problem because we happen to question the use of science and the necessity for the technology. Plus these people are absolutely opposed to anything which has the word organic or permaculture attached to it. Supporters of GMO's tend to see everything in purely scientific terms, whereas those who oppose GMO's have a much more holistic and joined up approach. Plenty of scientists say we can assess GMO's on a case by case basis. I say **no**, they will let in by stealth, ban them outright, break up the industry, investigate both individuals and organisations and bring criminal charges where appropriate. I also advocate diverting the cash tied up in GMO's into genuinely equitable and sustainable agriculture. The question again for the reader is to ask who you stand with and why. To see where the blinkered and isolated attitudes come from it is necessary to present an overview of the construct we know as big agriculture.

Chapter 6: Patents, Bio-Piracy, Big Agriculture, Pesticides, Yields And Hunger

As of the 21st Century agriculture is the largest business concern in the world. The exact turnover or indeed profit figures are impossible to quantify. Globally, agriculture generates in its entirety over several trillion dollars annually. Correct me if I am wrong, but we do live in a profit driven world, yes? To remain viable any component of the system must return a profit, if it is going to survive as part of this abnormal and abhorrent economy. Now you may be thinking something on the lines of *"So what? People have to eat and farmers have to get paid, it's a business, what's the problem?"* Well, at this point we can begin to input some of the realities of the construct which is known as big agriculture. If you start to feel concerned then you are eliciting the right response, if not then you need to keep reading. Big agriculture, as with big pharma, indeed as with "big x", is a huge global business oligarch [1] which is analogous to the cartel we know as OPEC. The players in "big agriculture" include names such as Nestle, Bayer, Kraft Foods and Monsanto which you may recognise and others such as Cargill, ConAgra, General Mills and Archer Daniels Midland which you may not. These are huge transnational corporations which control [2] most of the food produced, distributed and sold across the entire planet. They also control the sale and distribution of seeds, pesticides, herbicides and fertilisers. The term big agriculture includes chemical companies such as BASF and DuPont and Dow Chemical. They are all interconnected and intertwined with each other and they all exist to make profit and consolidate their position. The prospect in 2018 of the UK supermarkets

ASDA (part of Walmart) and Sainsbury's merging is yet another example of those manoeuvrings. It is from the organisations which make up big agriculture that GE came to be winging their way toward every single viable organism alive on the planet. By viable I mean the organisms big agriculture seeks to extract profit from. We are supposed to celebrate it all as a great leap forward and you the reader are repeatedly told somehow the likes of me are wrong for standing up to such realities. For these companies the pursuit of GM foods via the biotechnology industry is a global strategy to increase their already astronomically huge and obscenely bloated super normal profits [3]. They will tell flat out lies about or deliberately water down and / or sugar coat what is being done in our name and without our consent. By "our name" I mean every single living person on the planet. It is not an understatement or alarmist to label the big agriculture construct as an organised mafia. The classical definition of a mafia refers to gangs of organised criminals who act ruthlessly in the pursuit of wealth, power and influence. In concept, I see no real difference in organisational structure and concentration of power. The methods may be less brutal, although when it comes to it, they often are not. Death threats [4] against and actual killings of people who call themselves activists of all hues are on the rise all over the world. From journalists who speak out in Malta, to those campaigning against trophy hunting and for conservation in Africa and Asia, back to the draconian laws which exist all over the world, it seems as if war has been declared on those of us who have the audacity and temerity to speak out. In the US big agriculture regularly [5] employs tactics of flat out intimidation and demanding money with the threat of menace or violence when it comes to toeing their line, once you have signed on the dotted line. It all happens in tandem with the consummate pressure brought to bear in the form of lawsuits [6] designed to reinforce their power further. Think I'm wrong? Just as Eric Lungden what he thinks of Microsoft! The intimidation has also apparently extended into regulatory bodies including the US FDA, such that conclusions from the primary literature have been skewed to favour the Industry. I dread to think what happens elsewhere, where perhaps democratic norms are even weaker than they are here in the so called civilised west. Having said all that, the resistance mentioned in chapters four and five, to this kind of depravity is absolutely strong, fertile and growing.

Concentrating Power

The food mafia oligarch controls the global markets for pesticides, seeds fertilisers, and animal feed. The oligarch additionally dictates the how, when and where of the crop varieties grown. It determines the price a farmer can expect per unit of agricultural produce, i.e. the food most of us eat on a daily basis. In short the agribusiness oligarch controls what you eat, the price you pay and the nutritional content of the food itself. I believe this construct needs to be broken up and dealt with in much the same way as the biotechnology and life science industries which have emerged from it. Still not convinced? How do you explain the 2015 furore [7] over the price of milk, or the flagrant lies dressed up as special offers in UK supermarkets? For the record I do not think we should pay an extra 10p for the milk produced by farmers, I believe passionately the industry itself should be paying a fair price at the outset for **all** agricultural produce. This should be paid from the coffers of the oligarch and **not** by the environment, or the growers and producers themselves and certainly **not** from the meagre contents of our wallets. This is merely a foundation for breaking up the whole organisational structure. In a sensible world farmers and growers would be working with each other and the communities they should be supporting. They would have already would cut the middle man we call the supermarket and its associated tentacles entirely. The supermarkets are the benign front end face of the whole global enterprise. These particular stories are trivial in comparison to their behaviour in other areas, but they do exemplify how they operate and what their priorities are. The advent of GM foods has laid out clearly how the agri-business oligarch (big agriculture) has been determining the direction of global agricultural policy for decades. A time scale which begins roughly with the onset of the green evolution mentioned in chapter one. The institutions which make up the big oligarchs are not benign institutions or pillars of the community; they represent the foundations of global capitalism. They exist to make as much cash as they can, however they can and wherever they can, end of story. As the flavr-savr tomato discussed in chapter five indicates GMO's and supermarkets are inextricably linked. If GMO's are ever adopted wholesale, the supermarket chains will be the main retail outlets. After all, they are **all** as of 2017 selling food products made with substances derived from GM plants, which does not have to be declared (see below). They are also **all** selling meat, fish and animal products from animals [fed] feed loaded with GMO's, which does not have to be declared or labelled [8] at all. The question again presents itself, *"who do you want to be running and organising food and its distribution and what types of organisations do you want your increasingly hard earned cash going to?* So, playing devil's advocate, what is wrong with having a few transnational corporations controlling most of the global food supply?

The whole market is controlled by a few transnational corporations who work together to fix prices for their mutual benefit at the expense of all other actors. For example, in 2007 mergers and acquisitions between Nestle, Tyson Foods, Pepsi Cola and Kraft allowed for the creation of four multinational food processors who sold $23 BN [9] worth of processed foods, **each** in the US and Canada **alone**. In 2016 an equivalent merger [10] between Bayer and Monsanto would similarly concentrate economic power and make shareholders, hedge fund managers and their ilk, considerably better off than they already are too. In 2015 between them Monsanto and Bayer generated some $60 billion in turnover. Should this merger pass, and it is on the cards, the new conglomerate [11] will have control over 24% of the world pesticide market, 29% of the seed market and 70% of the global cotton seed market. Sadly the merger proposal has in spring 2018 been given the green light. This is not an isolated example, identical mergers [12] between the big players in agriculture are definitely on the way. The total value of such mergers is measured in hundreds of billion dollars and they can only concentrate further big agricultures control of the global food supply. According to those who support GMO's such manoeuvrings are of no concern and so, as usual, they are ignored. Environmental and economic crime, abuse, slavery, devastated and impoverished communities, destruction and outright disaster go hand in glove with big agriculture [13]. The system is characterised [14] by soil erosion, excessive pesticide use, eutrophication, ocean anoxia (dead zones), algal blooms, intensive production and animal husbandry methods and now GE. All of this to sustain the cash crop and/or mono cultured systems which generate the huge profit margins for the business. For example, in 2015 [15] the US FDA gave approval for the first GM animal for human consumption. The animal in question is a GM salmon created by a biotechnology company called Aqua Bounty [21], (see chapter seven).

Bananas, Legalised Theft on a Global Scale?

A practice known as bio-piracy (theft, mentioned in chapter two) is hardwired into the GM food construct. It is one method by which the industry maintains its profits. This wholly disgusting practice of stealing the intellectual property rights of indigenous peoples, farmers and growers wherever they are located ought to be illegal under international law, sadly the opposite holds true. In two sentences bio-piracy involves the exploitation of a naturally occurring biochemical, protein or genetic trait for commercial gain without paying full compensation to the community or culture from which the substance or gene comes from. The process is facilitated by the World Trade Organisation (WTO) and other corporate talking shops under the banner of Trade Related Intellectual Property [16] Rights (TRIP's) legislation. [17] The text book example is the plundering of beneficial traits from the Indian Neem [18] tree. A more recent example concerns the behaviour of the biotechnology industry around GM bananas; on those alone I could write another book. At the outset, one cannot deny reality; the banana is a staple food crop for about 500 million people in Africa and Asia and is vital for their future security. Entire fields have been wiped out by insects carrying disease. In response to decimated harvests bananas have been engineered to produce their own pesticides [19] courtesy of genes from sweet peppers. It doesn't work with the Bt cotton mentioned previously, so there is no reason to suppose it will work with bananas. Similarly, it will not work for those which have been engineered [20] to boost their mineral, nutrient or vitamin content. We need to address why so much food on this earth is just not fit for purpose. There are plenty of bananas being grown all over the tropics which are loaded with nutrients. And it is from these cultivars the various G'sOI for the GM bananas are stolen. Yet, there is no way I'm going to tell farmers in other parts of the world who have lost everything what to grow **or** how to grow it. In the long run, GM bananas are not the answer and I say that for the reasons mentioned in this writing and plenty more besides. Plus, the farmers themselves will, once again, be taken to the cleaners by those they see as their benefactors. The answer **is** to promote biodiversity and sustainability in food production as well as minimise pesticide and water use overall. The answer is **not** to create the kind of circumstances which allow pathogenic microbes to destroy the livelihoods of millions and compromise the food security of entire regions of planet Earth. Mono-cultured systems do **not** cause disease, but they certainly facilitate it, when disease hits; its spread is pretty much inevitable, which is **not** the case with organic and permaculture systems. The classic examples are Irish and Highland potato famines of the 1840's. The biological cause was a microbe called Phytophthora infestans. [21] This highly aggressive bacterium can devastate entire crops in a matter of hours, in much the same way as has happened to the banana crops in Asia and Africa. The microbe was helped in its destruction because Ireland was growing just two varieties of potato.[22] This policy was encouraged because the varieties concerned were high yielding, meaning more profits. Again, exactly what happens with most of the food crops grown on our planet. When the P. infestans [23] microbe arrived in 1845/6 the current crop was utterly wiped out as were the next three harvests to 1849. British government policy toward Ireland further augmented matters; they left the population to their own devices. The social and population upheaval was exacerbated by the ideas of The Reverend Thomas Robert Malthus (1766-1834). He believed starvation was inevitable and the lower classes (due to their fecklessness and proclivity to breed) should bear the brunt of its occurrence. Ideas which make perfect sense to our lords and masters and mistresses too! The onset of the famine was also used as a political tool by the British establishment to crush resistance to the Empire. Consequently, over a million people starved and millions more were forced to migrate. A similar blight affected the highlands of Scotland; it killed hundreds of thousands and caused equivalent levels of social upheaval. During the famine other regions such as South America which grew different varieties of potatoes were relatively unaffected. These varieties were used to restock Irish and European farms after the famine. If you are thinking things have improved since then, take a look at what the UK government is doing as regards Yemen. If more varieties of potato had been grown and if the politics of the time had been different, likely the famine would not have occurred. It certainly would have been much less intense. Similarly, if there was more diversity in banana cultivation; crops would be less vulnerable to disease. And if the organisation and objectives of big agriculture were modelled on permaculture and organic systems, there would be more diversity and resistance in the global banana crop. Despite the stated good intent and laudable objectives, in the long run GM bananas are just not going to work. Plus, the whole enterprise is being driven by some of the richest people on the planet. The motives of such people are questionable to say the least. GM bananas represent a quick simple fix to a problem of the global food systems own making. As usual, the key drivers behind GM bananas are ignoring the already present low tech alternatives, and rubbishing them into the bargain. Simultaneously, since the mid-1980's thousands of patents have been granted to biotechnology firms all over the world, including those connected with GM bananas.[24] The genes used to engineer the nutrient loaded bananas already exist and are grown the world over, but genes can only be patented when they are seen as a GOI, which is how biotechnology profits from them. So the genes or GOI have been identified and inserted into the genome of the transgenic variety. The point is missed entirely, but as far as I know not one cent of recompense has been paid to the regions [25] of the world, from which the genes of interest are stolen. Aside from a few landmark victories, [26] full compensation has yet to be paid for the majority of the patents granted. The majority world or global south endures the brunt of this theft. It has cost the people who live there, at the absolute very least hundreds of millions of dollars. In tandem with the resistance mentioned previously organisation and fight back is occurring. It will carry on so long as the vultures in biotechnology and big agriculture think they have the right to steal property which does not belong to them. With all of this in mind I am not surprised to read of trials of GM potatoes,[27] funded and developed by the chemical company BASF in both mainland Europe and Ireland.

GMO's The Iraq War, Subsidy and Human Rights

In 2004 at the height of the violence caused by the Iraq war, the Presidential Medal of Freedom was awarded to Paul Bremer.[28] In my view this person along with everyone else responsible for the current catastrophe in the Middle East is guilty of crimes against humanity and should be tried and then ideally locked up forever. This particular mandarin of US genocide was head of the Coalition Provisional Authority (CPA [29]), for 14 months. His title "American Pro-consul for Iraq" says it all. From 1990/1 Iraq, was and still is, a flat out colonial, expansionist and resource driven war, as they all are. The only objective was plunder the whole country and cement US, Saudi and Israeli power in the Middle East, ditto with Russia in Syria. The CPA was the agency set up to administer the disastrous and deliberately incompetent Iraq occupation. If the reader is looking for some understanding as to where organisations like Da'esh come from, the Iraq war is one place to start. Another good place to start looking would be the Red Army invasion of Afghanistan in 1980. Ancient Iraq formed one foundation of the Fertile Crescent.[30] From where wild wheat and other essential crops originated, crops which went on to form the foundation of the Neolithic revolution, again see chapter eight. In 2004, during the chaos, carnage and free for all mass murder which underpinned the occupation, the CPA was seeking to determine the future of Iraqi farming. The Iraqi people and farmers themselves had no say in the future proscribed for them, the baseline of **any** imperialist venture. Prior to the 2003 invasion and subsequent occupation Iraqi farmers kept and distributed seeds as they had done for hundreds of generations previously. This age old practice also occurred in the face of an absolutely criminal sanctions regime, brokered principally by the governments of the US and UK. The sanctions are reported to have deliberately killed about a million people, half of them children. And according to the then US secretary of state Madelaine Albright, [31] the price was worth it. Well alright, no drama, OK then! During his 14 month tenure Paul Bremer issued about 100 orders or statutes. All of them were designed to transfer ownership of the Iraqi state, its oil and other resources and infrastructure, wholesale to US corporations. No other country, even the UK even got a look in, even on its own terms a one-sided special relationship indeed. Two months before the invasion George "dubya" bush issued executive orders [32] giving the US absolute authority in this endeavour. These orders were renewed every year until 2008, as far as I know Obama has not rescinded them and Trump certainly hasn't. These orders exist to colonise Iraq and enslave the Iraqi people. As far as GMO's are concerned Paul Bremer is quoted as saying "farmers shall be prohibited from re-using seeds of protected varieties". This forms the bedrock of order [33] 81 which is also known as the plant variety protection (PVP) order. It opened the door for patented seeds and gave the green light for the imposition of GMO's on Iraqi agriculture. Under those auspices Iraqi farmers would have been forced to buy everything from big agriculture, including fertiliser and pesticides. Plus, growers would have been boxed into the kind of agreements [34] which are stoking so much resistance in the rest of the world. Iraqi farmers would have been sued for deviating from the agreements, which are exactly the same as those the likes of Monsanto celebrate as both necessary and essential. Farmers would have been compelled to pay a premium for the new seeds and saving them for next year's harvest, would as usual have been forbidden. They would also have been forbidden to cross breed other varieties and grow them on their land.

Conversely, the corporations would have been able to use these varieties as they see fit and be required to pay no compensation. All of this flew in the face of the original 1970 Iraqi patent law, a statute which forbids private ownership of genetic and biological resources. At time of writing amendments to the 1970 law allowing exactly that are enshrined in Iraqi law. Until they are repealed the country will never have genuine food security. The nightmare situation now playing out (entirely caused by decades of intervention and support for despotism) makes such statutes a moot point, but the fact is they exist. Never forget, the main drivers behind the whole criminal venture in Iraq were, corporate theft, rape and plunder of the country and its people. The usual vested interests merely allowed their stooge Saddam Hussein to do the same previously. It became official US policy to overthrow their former ally in 1998 [35], and install another pro-western dictator in his place. As of 2012 Iraq is importing some one billion dollars of agricultural produce ever year, in 2017 the Iraqi nation is still importing staple foods from the US. For instance Cargill and Archer Daniels Midland between them export [36] 450,000 tonnes of wheat a year, into a country which should be growing more than enough to sustain itself. Unbelievably, the nation has been stung with a $54 billion dollar war reparations bill to Kuwait, the last tranche of which is due to be paid by the end of 2021. [37] Sarcasm alert! Not bad going for a country which was food self-sufficient prior to 1990/1!

Agribusiness, along with **any** other concern global business wishes to control, enjoys a very generous subsidy [38] from its backers in various governments. These handouts total hundreds of millions of currency units. Consequently, cash and expertise which should be directed toward the alternatives to mono-culture and GMO's sits in the coffers of big agriculture. This structural adjustment is used to price food derived from organic and permaculture systems out of the reach of the majority of the world's population. The system leaves most of us with no alternative but to purchase foods derived from farms connected to the agri-business oligarch. For example, the European CAP subsidy is approximately 40 Billion euros [39] which is about 35% of the entire EU budget. In the US an equivalent subsidy runs into tens of billions of dollars. This cash should be ploughed into alternative strategies. For the future we need an agricultural equivalent of the million climate jobs campaign,[40] and we need it to happen globally [41]. So the next time someone you know asks you why "organic" (meaning real) food is so expensive, you now have an answer. As the UK lurches from one Brexit related disaster to another, the food security of the country can only get worse. And with the scene well and truly set for another drive in the GMO direction, such bleak realities are, on the current path only going to intensify. Big agriculture is a direct threat to global future food security and GM foods will only exacerbate and intensify an already dire and precarious situation. A global implementation will do absolutely nothing to alleviate world hunger; in fact the opposite is more likely. The whole premise of GMO's feeding the hungry ignores the real reasons why hundreds of millions of people all over the world are going without the basic human right to a full belly. Furthermore, GMO's will not provide a solution for hundreds of thousands of people in the Western world who have to make an invidious choice between heating and eating and / or require foodbanks. In 2014 about 2 million UK households [42] were in the same state, in late 2016 the figure is 2.3 million households,[43] a tenth of the total number of registered properties. This obscene, criminal and heart breaking issue will not be solved by the unfettered uptake of GM foods; it will make things a whole lot worse. I have yet to hear from the GM food lobby how their crops are going to alleviate the need for food banks, keep prices down, promote biodiversity and sustainability, encourage healthy eating, and improve the food security prospects of the UK in particular and the rest of the world in general. The role of global agri-business in facilitating the prevalence of food borne diseases as well as the resistance of known pathogens is well documented. Public health is somewhere near the bottom of the list of priorities for the corporations involved. All over the world, they have used their political and economic clout to undermine both the legal frameworks which are supposed to protect us and the environment. The TTIP [44] agreement was defeated by concerted and coordinated effort and NVDA. However, the Trump presidency is doing everything it can to undermine [45] the food safety standards, unfortunately with some success. Tragically, Hilary Clinton would not have been much better. Similarly, as the non-government led by the loathsome Theresa May and her sycophantic stooges continues on its current (highly entertaining), self-destructive path, such standards in the UK will continue to collapse. The furore over chlorinated chicken is just one relatively benign example of what is in the pipeline. If Brexit does actually happen the rules, such as they are, for food processing, intensive agriculture and GMO's will become increasingly weighted toward industry objectives and not the population that these activities are said to serve and benefit.

This point is for any reader who has, or knows someone who has a problem with migrant labour. A migrant is any person who lives and works in a country not of their birth. I don't care how you dress it up, if you have a British passport and you work, or have, in a foreign country, you are a migrant, end of story. The front end of agri-business is your local supermarket and it is almost certain the people who picked and packed those foods were migrants. The same cohort whom as of late 2017 is leaving in droves [46] and I for one can't say I blame them, I would. The basic rights of these human beings who have the same hopes dreams and aspirations as anybody else are violated to a lesser or greater extent the world over. For instance, there are plenty of people in foreign lands working plantations for a daily pittance to pick those lovely clean vegetables and pack them into pretty little packets, which then end up on the supermarket shelf. I'm **not** apportioning blame; we have a black bin bag filled with about 3 months of plastic packaging. The contents represent a reality of cost in terms of food miles, water use, dodgy labour practises and land grabbing. Bottom line, the land those pre-packed vegetables come from does not belong to the supermarket, or big agri-business, it belongs to the people of the country in question. The land should be used to grow food sustainably for the population first and exactly the same should be happening at home too. Plus I'm sure plenty of the people working in the plantations are not doing it through choice. I'm sure the young people would rather be at school or university and others would rather be working their own small holding in cooperation with their peers. The complete antithesis of everything big agriculture represents. It is not much better closer to home; in some areas it is in fact worse. The supermarket supply chains are known to treat migrant labour as little more than modern day slaves, well serfs on a good day. Amongst other profit driven strategies, the flagrant exploitation of these workers allows the supermarkets to

135

undercut smaller scale and / or independent producers. It does **not** mean a good deal for all, it means more wealth and power are further concentrated into the oligarch. It most certainly does **not** mean sustainable food production, how can it? The growers and farmers are not in control, big business is. You can be assured, the more the supermarket chains can remove the competition the more they will behave as the worst kind of organised criminal cartel, a mafia in all but name. For instance, should Brexit carry on as it is, then plenty of people in this country will be forced to work for their benefits. Such a strategy will allow the big players to syphon off the difference between "wages" and "benefits" to their collective bank balance.

Is There Any Good News?

Clearly, in terms of yield and productivity, modern agriculture has garnered great benefits. Unfortunately, there is more to it, if there wasn't I would **not** be writing this book. The environmental, social and human cost has been severe to a point well in excess of criminality. The practices of big agriculture, monoculture and / or intensive farming are known to impact on the environment in which a particular facility is situated. They also have documented detrimental impacts on community cohesion, communities themselves and other businesses which become entangled into its activities. In addition, the negative impacts on other aspects of "the countryside" from tourism and recreation to property values are similarly well documented. For instance, the 2001 foot and mouth[48] epidemic created financial losses for rural communities of between £2-3 BN. The same epidemic is thought to have cost farmers themselves almost £4 BN, about 0.5% of the GDP for the entire country. The series of shortcuts which led to the BSE scandal in the late 1980's are another case in point. We are not talking small beer here and I see **no** credible evidence that GMO's in the food chain **will** preclude future calamities. Increasingly, these agricultural calamities are making the current system evermore untenable. Similarly, with GMO's, costs are legislated toward us and not to those whom created the chaos around us **all**. Think of the extra 10 pence on milk argument presented earlier in this chapter, add a few zeros and you'll get the idea. If you don't think this is true have a look at the implementation of austerity economics and bank bailouts. The peoples of the world did not create such circumstances; we had, and still have, no control over how the economy works, so why are we being expected to pay for the deliberate policy failures of those who do? If we assess the impact of policies such as the green revolution (see chapter one) purely in terms of productivity then it is a resounding success. The figures speak for themselves, in 1960 India produced roughly 10 million tonnes of wheat but by 2012 the quantity was nearer 100 million tonnes. At first sight any sane and rational person will look at such figures and think something on the lines of *"Wow, amazing, what are the activists complaining for? People are getting fed and we have huge surpluses of staple food crops, what's the problem?"* An absolutely fair enough question, the best answer to be given here and now, is *"things just aren't that simple"*. Such figures can be recorded from all over the majority, world or global South; indeed equivalent figures can be cited for the minority world, or global North. However, either way or irrespective of location such figures mask the negative consequences which include:

- Failing to address the question as to why people are still malnourished in a world which has an overall food surplus. Overall, questions and the realities concerning food security and poverty have yet to be addressed by big agriculture.

• Excessive demand for water which is raising the prospect of intense future water shortages. To put it bluntly, if you think the current cycle of conflict based on oil is catastrophic, then when it comes to water, you will see those in charge attempt to drag us all down into new lower depths of depravity.

• Most of the crops grown are of a single variety, depending on the region where the food is grown, hence the term mono-culture. Rice growers could have access to tens of thousands of rice seed varieties [48] which ought be cultivated, yet modern agriculture as of 2017 grows only a maximum of 22 different varieties.[49]

The huge increase in yields across the board has only been possible by the prolific use of pesticides, herbicides and insecticides [50] and big agriculture wants to keep [51] it that way too. The whole range of chemicals involved include some you have probably heard of such as (dichloro-diphenyl-trichloroethane) DDT, [52] but this is but one molecule in a family of chemicals called organochlorine compounds [53]. They number several hundred in total and the environment is awash with them. The negative biological impacts include endocrine (hormonal) disruption and carcinogenesis. From an environmental perspective they are an unmitigated nightmare, [54] they are persistent and so dangerous for several reasons. They are volatile but chemically stable and so are easily distributed through multiple environments. They are not soluble in water but are soluble in lipids (fats and oils), this means they concentrate and bio-accumulate rapidly. Consequently, they travel upward through the planets food chains and webs. Organisms at the top of ecological structures (including ourselves) have hundreds of these chemicals encased in the fat cells of our bodies. They are also known to inhibit the processes which enable female birds to produce solid egg shells. They produce abnormalities in chicks which are equivalent to birth defects in human infants. Generally, they are genotoxic, so they interfere with genetic processes across the board. They can be present in animal (including human) breast milk and are known to traverse the placenta and poison the developing foetus. The devastation of bird populations all over the world was the catalyst which lead to the Rachel Carson book "the silent spring" mentioned in chapter one. In short the organochlorides are *nasty* with a capital "N" and are present in every environment on the planet. The main players involved, (which include Monsanto) in this manufacture, did not stop or curtail production because they developed an environmental conscience. They stopped manufacturing each substance when the target organisms became resistant to its effects. Even today, and in the face of this knowledge, some of these chemicals are still being manufactured. Such chemicals are known as persistent organic pollutants (POPs) and fall under the remit of the Stockholm convention. There are literally thousands of individual pesticide chemicals and they are in turn broken down into a myriad of different categories. Almost all are synthetic, novel and completely alien to the environment. All have some kind of detrimental impact on the biosphere and most are continually cycled through the planet and the life upon it. Furthermore, the same actors involved in GM foods are the same companies [55] who see no problem with the bee killing neonicotinoid [56], insecticides.

The soil which allows plants to grow is undeniably the most important resource on the planet. It takes several centuries to make about one centimetre of soil. As far as human beings are concerned the resource which allows plants to grow is non-renewable. Once a given soil has been degraded it cannot be replaced quickly, natural processes need time and long term stability to regenerate depleted resources. The crops grown today are dependent on fertilisers and other chemicals. When we realise most fertilisers contain chemicals derived from crude oil as part of their make-up, the implication should be obvious. In terms of actual impact on the soil itself the day to day reality is shocking but under capitalism not surprising. For instance, according to the World Wildlife Fund (WWF), Brazil loses some 55 million tonnes [57] of top soil every year. One way or the other such criminal waste and abuse is **NOT** going to carry on. As a species and as a system we are approaching more than several global tipping points. As far as soil is concerned evidence suggests we are approaching end game territory. If the current food system is not removed we are looking at between 60 and 100 harvests [58] before the soil can no longer produce the necessary yields. Hydroponic systems will not able to compensate, a notion which is delusional to a point well passed insanity. We need to be moving away from big agriculture and toward sustainable methods, and we need to be doing it **NOW!**

As a discipline GM is occurring at the frontiers of our scientific knowledge and the science itself is ground breaking. For example, the potential for it to "do good for humanity" through gene therapy is obvious. However, GM crops and animals represent an answer from the construct which has caused the problems in the first place. For instance, big agriculture is a huge contributor to climate change. Modern agricultural practices are responsible for over a quarter of all emissions of greenhouse gases. The principle gases involved are (Carbon dioxide) CO_2 (Methane) CH_4 and the nitrous oxide gases. The real answers to dealing with climate change mean adopting mechanisms which do not emit greenhouse gases (GHG's). For instance, we need to stop wrecking what is left of the rainforests to grow palm oil. There is no point in developing grasses which GHG's from the atmosphere if nothing is done to stop emitting them. GMO's are **not** going to solve these huge systemic global problems, only we the peoples of planet earth can do that. Overall, creating novel transgenic organisms really a complete waste of time money and expertise. They will do **nothing** to solve the problems of our rulers making. For instance:

- Plants or microbes engineered to remove GHG's will serve no long term purpose when the carbon cycle is on the point of collapse. The same is true of all other cycles which make this planet work properly.

- There is no point in developing salt tolerant rice if sea levels continue to rise. The marginal land the rice or other crops are to be grown on could well be underwater or polluted with salt in just a few decades.

- What is the point in such plants when countries such as the UK refuse to embrace renewable energy and the job creation [59] intertwined with it, as a stepping stone to the hydrogen economy?

- What is the point when governments and industry continue to ride roughshod over the objections of their own people by going ahead with fracking, nuclear power and unbelievably even more open cast coal mines [60]?

- There is no point in developing high yielding crop varieties while so much arable land is set aside for biofuels [61] or growing non-essential plants in the market [62] gardens of the western world and global south.

- What is the point when we are systematically polluting and misusing the entirety of the water which has existed on our planet for billions of years?

- There is no point in developing [63] crops which produce vitamins [64] if we do not deal with the real reasons why so many people are malnourished [65] or otherwise nutritionally deficient [66] in the first place.

- There is no point in developing non-leguminous plants which can fix nitrogen from the atmosphere when the soil itself is so degraded and the nitrogen cycle itself (like all the others [67]) is on the point of collapse.

Against this backdrop non-GMO varieties are known to consistently out-perform [68] their GM counterpart. The reader is absolutely advised to investigate this statement themselves. Do **not** take my word for it, go find out for yourselves and then ask yourself again *"who am I going to believe, why am I going to believe them and what sort of future do I want?"* The above list is endless and ever expanding. We as a species are in deep trouble and the examples mentioned represent merely the tip of a huge planet sized iceberg. It is not so much the "science", but the need to implement the policies which will give some chance of extricating ourselves from the mess we are **all** in. GMO's are supremely likely to make matters in the world of food security even worse than they currently are. The above points do not constitute an exhaustive list of what continues to go wrong. These issues in their entirety can be applied in different frames and will hold in a range of contexts. As such, GMO's will only exacerbate the above realities [69]. These issues are **not** going away and if the current system is not changed to prioritise sustainable food production and feeding everyone, there will be dire, even game over level consequences for all of us.

Agribusiness as a construct emerged out of the green revolution. Its biggest defining feature and characteristic is the practice of monoculture, or the growing of one crop variety in large farms. The average size of which has doubled [70] since the 1980's. A monoculture is characterised by the intensive use of machinery, fertilisers and pesticides, to produce as much of the variety as possible from a given area of land. Mechanisation has also facilitated such a profound decrease in employment "on the land" that it threatens the future of farming the world over. Increasingly, the corporations who constitute big agriculture are taking more control of the distribution, supply, marketing, final sale price of seeds, plants and the substances derived from them. Agri-business encompasses the entirety of activities which compose modern intensive farming. The fundamental problem with the entire structure is the pursuit of profit above **all** other concerns. The profit is only possible via huge economies of scale [71]. It is the sheer volume of yield which succours the lie that mono-culture is more productive than alternative and sustainable systems. Big agriculture cares not a jot for the quality of food it produces, the welfare of animals or its negative environmental,

143

community, human and social impacts. In 2017 practically every farm in the industrialised world is directly connected to the agribusiness construct. As the current situation stands the rest of the world is being dragged into following suit. All points considered insanity is an accurate description of big agriculture. The above issues are as complex as they are intertwined as they are downright frightening. As humanity has become ever more urbanised we have all lost a connection to the natural world as well as our inclination to grow our own food. Overall, the local noisy food-market has been replaced by supermarket chains that distribute and sell processed and packaged food stuffs produced from large mono cultured farms, orchards, groves, ranches and abattoirs. Midway through the second decade of the 21st century practically most of us are dependent on the skills and expertise of others to provide our health and nutritional needs. A clear cut definition of unsustainability if there ever was one, I think I'll wash it down with a slug of dysfunction too! Intensive agriculture has undermined, compromised and destroyed many of the relationships which characterise sustainable agriculture. GMO's represent a cognitive dissonance on a global scale which if allowed to continue will most definitely end in more tears, streams of them, from hundreds of millions more people who are still suffering for one reason or another in the 21st century world. If one throws in the overriding profit motive then we have a succinct definition of "impending collapse". So, to answer the question posed in the last heading, no there is no good news in the world of big agriculture.

Chapter 7: Value Free Judgements And Natural Genetic Engineering

Science like any other human endeavour is not a static process; it is an organic and dynamic mechanism by which we make sense of the world around us. For an enquiring mind an observation becomes a hypothesis which in turn becomes a theory. The theory holds until it is replaced by another. If new observations lead to a new hypothesis then a new theory will likely present itself. Every time new evidence is presented the existing theory is re-assessed and if necessary replaced. Within this paradigm there are countless examples of where science can and should be framed as a value free process, a phrase which has different meanings in different contexts. Any aspect of science which has **no** consequences in the real world as it is today is said to be value free, or genuinely and totally objective. The application of science and / or technology in the real world must **no** impact, good or bad, at all. A personal opinion or perception of the application must equally have **no** consequence for other people, their community or the natural world. The only way science can operate in this manner is by separating itself from the world it is part of. I do not believe any agency operates in isolation from the others. No single structure can implement a given policy or move in a given direction without it having impact on the others. Clearly, as far as GMO's are concerned, there will always be an impact on the wider world. Hence we as human beings are going to make a value judgement on whether we agree or not. According to those who support GMO's this is not the case. We are supposed to accept without question GMO's because supporters say the science is sound, even though it isn't.

Concurrently, the organisms themselves touted as being are equivalent to those already here, which they are not. We are supposed to ignore all other considerations. We are supposed to agree solely on the basis of results presented in a given set of primary science papers. In one sentence the community of practising scientists who support and / or develop GMO's want hundreds of millions of people to drop their opposition because of results presented in research they have produced. We say perhaps they ought to stop and engage with the reasons why there is so much opposition. This engagement does not mean ridicule and grinding down opposition, it means talking with the people you are supposed to serve.

Achieving objectives of improved food security, reduced pesticide use and increased biodiversity are supposed to benefit all living organisms on the Earth. So, the how, why, who and where and the mechanisms to achieve these goals ought to be continually assessed. The development and implementation of GMO's cannot be framed in anyway as a value free process. Such issues connect to questions of the "ethics of science", meaning there is no right or wrong answer. It really does depend on what kind of future you want and what kind of planet you wish to live on. For example, I have been opposed to GMO's from the outset. Since the early 1990's I have seen nothing to make me change my mind. I consider the current situation in the Middle East and North Africa to be crimes against humanity, for which there will be some future reckoning. As it stands, I do not support nuclear power in any sense and developments such as fracking represent a complete disregard for the coming climate catastrophe. Others have the opposite view on these and other systemic global problems. It is up to the reader to decide where they stand on such issues and for most, there is no middle ground. For instance, you either:

- Want to live in a nuclear free world or you don't.

- Want to end poverty, inequality, conflict and global war or you don't.

- Want fracking to go ahead here in the UK (or anywhere else) or you don't.

- Want to push for a renewable energy portfolio or you don't.

- Want fossil fuels to remain in the ground or you don't.

- Support the Palestinian cause or you don't.

- Oppose deep sea mining or you don't.

- Want to eat food produced by means of GE of plants and animals or you don't.

- Think the techniques used to produce GMO's are substantially equivalent to those already present, or you don't.

These are not value free subjects and your viewpoint on them indicates exactly the values you hold. Perceptions and opinions vary, but one point is 100% cast iron guaranteed, once you have embarked on any of the above examples, there is no going back. Either way, warts and all, you have to stand up and be counted. There will be consequences, meaning your value system will come to the forefront of your thinking. In contrast, value free means the matter can be settled by the evidence alone and the subject is closed, there is no consequence, the answer just is. The supporters and drivers behind GMO's want us to believe exactly the same thing. Hopefully, the following example will demonstrate, yet again, why opponents to GMO's **know** this is **not** the case.

What if Tyrannosaurus Rex (T-rex) was not the majestic predator we like to think it was? Within palaeontology T-Rex is accepted to have been an insatiable predator. However, another theory suggests T-rex was a scavenger, living off carrion where ever it could find it. The question for us today is to ask *"does it really matter?"* Well, it does in the sense of using palaeontology to construct an ever more detailed picture of the prehistoric world. The more blanks we can fill in the more detailed picture we have of evolution and the processes which drive it. On the other hand does it really matter to you, me or anyone else outside of the disciplines of Earth science and palaeontology, whether T-rex was a scavenger or not? Will the outcome of this debate influence any of the decisions you make during your lifetime? It might, but probably not. Did you even know this T-rex debate was even happening? You may have done, but the chances are you didn't. Either way, T-rex on the balance of good, solid and objective science, appears to have been a predator, so what of it? Will the answer help you pay the mortgage? No of course not. The answer will satisfy our thirst for knowledge and need to construct a picture of the past and rightly so, but there is no impact on life today. The scavenger or predator discussion for T-rex **is** a value free scientific debate. Does the scientific evidence either way make any difference to us, the biosphere today or the future direction of evolution? The answer is of course a succinct **no**. I mean to say do you really care whether T-rex was a predator or not? Without belittling the science in anyway shape or form, I don't. Even the chief protagonist for the scavenger theory is reported to have said words to the effect of *"look I don't care either way, let's just do the science and find out"*. Bang on and no argument from me!

The presence, or not, of GMO's is absolutely pivotal for any strategic discussions concerning our impact on what is left of our rapidly diminishing biosphere. I would love to live in a world where just a fraction of the obscene amounts of money and expertise tied up GMO's was diverted to worthwhile endeavours such as palaeontology, earth and environmental science along with global solutions to climate change. Indeed I would love to see the finance tied up in GMO's and big agriculture immediately diverted to organic and permaculture systems. And I would love to see it on a global scale. I would like to see a full global moratorium on every aspect of GMO's in agriculture. I would love to see the whole enterprise properly regulated and thoroughly investigated. Where appropriate I would love to see criminal charges brought against the corporations and the key players within them. Overall, to settle this whole self-inflicted nonsense, I would like to see GMO's banned outright. The supporters of GMO's have not (in my experience) even acknowledged this point of view as legitimate. In many ways, they do not even know it even exists, of such realities are schisms made. In contrast, my value system says the above opinions represent part of the framework for achieving a genuinely sustainable future for ourselves and all the life on planet Earth. Sadly, for opponents of GMO's and other issues, such a shift is not going to happen anytime soon. Plus, it will only happen if we demand it, campaign for it and make it happen.

The subject matter of GMO's is arguably the most complex, intertwined and convoluted issue facing humanity today. Discussing (or more likely arguing) around it makes the discourse on nuclear power, global war, austerity and climate change appear as if you are explaining "the cat sat on the mat" to a five year old. The whole framework concerning GMO's is occurring right at the frontiers of our knowledge, meaning perceptions and strands of discussion change. For instance, when this book was first published I ran into a whole barrage of very heated discussion about how genes interact with each other. At its heart, the information salvo presented the case of natural gene swapping which has been happening for millions of years. In pro-GMO circles, gene swapping is called Natural Genetic Engineering (NGE), from this perspective, we opponents should basically shut up now. The factors hitherto highlighted were ignored or downplayed as they always are. However, the point remains; in the early part of 2017, I was presented with a corpus of knowledge which I was unaware of. I had dropped the GMO ball and at the time there was not much else to be said. I guess this sentence sums up what I mean

Opponent: *"Look, Mark, I used to oppose GMO's just as you are today, but things have changed and your arguments are no longer relevant. I am now satisfied that GMO's are safe and I have no problem with them."*

Me: *"OK pass me the information that has led to this change of view"*, which is exactly what happened.

Some of the references and sources cited in this chapter are from the conversation. I truly thank those people (and you know who you are) for forcing me to look deeper into the subject. They compelled me to look at the whole subject again, which is why this chapter exists. I can honestly say, upon considered reflection, additional research intertwined with matters of ethics, morals and perception that nothing has changed. Well, truthfully, not so, as a result of actually engaging with this issue in its widest possible sense; my own opposition to GMO's has become more entrenched. My aim here is to explain why, so here goes.......

One of the many good reasons for opposing novel, human made GMO's, is we don't know how the genome of a given GMO (see chapter 1) is going to interact with the environment it is placed into. We do not fully understand the complexities and environmental interactions of the genetic code we refer to as DNA (See chapter 1). Personally, this alone raises enough mental alarm bells to oppose the release of any GMO into the natural world. The acronym GMO refers to millions of **individual** organisms, within a given variety, they really should be seen as a whole set of new invasive species.[1] I am not alone in expressing concerns or questions. In the summer of 2016, I met someone at a 3 day music festival. During a campfire conversation, the subject of GMO's came up. By his own admission, the person has no science background. I asked what he thought of GMO's and the response was sublime in its perfect simplicity. Here is the conversation ad verbatim:

Him: "What GMO's, that's those genetic things innit?"

Me: "Yes," I said

Him: "What like DNA and all that stuff?"

Me: "That's the one," I said.

Him: "Well, you can't go effing about with that"

Me: "Why?" I said

Him: "Because it's DNA innit! We don't know what it is or what it does ooooo no; I don't like that, Effing silly idea."

At which point I walked around the camp fire gave him a big hug shook his hand and said: *"well done dude I couldn't have put it better myself"*. Clearly, the reader was not there and it is an anecdotal piece of evidence against GMO's. However, as with the rotten bollocks, in chapter four, that is what happened, exactly the conversation which is routinely dismissed by supporters of GMO's, because it is not scientific. I call it basic human intuition! I know this because they always do. It also, again, underpins who I will stand with and why. In one conversation the entire case for GMO's was demolished. All the scientific literature in support of GMO's makes **no** difference. The academic person in the conversation who supports GMO's had no answer. If you think about it, the dialogue makes perfect sense, the conversation **is** the PP. The total opposite of the drive to implement GMO's expressed verbally.

Attitudes and Genetic Migration

One tenet of opposition to GMO's considers the possibility of HGT and other forms of genetic migration between organisms. The first GM plant came into existence in 1983. Ever since GMO's have been opposed on the understanding that genes from different species were unable to cross the species barrier, (see chapter four). So, the thinking went, we should not be transferring genes between different organisms across the barrier as it will violate the laws of nature. Fast forward 35 years and we know this form of gene transfer does occur. Unsurprisingly, the industry is very keen to promote this reality. However, until gene transfer was discovered the same industry dismissed the possibility. A position it used as good reason to **support** GMO's in agriculture. A virus completes its life cycle by inserting its RNA or DNA into the cell nucleus of host organisms and they have been doing so for aeons, this is how viral life-forms reproduce themselves. The comparison with genetic engineering is clear and obvious. With GMO's viral DNA is almost always used to carry the desired traits into the genome of the engineered organism. This reality also explains why the human genome contains about 150 sequences of DNA which are **not** human in origin. At this juncture the reader must be absolutely crystal clear; the agency behind GMO's initially **denied** outright the possibility of gene transfer between species. This shows the complete lack of scientific literacy the real drivers behind GMO's have, or they have been lying since the outset. Way back in the late 1990's and early 2000's I remember being lambasted as being alarmist for suggesting the possibility. Now the drivers behind GMO's see gene transfer as a reason for their technology to be accepted. From their perspective, the proponents of GMO's have an opportunity to strengthen their case. The implication being, if nature has been swapping genes between species for many thousands of years and longer, then there is no intrinsic problem with 21st century biotechnology doing exactly the same. According to supporters of GM foods, those of us who oppose the technology should now just stop our opposition, as gene transfer is an entirely normal part of evolution. Biotechnology should be given carte blanche to move which ever genes it wants, whenever it wants and however it wants to achieve its objectives. Those of us who oppose GMO's should now shut up admit we got it wrong, go back to yoghurt weaving and let the industry big boys get on with it. From the opposite perspective, nothing has changed and once **again** the industry is manipulating "the science" to suit its own ends.

To reiterate, it is absolutely spurious to compare processes which have taken tens millennia or longer [2] to evolve [3] and the hybridisation which continues to this day, with 21st century techniques which result in GMO's. In GE different genes from different genomes are spliced at precise points into the genome of what becomes the transgenic organism. The aim is to produce a novel organism which expresses previously defined and from the industries perspective advantageous genetic traits (see bullet list in chapter three). This is **not** how evolution functions and it is **not** how hereditary or inheritance (See chapter 1) works. They are in fact opposite propositions; mutation (see chapter 1) and evolution are both random processes which do not always produce a viable progeny. However, the continuing work of James Shapiro [4] and others could in time, mean this statement is not so clear cut. Even so, artificial GM is a precise and delicate process using specific equipment, technology and expertise. Additionally, the engineering occurs in the laboratory and the novel organism is eventually released into the "real world". The immediate genetic environment and wider biosphere is then obliged to adapt to an organism which only exists because of GE, exactly what happens when invasive species are introduced. New organisms produced via GE in a laboratory are released into the environment. The GMO is trialled first and if it performs as expected it is grown or farmed commercially. As usual the environment is seen merely as an economic externality or repository for our activities. We are **not** discussing cross breeding or the principles of inheritance which were first set

154

down by Gregor Mendel. We are **not**, discussing the difference in wheat as it is today with cultivars present during the Neolithic revolution (see chapter eight). We **are** discussing GMO's and I fail to see how "natural" and "artificial" GE can be compared on a like for like basis. The two propositions are anything but more or less equivalent. NGE, like SE before it, is an industry brokered term. Neither are reasons or excuse to accept artificial GE conducted by human beings without question. We have the same clear distinction between GE carried out in the laboratory and the genetic interactions which occur in the natural world. GM in a 21st century laboratory is **not** the same as evolved and / or random gene transfer which have been occurring since the aeons before the Cambrian explosion (see chapter eight).

Another strand of objection comes down to attitude and communication. The agencies involved in pushing GMO's have a tendency to frame their support solely in terms of science, cost or what is best for the market. All other considerations are relegated, distilled out and at best seen as less important. In this paradigm those of us who oppose this use of science and how it is applied are seen as the problem and not the other way around. It is about perception and attitude; I would rather not eat GM, processed or intensively produced food in any shape or form. The only reason we are **not** eating food grown in organic and permaculture systems is structural. The bottom line is as absolute as it is criminally dysfunctional. If "doing the science" is detrimental to alternatives which are proven to work, then surely in this context it represents a waste of time, expertise, money and resources. Again I reiterate, I am not anti-science, quite the opposite. The geneticists involved in producing GMO's know more about genetics than I ever will. I will **always** defer to their knowledge, if they say Gene X codes for protein Y, I won't argue. However, this doesn't mean their knowledge is somehow superior to other ways of interpreting or explaining how knowledge is applied in the real world. Unfortunately, far too many supporters of GMO's seem to think all other factors and attitudes are secondary to the science. Personally, I find the condescending arrogance and the superiority complex such people demonstrate deeply offensive. On that basis alone I won't stand with them. I am not in *"the quinoa-munching natural-is-best brigade*[5]*"* I am a human being. The likes of you, Michael Le Page can, do one by disappearing in ecstatic and jerky movement! Supporters of GMO's also use words like Luddite to deride their opponents. Well, I applaud the Luddites [6] and the Chartists [7] who came after them. The Luddites were not at fault, they were absolutely right. Given our current situation we need more of their principled militancy and we need it yesterday, ditto with the US equivalent the Molly Maguire's. [8] Their relevance today is clear and present, if the current drive toward automation and artificial intelligence is allowed to proceed as things are; billions of people are going to find out how right the Luddites truly were.

To those who support GMO's, I speak for all those who oppose you, the world over, when I impart the following. I am a concerned, in fact downright terrified citizen of planet Earth. I find your historical and political illiteracy and your wilful ignorance and disregard deeply offensive, a value judgement which I do not expect you to understand. I have just as much ethos as you do in the scientific realm. You keep rolling out the same tired platitudes, not I, which gives GMO's **no** extra credence. GMO's will eventually be detrimental to the future evolution of life and to what is left of the current biosphere. For good solid scientific, environmental, ethical and evolutionary reasons, we have no right to interfere with the fabric of life in such a fundamental manner. This is especially true if the **only** purpose is to profit from and control the global food supply. Gene transfer between different species was discovered in the early 1990's. [9] Plus, GM plants have only been existence since 1985, (see chapter four) another fact the supporters of GMO's conveniently forget. The industry does not acknowledge this, it prefers to use terms like SE or NGE / NGM. It also has an extreme proclivity of broadcasting as loud as it can in all media that we have been carrying out GE or gene manipulation for thousands of years. Along with equating cross breeding and hybridisation with GE, the mantra is in my view a clear cut lie. Back in the mid 1980's we had **no** definite notion of genes from different genomes intermingle with each other. We had **no** definite notion of genes adapting to the presence of novel DNA. Science has established that genome A will interact with genome B or vice versa. We **know** genes can be expressed in a single location or at many locations. We **know** genes can exist as different alleles, (see chapter one). We **know** a given gene can influence the activity of those next to it. We **know** genes migrate as they are inherited by different generations. We **know** genes can migrate through the genome and can be expressed in future generations. We **know** genes can be expressed in ways which are different from the initial GMO. There could be expressions going on right now which we have not seen. If unforeseen expressions were happening they would be covered up, or they could be in the post for tomorrow morning. However, the question remains, if nature has been swapping genes between different species for longer than Homo sapiens have been on the planet, why should we maintain GMO's are still from this gene swapping perspective, an exceptionally bad idea? A few real examples of current GM will hopefully demonstrate why they are.

The Aqua-advantage Aqua-bounty Salmon

The prospect [10] of GM salmon making its way into the marine food chain is nothing short of appalling. The presence of 35 different species of transgenic fish in aquaculture farms controlled by the life science industry is equally worrying. The GE salmon in question will be confined to aquaculture and so will ostensibly be separated from the environment a point which must be made clear. However, fish farming is not exactly known for its environmental credentials, by and large it has the same issues intrinsic to the factory farming of terrestrial animals, a reality dismissed by supporters of GMO's. The Atlantic salmon possess some 40,000 individual genes and the species grows **ONLY** in the summer months. The engineered and artificial aqua-bounty variety has a gene which codes for the expression of a growth hormone. Here, the GOI comes from a species of salmon called the Pacific [11] Chinook. Atlantic salmon is already extensively farmed and was apparently the first commercial transgenic fish. If true, GE animals have been in the pipeline from the outset. Something else the industry prefers to keep quiet about. The gene which codes for the growth hormone is the same in both species of salmon. Under SE banner, these G'sOI are identical because the code for the same protein, especially if they come from a related organism. Outside of SE no two genes are identical. A second GOI which expresses anti-freeze [12] properties is also engineered into aqua-advantage salmon. It comes from an eel species called the North Atlantic Ocean pout. Both G'sOI are inserted into the genome of what becomes the aqua-bounty salmon, producing a novel species of farmed fish. The resultant GMO is female [13] and sterile, the fish is engineered to grow continually and much faster than wild Atlantic salmon. The Transgenic salmon is larger than its wild counterpart and presumably produces a lot of fish per buck invested in the technology. This is exactly the same ethos behind developments such as the Belgian blue cattle and GM trout mentioned in chapter one.

As with the trout and the Belgian blue cattle (which is **not** a GMO) the objective is to produce an animal which is larger than the naturally evolved and wild species. Presumably, this is one reason Aqua bounty refer to their creation as *"the world's most sustainable salmon"*. I truly do wonder whether these people really think they know better than nature or those who have been practising genuine sustainability for centuries, or are they just plain deluded and arrogant enough to believe their own bullshit? Chapter eight imparts the current biosphere is the end point of aeons of evolution **and** that genes are the primary vehicle by which inter-species evolution occurs. There is no genetic rule book and to suggest, as the aqua-bounties of this world do, there is nothing to worry about, simply stretches the bounds of credibility and insults our intelligence. Furthermore, the aqua-bounty salmon is sterile, which begs the obvious question, how does it reproduce? Well, it doesn't, which begs the next question, "How are stocks of GM salmon maintained?" Well, its obvious isn't it? More GE, like DUH! The industry is at great pains to tell the world they have **never** developed "terminator technology" (see chapter one) for crop plants, (which they have) they have also been doing the same with GM animals since the mid-1990's. Further evidence that the GM food industry is riddled with deceit, lies and hypocrisy. In other words, I advise not to trust a damned word anyone connected with it says. The questions continue, the most obvious being, *"when have eel and salmon genes or genes from two different species of salmon ever met in nature?"* The Answer is never!

Plus, if the routine documentation of escapes [14] from fish farms is anything to go by, as this internet search suggests, then some form of genetic contamination is, in the long run inevitable. Are we seriously expected to believe farmed fish do **not** escape into the environment? When they have in the past, in February 2018 [15] and will continue to do so in the future. Are we truly to believe engineered traits will **not** be passed on to wild salmon, other fish species or other marine organisms? I say **no** and it appears the science [16] is in agreement with me. Even though aqua-advantage acknowledge their sterilisation procedure is **not** 100% effective, the company and supporters [17] of GMO's continue to rubbish such real and present concerns. The arrogance and disregard these people project is shocking but not surprising. They seriously state the engineered genetic safeguards [18] will prevent gene transfer in the wild, or they are **lying**; they can't be both, so I wonder which it is. Science now knows gene transfer does occur naturally, yet we are supposed to accept it won't with GMO's due to the apparent safeguards. These safeguards include terminator technology and breeding sterile animals. To avoid charges of lies and hypocrisy, "you can't have it both ways". Yet, the industry will continue to state from all aspects that it can eat whatever cakes it likes in pursuit of its profit driven aims. As always it is supporters and geneticists carrying out the actual science who continue to downplay all objections framed in environmental, scientific ethical, economic and political terms. Either way these people are deluded or in denial, they choose to hide behind their science and refuse to engage with reality. Furthermore, are we to seriously believe transgenic and farmed salmon is somehow a substitute for those already evolved? I say no, but the industry says yes. Surely a better option is to learn from past criminal mistakes. My phrase criminal mistake is actually a misnomer; the environmental crimes committed by the global elite are in fact a deliberate policy. If they were mistakes the crimes would have been allowed in the first place. The reality is as horrific and terrifying, we are heading toward environmental Armageddon, and our rulers know it (see chapter eight). We are witnessing the deliberate rape and abuse of an entire planet. A rape which is not only continuing but is intensifying and GMO's are a future component of such continued rape, if the industry gets its way. I believe the global elite to be guilty of environmental crime and rape of the worst kind, the total and systematic destruction of the biosphere of an entire planet. Now they are seeking to corrupt the very fabric of evolution. The members of the elite ought to be in an equivalent dock for environmental crime which exists in The Hague for war crimes and crimes against humanity. Again I ask the reader who are you going to stand with and why?

Instead of developing even more farmed and this time sterile fish, surely a better option is for all nations to work together to bring wild salmon and fish populations overall back to something approaching the levels they were before human activity decimated them, put simply:

GM fish will not improve marine ecology and the totality of its biodiversity.

GE fish will not stimulate a drive to make fishing sustainable.

Transgenic fish will not encourage certain members of our species to act with respect toward the marine and wider environment.

Quite the opposite will occur and marine conservation organisations such as the sea shepherd [19] are in agreement with this position. Once again I know exactly who I stand with. Some scientists involved in developing GMO's find such concerns "bizarre", "non-sensical" and even "stupid". Some have said publically we opponents should be held "accountable" for our opposition. OK then game on! You first though, after all this was your idea in the first place and I millions more don't ever recall being asked about it. You have imposed GMO's without regard or consultation in any capacity. You have put your own self-serving interests before the future of humanity and its immediate future. For that alone, this writer will never forgive you, ever. The entirety of the biotechnology industry involved in GMO's has yet to tell the complete and open truth about any of its activities or why they are happening. They also fail to comprehend or even acknowledge the problems GMO's are supposed to solve would not exist in the first place if the world were organised differently. Some who support GMO's come out with statements like:

Supporter: "Ah yes but that is a problem of capitalism and not of science"

Me: "Well, OK then, I expect to see your application to join an organisation such as the "Socialist Party" or Socialist Workers Party accepted in the near future. All you need to do is contact me and I'll get you the application form and for the campaigning organisations connected to them too, well? Perhaps we can start with the GM insects discussed below?

Yes, I thought so on both counts!

Such points are surely enough for a legitimate demand for the moratorium (if not outright ban) on GMO's, investigation and criminal charges mentioned previously.

As of 2018, the aqua-bounty company appears to be mired in various financial and equivalent troubles.[20] The absolutely dysfunctional regulatory process for GMO's is also coming under ever more scrutiny. As the furore over labelling becomes more contentious and intense more individuals are becoming aware of how the agency driving GMO's truly operates. Labelling is only one front of resistance which the industry ruthlessly attacks. Anyone who has ever campaigned in this area knows how relentless and merciless the drivers behind GMO's truly are. It is a pity far too many scientists have not woken up to this reality and they seek to justify their position and abdicate their responsibility by separating "the science" from the "real world". They hide behind the primary literature, the letters after their names and abuse the position they hold. A core reason for writing this book was to explain what the industry is up to and why. If you need industry objectives made clearer and where it places its priorities, this quote from a key backer of the aqua-bounty project should say it all. A deceased former Georgian oligarch Kahka Bendukidze, a man who admitted he knew **nothing** about fish farming, said in the New York Times on the approval process and objections to transgenic fish *"Salmon is salmon at the end of the day, economics will win."* The aqua-bounty example is not an isolated case; another 35 varieties of GM fish are in the pipeline. In the wider context of our current global situation, the prospect of unfettered GMO's is one reason for my regular, but thankfully rare, bouts of insomnia. GE animals across the board are very much in the post. Once again the reader is given a choice. Either to embrace engineered animals and precision agriculture (their term not mine) on populist and purely scientific grounds or you can ask serious questions [21] on the utility of the entire notion. A second example will hopefully continue to hammer these points home.

Genetically Engineered Insects

A UK based biotechnology company called Oxitec [22] have as early 2018 released some 70 million [23] GM mosquitoes into the natural world. The company specialise in controlling pest insect species by means of GE. In 2010 Oxitec gained approval to release 3 million [24] mosquitoes into the environment of the Cayman Islands. Since early 2016 Oxitec sought (but to date not been granted) approval to release thousands of GE mosquitoes into the Florida Keys [25]. The stated objectives of these and other releases are to combat viruses such as zika and/or to control pest organisms. Thankfully, Oxitec and their ilk are not having things their own way. This petition represents just one tiny part of the global resistance to the release of the engineered insects into the environment. It works too, for instance, in 2013 plans to release GM olive flies in Southern Europe were stalled.[26] Although Oxitec continues to lobby various Southern European governments [27] as far as I know there are no definite plans to release transgenic olive flies in the region. However, this could change at any time. So what kind of GM has been carried out and what sort of GE insects have been created? What could be released, (if they haven't been already in secret), if the industry gets its way?

The olive fruit fly (*Bactrocera oleae - B.oleae)* is a recognised pest. Hence mechanisms of control are going to be considered and rightly so. However, by any rational and long term standard the GM approach is **not** the way forward. Oxitec originally planned to release about 5000 GE olive flies per week into the olive plantations of Southern Europe. The male of the species is engineered to carry a femicidal trait. The engineered male flies mate with non-engineered, the evolved and already present, females. The femicidal gene is inherited by all male offspring. The inherited trait causes the female of the species to die at the larvae stage of their life cycle. It is a deliberate mechanism to ensure all female larvae die before they reach maturity. The G'sOI come from various species of bacteria, microbe, other insects, marine organisms and a substance called synthetic DNA.[28] The idea is to control, perhaps eradicate, olive fly populations by inheritance of the femicidal gene. To be absolutely crystal clear gene transfer is the present and deliberate objective of this mechanism of pest control. Gene transfer is the absolute core of the entire enterprise, a glaringly obvious double standard when compared to the aqua-bounty salmon. The transgenic fish developed by aqua-advantage are to have their sterility genes controlled as much as possible. To my mind you couldn't make such dichotomy up. Once again the industry is saying one thing but doing another; in the world I live in we call that hypocrisy, deceit and lies. Irrespective of the ethics of eradicating an entire species the gene transfer question has to be central to this mechanism of genetic control. I know we are discussing an insect but the organism is still part of the fabric of life on Earth. Do we have the right to eradicate yet another species? Again I say no. I would also suggest if the subject in hand were a "cute" animal then GM would be much more unpopular and the proposition would be common knowledge. Perhaps the genes contained within the engineered olive flies would have behaved as predicted in Oxitec's olive grove enclosures, but an enclosure is not the real world. All it takes is for one GM olive fly to escape, if that happens the femicidal gene will have escaped into the real world. From there not much if anything can be done. Nature and evolution will take its course, especially if we accept that genes can move by means of HGT or equivalent mechanisms. If each individual GMO and the millions of individual organisms which make up a given variety are considered as an invasive species, then we have been here countless times over the last several centuries. Every time an alien organism is introduced to a given environment the consequences for the natural world are generally devastating and always irreversible

The environmental history of planet Earth over the last 500 years represents a damning indictment of how things are done. Sadly most of the millennia before the 15th century are not any different. As for the time before the last ice age, there is nothing to be done, but we should be learning the lessons, unfortunately, as a species, we are not. The reader can choose any date or timescale they wish but however we choose to frame it, the picture is flat out ugliness laced with a healthy measure of dysfunction. For instance, two words spring to mind; two words which, like "nuclear weapons", or "sixth mass-extinction" should not exist in **any** language. The two words are "invasive species". Something the wildlife of Australia and New Zealand knows all about; tragically, these are not isolated cases, merely they are two of the more obvious. Acknowledgement of escape and proliferation on the art of sterile GM insects is factor at best marginalised by the likes of Oxitec. As for other releases which have been allowed, only time will tell and as I'm very fond of saying, "you better hope I'm wrong, because if I'm right......" There is no way to categorically state **any** organism will remain genetically stable (i.e. it **won't** transfer genes or **will** behave as predicted) once it is released into a real environment. And this possibility, well highly likely probability, is before any consideration of the economic and human health impacts are even mentioned. There is recent historical precedence in this area. In 1956 scientists tried to cross-breed African bees with the European honey bee and total failure [29] was the result? So, it absolutely staggers me (for all the wrong reasons) there is proper serious discussion on pursuing exactly the same course of action to deal with the collapse in honey bee populations, occurring as a result of neonicotinoid pesticides. I mean Helloo, is there anyone in there? Stop using neonicotinoids would seem to be the best precautionary option. Then we can look at cross breeding (**not** GM) between sub-species of insect again, **without** transporting different species thousands of miles away from their natural habitat.

The Rubisco Enzyme

Photosynthesis (PHS) is likely the most studied biochemical reactions on the planet, for any organism which requires oxygen it is also the most important. If for whatever reason PHS were to stop life as we know it would be snuffed out in short order. PHS (see chapter eight) is an evolved process, an evolution which is continuing to this day. The Rubisco [30] enzyme functions by catalysing the series of reactions which convert carbon dioxide (CO_2) and water into sugars and oxygen, i.e. PHS. Presumably it has been doing so since the very early history of life on Earth and been getting better at it too. However, for 21st century biotechnology, this is not good enough. According to the scientists involved in the research, [31] Rubisco is "a target for improvement" because it is a "highly inefficient enzyme". The inefficiency is probably why there is so much of it on the planet. Rubisco is everywhere around the chloroplasts of photosynthesising organisms and is the most common protein on the Earth. More than several strands [32] of research are seeking to establish mechanisms to make rubisco work harder, by making it more efficient. In 2014 increased [33] the rate of PHS by changing the structure and orientation of the rubisco molecule. Rubisco from an algal species called cyanobacteria (see chapter eight) were inserted into the genome of tobacco [34] plants and compared with existing organisms. The industry holds onto the SE mantra here too. I mean, sarcasm alert, the non-GM plants clearly contain genes from microbes inserted at a precise point on their genome don't they? And the Rubisco they contain is also SE to the molecules in non-GM plants isn't it? In this case the native genes were "knocked out" and replaced by the engineered form. The GM tobacco plants produced more sugars, fixed more CO_2 and produced more tobacco than the non-engineered varieties. Theoretically, if the rate of PHS can be increased the growth and productivity of food crops could well be increased. Great, what could possibly be wrong? Well I wonder? Err not! First things first this is corporate driven research from the DuPont chemical companies crop development division. Other chemical companies will be involved and be exploring similar lines of enquiry. The same companies involved in manufacturing everything from napalm, chemical weapons, pesticides, pharmaceuticals, food additives, synthetic and industrial chemicals across the board. Obviously, exactly the same agency needed to develop a sustainable agricultural model for the future! When it comes to it, the profit motive will inevitably over-ride all other concerns. To state otherwise denies the reality of the dying world we live on. Secondly, gene transfer concerns clearly apply to this particular strand of GE. The engineered varieties could only grow in a high CO_2 environment which we need to avoid. The engineered rubisco itself has a tendency to react with oxygen and not CO_2. In other words there are biological hurdles to overcome. As of 2017 we are in very early days. There will be no super photosynthesising plants in the foreseeable future. Likely by the time they are ready their utility will be irrelevant. Even so there is talk of copying GE forms of Rubisco and using it improves the yields of staple crops such as rice and corn. This area of GM certainly will be one to watch.

This example underlines totally what has gone so catastrophically wrong with food production and distribution in the world as it is today. If we are serious about improved food security and productivity for the peoples of planet Earth then surely we need to address the problems which have compromised it so badly. The organisation (see chapter six) behind global food production is so unstable that future food price hikes and more famine are inevitable. As just one example, look at food prices [35] since Brexit, here in the UK. Plus, can the supporters of GMO's explain how the science and technology is to overcome the current (2018) blockade of Yemen and Venezuela? Again what is the point in developing crops which can grow in the desert, when for political reasons the global elite are deliberately starving an entire nation, and enforcing untold hardship and borderline starvation on another **again?** This strand of science is one those areas where I would **again** say divert the finance, expertise tied up with plant and animal GE into the alternatives which have been shown to work on multiple occasions, you only have to look, so please do. The systemic problems are clear and present to any person who chooses to interact with the wider world around them. I see **no** evidence that GM crops or animals will ultimately solve such deep rooted and systemic problems. Put simply, on the current trajectory we are heading for a series of food related disasters which will make the Irish and Highland [36] potato famines look like two school children who have forgotten their packed lunch.

It would be interesting to see how the productivity of organic and permaculture systems compare with the above form of GE. I do not see any research in those areas being funded by DuPont or other chemical companies of the 21st century world do you? I wonder what the average small holder could achieve with the research budget and expertise tied up with **just** the Rubisco research budget. A further obvious question to pose is on the following lines. Perhaps in the evolutionary past, in the time of the Archean or Proterozoic (see chapter eight), evolution [37] tried different mechanisms of improving rubisco efficiency, perhaps they didn't work. Perhaps they caused unforeseen, disastrous and / or multiple biological impacts on the biota of the time. Perhaps on balance it is better from an evolutionary perspective to have lots of "inefficient" rubisco around the chloroplasts, than any of the "efficient" engineered form. Such are the questions the yoghurt weavers, quinoa eaters and carrot munchers of this world ask. The whole proposition that GMO's will **not** cause gene transfer problems is fatally flawed. We know genes are **not** individual structures and are **not** separate from each other. This reasoning refers to the probability of the genetic cocktail effect mentioned in chapter four. Those who support GMO's do **not** see the potential for harm in terms of individual GMO's. There are already hundreds of millions of individual GMO's interacting with the environment around them. The cystic fibrosis example mentioned in chapter two concerns a mutation of one codon on one gene. If that is all it takes for some negative consequence to present itself, eventually something will go wrong. When, **not** if, genetic pollution problems we cannot deal with present themselves, is the point being made here. As stated elsewhere a variety of GMO is an invasive species. The more engineered genes released into the environment the greater the possibility of something going wrong. Imagine a normal six sided dice, where 1 represents no gene transfer and 6 represents irreversible **and** dangerous gene transfer. If I roll one dice the probability of each outcome is going to be 1/6. Every time I have one more die I have one more chance of each outcome occurring. If I have 6 die and roll them, I have 6 more chances of each outcome presenting itself. Anyone who has ever played a board game called **RISK** knows exactly what I mean. The more individual GMO's developed and released into the environment, the more chances of rolling each number we have. So if **each** Oxitec insect, **each** Aqua-bounty salmon, **each** engineered form of rubisco and **each** individual GMO in existence is a dice we are going to get gene transfer of some kind at some stage. I would question the motives and perception (if not sanity) of any person and / or organisation whom suggested otherwise.

On top of rubisco research, plant geneticists can engineer the chloroplast (see chapter eight) and nucleus (see chapter one) in living cells. It is now possible to GE the mitochondria [38] (see chapter two) of many plant species. One area of research employs mitochondrial DNA which codes for male plant sterility. The G'sOI code for masculine sterility, these are inserted into the genome of crop plants which do not have the trait. Male sterility for hybridisation can be useful for commercial or big agriculture (see chapter six). The more male sterile plants in the total population of plants, the less self-fertilisation occurs. Concurrently, less of the offspring of the population plants will be hybrids, which adversely (according to those who know) affects diversity and yield. To my knowledge and as of autumn 2017, the only way to prevent self-fertilisation is to actually remove the stamen (male part) of the flower by hand. This, of course, requires plenty of labour as well as a degree of training and that means training and paying people money, which means reduced profits. This is another example of creating GMO's which code for male sterility. As a whole, this form of GM is nano-metres distance away from terminator technology. According to the industry, we are supposed to differentiate between this objective and terminator technology. I see no difference, do you? Again the point is beyond obvious. How about diverting a portion of the cash invested in agricultural GMO's to methods we already know work and are in terms of genetic pollution risk free? Once again are we seriously expected to believe a form of the original engineered gene cannot be transferred and then undergo mutation and then further migration in the real world?

Genetic Safeguards and the Need for Precaution

NGE and HGT are complex and interrelated processes. If we are artificially altering the genome of an organism **and** we accept DNA is not a passive molecule, it seems likely artificial

172

GE can disrupt NGE. All forms of GM involve altering cellular processes and/or cell organelles (see chapter 2) which have existed for many tens of thousands of millennia, or longer. The vector organism (see chapter 3) functions by carrying an engineered trait into the genome of what becomes the GMO. The vectors also carry sections of DNA called promoter genes which exist to force the expression of artificial and natural genetic traits. The initial promoter genes were derived from a deactivated form of a microbe called the Cauliflower Mosaic Virus,[39] as far as I know in 2018 this is still the case. A given engineering technique will elicit biochemical change at the cellular level. It is not possible to insert genetic material from one organism into another without causing some sort of disruption. After all, this is the **whole** point, isn't it? Engineering causes genetic stress which can destabilise the genome of the engineered organism. In other words, GMO's can be unstable because:

- The novel organism itself may not be genetically viable.

- The engineered genes can be more easily transferred and undergo gene transfer.

- Inactive (unexpressed) genes may become activated.

- Currently functioning, or expressing genes may become deactivated

- The genomes of other organisms are known to adapt to the presence of novel genomes and/or the promoter genes.

The truth is we simply do not know what the long term consequences of releasing GMO's into the environment could be? If you hear of any supporter of GMO's saying any different, you have licence to tell them to get their facts straight. Genetic material can be dominant or recessive, expressed in the first, second or any subsequent generation. Or it may not be expressed at all. In other words DNA is **not** a passive receptacle for us to experiment with, irrespective of the stated objectives. This is another difference between NGE and hybridisation as compared to artificial GE. There is no experimentation as such but a continual process of trial and error. Some degree of interaction and therefore future expression is inevitable. What form the expression may actually take is only limited by biochemistry (see chapters one and five) of DNA itself. The industry may have belief in safeguards and stringent testing for the GMO's it creates. Yet, there are no guarantees concerning genetic expression in future generations. I count myself amongst those people who raise their head above the parapet when I present this point of view to those who support GMO's. The response is as predictable as it is vituperative, vitriolic and on occasion borderline psychotic. I along with those biologists, scientists and geneticists who dare to publically question the aims and objectives of the industry, are attacked personally and ferociously. It is well known in the scientific community that you keep quiet about such objections, or else. In this frame "or else" means you don't get funding for your own research, your peers and colleagues could ostracise you and your own work and therefore career could well be scuppered. As a whole the GM food lobby has a terrible history of discrediting research it doesn't like whilst promoting that which it does. If you think this is unfair or I'm being unduly harsh or even residing in conspiracy theory land, then go ahead and try it. It starts off all nice, polite and civilised, but once you really start to challenge those who support GMO's, things soon deteriorate. Especially, once you start using science to present your challenge. It happens all the time; I have been called everything from a misanthropist, to a Luddite. I am also, either anti-science, far too emotional for this subject, or I don't understand what I'm talking about. Often I am called plenty more besides and combinations thereof to boot. My life experience in this area demonstrates totally, GMO's do not represent a value free science.

The olive fruit fly has a life span of about 6 months and females will lay approximately 500 eggs during this time. This translates into anything between 4 and 6 generations per life span per insect. For an insect, 500 eggs may not seem very much, but there are very large numbers of insects. If each insect represents a die, each of which can roll any number from 1 to 6, things will not stay static for long. The environmental chemistry of the hundreds of organochlorine compounds developed by big agriculture teaches us insects adapt very quickly and evolve resistance to the poisons thrown at them. An equivalent current comparison can be made with the growth (pun intended) of super-weeds [40] which have evolved resistance to agricultural chemicals and pesticides. This form of resistance and adaptation is another factor which the supporters of GMO's ignore, deny, deflect or water down by one mechanism or another. The GM industry is very fond of telling us that vector organisms are highly receptive and adaptable to their attentions, the primary reason why microbes are used as vectors (see chapter one). Simultaneously, they quickly inform of various safeguards which exist to prevent unintentional gene transfer (gene flow [41]). Safeguards which are not needed outside the GMO world! The latest safeguard incarnation is biocontainment. [42] Here, genetic information is constrained from spreading because key amino acids [43] (the building blocks of proteins) can only be manufactured by virtue of the synthetic DNA mentioned above. As the literature points out, these techniques are already used in closed systems, those which have no direct contact with the outside world. Obviously, a GMO is not separate from the real world; it is part of it, which is not supposed to be a problem. Biocontainment and other strategies are supposed to reassure us, but four obvious questions present themselves:

• Why are we once again altering the biology of the natural world to accommodate both potential and real genetic transfer problems which the industry has created in the first place?

• Has the reader ever heard of the need for biocontainment in an organic or permaculture system? No, I thought not. And guess what? They haven't either!

• What happens when the biocontainment or other safeguards fail? This is the fabric of evolution we are discussing, i.e. DNA. The nucleic acids which pass on genetic information will adapt to the presence of any synthetic DNA. It will accommodate it. Are the supports of GMO's seriously and truly saying DNA will **not** adapt? Still, I'd best get back to the quinoa hey?

• What about those GMO's such as corn and soy beans which are already grown on a commercial scale? Are transgenic crops somehow less safe than the ones in the pipeline? If so, how? Again this question simply does not exist in organic and permaculture systems.

The development of biocontainment and other safeguards tells me the industry knows there is a risk of gene transfer, but they are carrying on regardless. Biocontainment totally contradicts the PP, if we need to bring in protective measures for any technology then its necessity and utility, must by definition be open to question. Imagine I have built a wooden house which I wish to heat. To save money I'm not going to build a fire place, I am going to construct a fire in the middle of the front room and surround it with bricks. In the case of the olive fly, and aqua bounty salmon we are talking about GE animals. The science around rubisco is concerned with GE cell organelles. All three examples can be viewed as the fire. It is entirely likely (if not 100% certain) that individual organisms will escape into the "real world" (the house). Clearly the fire will escape from its safeguard (the bricks) and the house will burn down. Are we to seriously believe that **when** (not if) GMO's escape into the natural environment there will be no gene flow between species. Are the safeguards produced by a new industry really such a strong bulwark against processes which have been evolving for billions of years? I think **not** and it is supreme arrogance to suggest otherwise. Despite the efforts of those who run things and their supporters to demonstrate otherwise, we do not own or control the natural world we are part of it. The release of GMO's into the natural world makes some form of NGE and transfer of engineered genetic material inevitable. After all the more dice I have the more sixes I will roll. The industry admits it; science has established it and all the huffing and puffing in the world does not deviate one iota from this conclusion. If the industry were telling the truth about its intentions around GMO's, they would never have gotten off the ground. The next story represents many others in the same ball park and **again** demonstrates GMO's are not a value free subject. Concurrently, if I were an organic or permaculture small holder I would be taking this story as clear warning and definite reason to further oppose GMO's.

Mexico, Corn and Terminator Genes

In the year 2000, a community of small holders in the mountains of Oaxaca in southern Mexico was seeking to gain organic status for the corn they have been growing for centuries. They like any grower; they were seeking to gain as much income as they could for their crop. In pursuit of this objective, a microbiologist called David Quist was asked to help in the certification process. At the time of writing (2017/8) he studies gene transfer between different organisms, a sub discipline called transgene ecology.[44] During the genetic analysis of the corn grown in Oaxaca, segments [45] of GE corn were discovered. The corn in question was developed by Monsanto and was engineered to be resistant to Glyphosate (See chapter three). As of late 2017, no authority exists to grow GM corn or soy beans anywhere in Mexico, hopefully, it will stay that way. The transgenic genes are sourced from corn imports and/or from seeds planted accidentally by Mexican farmers. Likely, cross breeding and repeated pollinations between the original and GM corn led to the uptake of the novel genes by the original variety. At this point politics, vested interest and the kind of attitude promulgated by those who support GMO's again presents itself. The reader should be under no illusions on this. Supporters of GMO's as with those who deny climate change really do not like being challenged. Try it for yourself, it is a most illuminating if shocking experience. When David Quist published his findings the same sordid set of circumstances which always happens whenever anyone dares to even utter "just a minute" began to play out.

The findings were published in the well-respected scientific journal Nature. [46] According to those in the know, Oaxaca is the birthplace of corn cultivation. The crop is also considered sacred by the indigenous population. This reality represents another objection to GM crops which is well beyond intellectual scope of those who support the technology. Nobody has the right to deliberately genetically pollute a staple crop in any context, but in a religious context (I am an atheist and humanist) the opposition ought to be obvious. For the people who support GMO's it isn't, or if it is, it is ignored and I'm not sure which position I despise most. As well as other unscientific factors, religious and spiritual beliefs are continually ignored by the pro-GMO lobby. When David Quist and Ignacio H Chapela (his supervisor) published their paper in 2001 it was comprehensively savaged. GM supporters ensured all objections were framed exclusively in terms of the scientific techniques and methods used. They also discredited the degree of gene transfer. At the time they said cross pollination was not possible because the corn pollen is "characteristically heavy" and could not be blown "far away from the corn fields" by the wind. Very scientific assertions then! The research carried out by Quist and Chapela apparently discovered signs of genetic transfer in the form of a sequence of DNA called nopaline synthase terminator sequence. [47] This particular terminator gene was vectored into GM corn by means of the microbe Agrobacterium tumefaciens (see chapter three). So, if the GM industry is not employing terminator technology did the space pixies from Alpha Centuri put it in the genome of the natural corn? Just for a laugh like, to see what would happen? Other tests detected the presence of the Bacillus thuringiensis (Bt) gene called cry-1A (see chapter four). This sequence is part of the genome of those plants which have been engineered to code for its manufacture. Contamination was found at multiple sites in the sample population of crop plants. The industry in the 21st century is using gene transfer as an excuse and reason to promote its technology. The clear cut hypocrisy and flagrantly blatant lies leave this writer speechless with fury and incandescent with rage. The GM lobby applied so much pressure that Nature felt compelled to "withdraw support for the paper". Although not a complete retraction, the implication here ought to be obvious. The withdrawal was issued in 2002 and since then very little research on the corn grown in Oaxaca or anywhere else has occurred. The bottom line is we know gene transfer occurs; we just don't fully understand it and therefore don't know how prevalent it is in nature.

Be assured once a GMO is released into the environment there is no going back. Once applied the technology is irreversible. Overall, GMO's must be opposed because they will not solve [48] any of the current food related issues which are blighting the planet and its people. They will intensify them and create a whole host of gene transfer (and other) problems. There will be no plan and absolutely no strategy to deal with them because we will be in uncharted territory. As our global situation stands we are on the cusp of moving from the current Holocene epoch (see chapter eight) and into a new time period called the Anthropocene.[49] The presence of GMO's and the impending climate catastrophe are merely two key drivers which will take us into this new epoch. If you ever see a proclamation "we have entered the Anthropocene", then all bets are off. There will be no base line or point of reference; it will be all change on all counts with no ability to make any meaningful predictions of any kind. Given the way our affairs are currently organised the changes will **not** be good or beneficial for the majority of life on Earth. This is not scaremongering or framing GM foods as Franken foods or some such drivel. This is cold hard science shouting as loud as possible in all directions from a very high Babelesque tower called the **precautionary principle**. As such I have no hesitation in imparting the following. Should we ever experience the application of unfettered GM crops and animals I will **refuse** to take the blame for any consequences. In such a circumstance when things do go wrong the blame will lay with those who have funded, developed and supported the science and technology in question. **You** will be responsible for the negative biological and genetic consequences for the organisms you have produced. I have said as such to every GMO supporter I have met. It will be **their** fault and **not** mine. I have been saying this since the mid 1990's and since then I have seen nothing to compel a change of mind. GMO's are being developed without the consent or consultation of humanity. The **only** agency which is driving them is that which seeks to profit from it. All other points are distraction, smoke and mirrors. Within this argument is the reality of total unawareness of the issue at all, surely, another reason to wait. For supporters the lack of awareness is of benefit because it means they can perpetuate the lies and disinformation which emanates from the industry. Similarly, it is not my fault if supporters refuse to comprehend, or they deflect understanding of, the irreversible nature of the technology. I do **not** agree GMO's are needed. I and everyone else who opposes the technology object in the strongest possible terms to its imposition. In my view science as an entirety of knowledge is in great danger of losing its status if it continues on the current pro-GMO course. GMO's will not I believe (based on evidence) deliver the goods or live up to any expectation. In short whichever way you cut the cake they simply do not work.

GMO's are replete with external issues to science which simply do not exist with non-GM and organic/permaculture alternatives. As with the push for fracking and nuclear power, if you support it, then at some stage you are going to have to go along with the climate and other environmental consequences, the undermining of local democracy and the riding roughshod over those communities which stand to be ruined by it. Truly, it really is that clear-cut, do you support or not? To borrow from the Stop the War Coalition, GMO's are a "not in my name [50]" or red line issue. The statement means what it says with no ambiguity or grey areas. **When** it goes wrong any supporter or agency which drove the transgenic organisms will be at fault, it will **not** be on me or anyone else who didn't. Supporters and drivers will be responsible not opponents. By the same token if I'm wrong I'll be eating huge portions of humble pie. I will even let them walk me to the village stocks and you can throw as much GM food at my face as you like. The question is "how will you respond if I am right?" will you admit culpability? I doubt it, because you never do with anything. I suppose this writing is an appeal to the reason and critical faculties of the undecided or concerned. To the scientists driving this I ask (nay beg), are you **really** so sure of your science and technology? I'm not. I don't think it is worth the very real risk and probability of total and complete global disaster, on top of everything else which is going so horribly wrong. So dear reader, what do you think? Full steam ahead with GMO's with no regulation to speak of? Or, hang on a minute can we go over this again? What is it to be? The final chapter will I hope explain why there is no "oops that didn't work" option.

Chapter 8: A Sense Of Perspective

In the summer of 2003, I was enjoying the rarest of beasts, a paid and highly enjoyable job, which also and made a difference. As the debacle of the Afghan invasion bled into its equally catastrophic bedfellow known as the Iraq War, I was employed as a fundraiser. Each of us had to obtain a minimum number of daily sign ups but our remit included raising awareness about GM crops. In early 2003 the prospect of GM crops being grown on a commercial basis was becoming distinctly likely. Unfortunately, the same held true in late 2015, when the first edition of this book was written and the same is true in early 2018. The EU has given the green light for GM crops to be grown on an ad-hoc basis. In conjunction with this reality the UK general election of May 2015 saw 11 million people vote for a government headed by a man who by his own admission wants to put "rocket boosters under TTIP" [1] (Trans-Atlantic Trade and Investment Partnership). After the 2015 election David Cameron re-affirmed his personal support and therefore that of the conservative party to a trade deal which have destroyed what is left of democracy in Europe. The same goes for equivalent trade deals such as TPP (trans-Pacific Partnership) and TPSEP [2] (Trans-Pacific Strategic Economic Partnership). All discussion pertaining to these wholly undemocratic policies (TTIP and GMO's) is occurring behind closed doors. We only know about them because you cannot keep something that big under wraps for ever. Secondly, in the UK, a flurry of freedom of information requests have brought both polices into the public domain. I'll put it bluntly GMO's, TTIP/TPP and equivalent trading arrangements are inextricably linked. Resisting one augments resistance to the other; conversely support for one strengthens support for the other. Although TTIP has been stopped the Trump administration and others are concocting even worse measures. A post Brexit UK could find itself caught up in such trade agreements.[3] GMO's is merely one area which the British establishment seeks to fastrack.[4] If GM crops are not stopped I predict as the third decade of this century proceeds we will be eating a diet laden, (if not completely contaminated) with GMO's. If such an eventuality occurs there will be dire consequences for all of us.

As the Shirley Bassey song imparts, history is, in fact, repeating itself. When the New Labour government headed by Tony Blair was dragging the UK into the catastrophic debacle we know as the inter-related Afghanistan and Iraq wars, the whole discourse on GM foods was relegated to the back seat. Back in 2003, the British establishment, with the personal support of Tony Blair [5] saw an opportunity to pull a fast one and proceed with the commercial growing of GE crops. Thankfully, it never happened, my tiny contribution to this clear defeat for the new labour project [6] and supporters [7] of GMO's in the UK, was the fundraising and communications role mentioned above. Unfortunately, the same fight is coming and soon too. Whether you like it or not GMO's are again raising their ugly head, this issue is not going anywhere; in fact, it is well and truly in the post, the primary reason for writing this book. Recent polls in the UK appear to indicate a softening of opposition to GE foods. However, the ideological covenant I am in says the surveys and questioning regimes were somewhat biased and misleading. Again the reader is reminded that GMO's are irreversible, novel and is again asked who they believe and why. Therefore it seemed pertinent to ask the questions which cut right to the core of the whole issue:

- What are GMO's?

- Where have GMO's come from?

- What is agricultural GE?

- Do we need it?

- Does it work?

These and other questions are a mechanism by which to remind ourselves of the very real dangers intrinsic to GMO's in agriculture. Hitherto this book has provided a solid foundation for answering the first three questions and presents resounding "No" by way of answer to the other two. A huge part of your point of view on GM foods (and other issues) is perspective dependent. Have a look at the questions posed at beginning of chapter seven, to see what I'm driving at. Personally, I view our world today and see a ball of conflict, destruction, madness, total insanity, denial, apathy, acceptance, confusion and dysfunction. All of it completely unnecessary and fuelled by the venal desires of a childish, selfish, greedy, psychotic, sadistic, sociopathic, misanthropic, lying, thieving warmongering, plutocratic elite, a cohort that will say and do anything if they can profit from it. Those who identify with the use of the above adjectives **are** going to have questions on the motives and attitudes around the mandarins of global power. Conversely, far too many people seem oblivious and apathetic; whilst others equivalently go along with the depravity. If you're thinking all is well, normal and acceptable, the chances are you're **not** going have a problem with GMO's. You are also unlikely to have questions concerning "how things are done in this world". If you're of this latter persuasion I would argue you need to wake up both for your own sake and for your children. If after some thought you still think things are "going well", then I would present the case that you have a major attitude problem. GM foods are **one** product of the commercialisation of science. Along with the obscene amounts of resources diverted toward military and weapons research, GMO's represent an abuse of the scientific endeavour and its achievements. On that basis alone J'accuse [8] in their entirety and with all personal power I can muster, the movers, shakers and supporters of GMO's of being anti-science. The science conducted in the laboratories which produce GMO's is technically brilliant and of an impeccable standard. I am **not** suggesting or arguing otherwise, but this is **not** the point. I am inculcating GMO's do **not** work, **alternatives** exist and GM foods are wholly **unnecessary**. GMO's represent **one,** if not **the,** prime candidate for the PP, which implies that as a species we interfere with DNA at our peril. On the other side of the coin, those who support GMO's do not agree. [9]

Consider the attitudes toward the science behind climate change and that displayed toward GMO's. They are the antithesis of each other. On one hand the response of the capitalist classes in the industrialised world toward climate change has been inadequate well passed criminality. Their ineptitude and intransigent denial, occurs against the sense of urgency displayed by the global community of climatologists, the wider scientific community and the peoples of the planet. Conversely, the global establishment appears to have embraced GMO's wholesale despite the subjective and downright spurious science. Objections on the part of hundreds of millions of people all over the world are also ignored. If this reality does not represent a systemic contradiction (if not dysfunction) as well as a threat to global democracy then I don't know what does. With climate change and GM foods there is no reverse switch. Once a GMO has been released into the environment there is no rescind option. The same is true of greenhouse gases emissions, once released it is impossible to retrieve them. With both of these huge issues the answer is very simple, for GMO's we don't need them and they don't work in the real world. For climate change the energy we use has to be derived from renewable technologies at least until we can bring hydrogen and / or fusion on stream. The one course of action **NOT** open to us is to say "oops, that didn't work" and expect no consequences. As far as GMO's are concerned, to see what happens when "things go wrong" the reader need only look at the litany of environmental disasters caused by invasive species across the world. The text book example is the transport of African bees to South America in the 1950's. If we are paying attention the consequences teach us what happens when nature reminds us who is in charge. Communities in the affected areas have since adapted and by and large dealt with this problem, but they shouldn't have had to. An equivalent example would be the cane toads introduced to Australia. Closer to home, Japanese knotweed here in the UK represents a problem which could disrupt the flora of the entire country. I argue GMO's fall well and truly into the precautionary category and have a real potential to cause severe and irreversible damage to both human health and the environment. Despite the industries protestations to the contrary GM foods come with an inherent risk to people and planet.

Back to the Beginning

Conspicuous in its absence from the so called debates in mainstream media on GM foods is any mention of the "where", "how" and "when" of agriculture. To appreciate the gravity of the forces supporters of GMO's wish to manipulate, some reference to the time scales involved in the accretion (formation) of the Earth is essential. To omit this perspective, would be akin to discussing fermentation without explaining how yeast converts sugar into ethanol. Any individual who has even the most fleeting interest in any aspect of science would have heard of the geologic time scale [10]. The scale is a very helpful point of reference which helps to explain the relationships between biology, chemistry and geology, these sciences are intertwined in a scientific discipline called bio-geo-chemistry [11]. When a real scientist (i.e. one not involved in GMO's) speaks of "geologic time" they mean the history of the earth. This refers to the aeons, eras, periods, epochs and ages which constitute the time line of evolution of our planet and the life upon it. These periods of time are organised based on the characteristics of life on Earth at the time and the events which have shaped its evolution. An aeon is a period of time measuring 1 billion years (10^9 years) and a period enables us to break such a long time frame into hundred million year sections. It is impossible to pin down an exact date for when a given aeon and the subdivisions it contains truly starts. Hence, events like mass extinctions [12] (ME) or other less catastrophic episodes are used to differentiate between different sections of geologic time. In a ME the impact on the biosphere is so severe and destructive that evidence is recorded in the fossil record and the chemistry of the rocks themselves. Periods are further divided into epochs based on global environmental changes. Other techniques include sediment, ice core and isotope analysis. The story of life on Earth is as fascinating as it is often frightening. We will probably never know for sure how and where evolution kicked things off, but we can present the broad strokes.

Our planet began to form 4.6 aeons ago. The first 500 million years of our planet's history is called The Hadean [13]. We know very little about this period of time except that it was hot, violent and absolutely inhospitable to any life, at least as we would understand it. The end of the Hadean is generally believed to be marked by the beginning of an event called the Late Heavy Bombardment (LHB[14]). There is no definite consensus on the causes, duration or ferocity of the LHB, likely there never will be, but the term LHB is absolutely appropriate! We can say with confidence that from about 4.1 to 3.8 aeons ago the boiling Earth was pummelled almost constantly by objects from outer space. The objects ranged in size from a few metres to dozens of kilometres in diameter. A 300 million years long rain of impacts which never stopped! In credible scientific circles, it is hypothesised some of the microbes and amino acids which made the evolution of life possible were transported to the Earth on comets and meteors. The notion has very strong weight and is not the domain of cranks or mavericks, it is a serious proposition. If a proportion of the precursor chemicals which enabled life to evolve were of extra-terrestrial origin, then the LHB would have been a prime conduit for their arrival. Irrespective of this supposition, these objects pummelled the Earth for several hundred million years. The Earth was a boiling mass of liquid rock which began to cool and stratify into the form we know today. During this time an object the size of mars is believed to have collided with our forming planet. The result is the moon and its geostationary orbit around the Earth.

The Archean, is where life began, for the next four aeons it was microbial, bacterial and viral. Some were multi-cellular whilst other forms were uni-cellular. The microbes which facilitate the GE outlined in this book are very likely descended from those present hundreds of mya, possibly aeons ago. Irrespective of what happened in deep geologic time [15] and the mechanisms by which they came to occupy their current position, the microbes are omnipresent. Microbes have been here since the beginning. Hence, GMO's represent an interference with the oldest forms of life on the planet and certainly their descendants. The modified forms are released into the environment which supports us all. Each GMO is an individual, separate from, but with the same genome as its peers. There are millions of these organisms, they **will** eventually find a way to interact with the natural world and the evolved organisms (well what is left of them) it contains. In a related frame the melting of ice caps, the prospect of deep sea mining, the drying of wetlands and peat bogs all over our planet, could all release microbes which have been in stasis for longer than we have been here.

The end of the LHB marks the beginning of Pre-Cambrian time which lasted from about 4.0 aeons to 542 mya. This constitutes approximately 90% of the history of the Earth and we know very little about it. Precambrian time is divided into three broad aeons:

- The Hadean

- The Archean

- The Proterozoic

The aeons of the Archean [16] era began with the **end** of the LHB. One of the many obvious differences as compared to the Earth today was the composition of the atmosphere. The Earth of 4 aeons ago was (due to the pull of gravity) covered in a mixture of methane, ammonia, water vapour and very small amounts of nitrogen and carbon dioxide. The impacts of the LHB were very likely to have brought additional quantities of the above compounds. The Earth was, and is, kept molten two primary forces, first the impact of trillions of extra-terrestrial objects. Second, the heat generated by the decay of radioactive elements deep underneath us. The residual heat left over from both of these sources is the reason our planet still has an active geology and therefore the capacity to maintain life. The Archean era was also characterised by intense global volcanism, increasing the CO_2 concentration in the atmosphere. The sun of the Archean Earth was about 30% less bright [17] than it is today. This is crucial because as the Earth cooled it was able to maintain a temperature conducive to the processes outlined in the sections below. In the millions of years after the LHB the Earth began to cool. The temperature dropped from several hundred degrees down to less than the boiling point of water. There is massive debate on the duration and ferocity of the volcanism and where the water we depend on came from, but at less than 100°C, water vapour condensed out of the atmosphere. The result was a planet wide and continuous deluge of water, which lasted for a minimum of several million years. The downpour formed oceans and provided the water for life on Earth to evolve in.

The same water which has been so violated by the big agriculture construct outlined in chapter six. In the Archean world, a whole menagerie of complex physics and chemistry began to play out. Atmospheric pressure decreased as the rain fell and water began to dissolve the ammonia and methane mentioned above. Simultaneously, the volcanism ejected huge amounts of sulphur dioxide (SO_2) which along with CO_2 formed acid rain of varying potency. Other acidic gases were also ejected. Collectively the acid rain kick started planet wide chemical weathering, creating huge flows of dissolved inorganic chemicals into the growing oceans. Simultaneously, the sun steadily increased in luminosity and more heat and light came into the contact with the Earth. Consequently, the reactivity of the dissolved compounds increased. These and plenty more processes, combined to create oceans, which became filled with the precursor chemicals to self-sustaining macro-molecules, i.e. life. Possibly, our most feared diseases (for instance HIV [18] and Ebola) represent the evolution induced by biochemical reactions which occurred in the primordial oceans [19]. In the case of Ebola, the events of late 2014 and early 2015 demonstrate how little we really know about the ability of microbial genetic material to adapt and mutate in new environments.

The lower atmosphere of the Archean contained very little if any oxygen. Scientists think very low amounts of oxygen may have existed in the upper atmosphere. The onset of photosynthesis (PHS) changed everything. In terms of the evolution of life and our place on Planet Earth, the **single** most important event was the appearance of photosynthesising bacteria about 3.5 aeons ago [20] . For these microbes oxides of sulphur were the main waste products of their metabolism. They used infra-red as opposed to visible light as an energy source. The Earth would have had a distinctly red even Martian hue. These microbes dominated the biosphere for the next 800 million years or so. The first oxygen producing bacteria appeared somewhere between 2.7 and 2.45 aeons ago. [21] Known as cyano-bacteria, these microbes are accepted to be the ancestors to the chloroplasts found in green plants today. The structures being used the Rubisco research mentioned in chapter seven. Still think there is **no** issue here? I don't, quite the opposite. The onset of PHS was a wipe-out catastrophe for **all** other microbes which constituted the biota on Planet Earth. Through cyanobacteria metabolism oxygen was released into the atmosphere. Strange as it may seem, as the gas began to accumulate the previous biota was wiped out. The evolution of PHS represents the first known mass extinction in the history of our planet. Oxygen gas still is poisonous to every form of life which has not evolved to metabolise it.

All Change!

In the parlance of environmental and Earth science at about 2.7 aeons ago the Earth moved from a chemically reduced or anaerobic state to an oxidised or aerobic state. Microbes which could not adapt perished, or they were left to a life in the most extreme of environments. Today, these microbes only exist in environments such as mudflats or the anoxic zones of the deep ocean. Speaking of the deep ocean, I am absolutely disgusted to read of mining corporations seeking to plunder the seabed for resources; everything from minerals and fossil fuels is in the offing. From their position, deep sea coral reefs and hydrothermal vents are merely an externality to ignore. Aeons ago, these structures had yet to form, but the deep sea environment is widely believed to be where it all began. In my view, while such criminality is allowed to continue we **cannot** be allowed to explore other planets. If it exists, now would be a good time for the galactic club to intervene. In the geologic time scale, the presence of oxygen delimits the boundary between the Archean and Proterozoic [22] eras. Both eras are characterised by life which was completely microscopic and almost totally unicellular. It took at least two billion years for oxygen to accumulate in the atmosphere. The reasons for the time lag are intertwined with the definition of bio-geo-chemistry mentioned above. The accumulation of free atmospheric oxygen set the scene for the progression of life from the sea onto the land. In turn, only the formation of the ozone layer made that particular evolutionary leap forward possible.

The Cambrian Explosion

About 600 mya the biota of planet Earth consisted in its entirety of microbes, plankton and a few species of multi-celled algae. According to the fossil record life began to diversify at around 570 mya. By about 543 mya complex plants and animals with a biological organisation (shape) appeared. In addition this complex multi cellular life began to move out of primordial seas and on to the land. Both pivotal events characterise a period of time known as the Cambrian explosion [23], which delimits the point between Cambrian and Pre-Cambrian time. In a blink of a geologic eye (about 30 million years) large multi-cellular flora (plant) and fauna (animal) firmly took their place in the evolution of life on

Earth. The presence of free oxygen and the formation of the ozone layer set the chemical and atmospheric conditions to make such a great leap forward possible. However, the absolutely fundamental biological driver to this event was the evolution of DNA. The double helix discussed in chapter two, enabled the most efficient biological processes and beneficial traits to be rapidly passed on to the new families of organism. The DNA subject to all forms of GM has been with us for hundreds of millions of years. It is also the result of aeons of evolutionary trial and error. Again, according to the supporters of GM foods we are **not** supposed to view the development and application of GMO's from this perspective, apparently its alarmist! Well, I call it common sense and a respect for the Earth and the biosphere. The fossil record shows us many late Pre-Cambrian forms of life simply disappeared. It seems the organisms of Pre-Cambrian time were displaced by the newcomers. The mechanisms which facilitated the explosion of multi-cellular life are the subject of animated discussion. Irrespective of the why and how, the Cambrian Explosion set the scene for the evolution of modern human beings.

The Cambrian explosion delimits the point in time between the Proterozoic aeon and the Phanerozoic aeon. [24] The latter aeon is where humanity finds itself and is broken down into three eras:

- The Palaeozoic (ancient life) era,[25] ran from 542 mya to 251 mya. Its endpoint is marked by the end Permian mass extinction event. [26] This pivotal event is by far the worst environmental catastrophe to befall the Earth, since the Cambrian explosion. Approximately 250 mya, on a Tuesday at 10.00am, an inter-related series of processes was set in motion by the geology of Planet Earth. About 100,000 years later the collective of processes had fully run their course. By which time up to 90% of all life on Earth had been eradicated. In everyday language, the event is known as "the great dying" or "the day the Earth nearly died". For good reason, words phrases such as "wipe-out" characterise this extinction event. We don't know what started the catastrophe, but the culprit could a meteor impact. Way back in 2004 I recall the evidence for a meteor impact being cherry picked by the fossil fuel industry. Again showing is **not** a value free process. But the point remains a meteor impact could have upset the geology of the earth, setting the Permian mass extinction off.

- The Mesozoic era [27] (Reptiles and dinosaurs) ran from 251 to 65 mya. It is now almost universally accepted to have been ended by a meteor impact. The collision wiped out some 60% of all life on Earth, including the dinosaurs. It created the evolutionary space to usher in the age of the mammals. In a few weeks, most of the dinosaurs were removed from the biosphere. Only some of their descendants exist today, but industry driven activity across the board is doing its utmost to kill them off too. For instance, just ask the whale sharks, the organisms which call the deep ocean home, komodo dragons as well as the crocodiles and alligators. As well as a meteor impact the fossil record points to a whole host of climate phenomenon which was already putting the dinosaurs in serious trouble. The cretaceous tertiary (K/T) meteor impact merely catalysed, intensified and ultimately overwhelmed events which were already unfolding.

- The Cenozoic (recent life) era runs from 65 mya until the present day. This era is divided into two periods called the Tertiary, and the Quaternary. The tertiary period (now referred to as the Paleogene [28] period) ended approximately 23 mya. The Quaternary period is now termed the Neogene [29] period and extends to the present day.

The Paleogene period is itself broken down into 3 sections we term epochs, a random division which is shorter than a period but longer than an age. An epoch is generally measured in millions of years but an age can wax and wane within a few thousand or even hundred years. The oil age where Homo sapiens currently live is very likely to be an instance of the latter case. The Anthropocene epoch will likely be recorded as lasting a few decades, if of course there are any people left to record it. The three epochs which compose the Paleogene period are:

- The Palaeocene [30] (65-55 mya)

- The Eocene [31] (55-33 mya [32])

- The Oligocene [33] (33-23 mya)

The Neogene period is the next segment in the geologic time scale and is composed of two epochs:

- The Miocene [34] (23-5.5 mya)

- The Pliocene [35] (5.3-2.6 mya)

The Paleogene and Neogene division is down to environmental changes as evaluated from the fossil record, the analysis of the rocks by radioactive dating [36] and other techniques. The climate aspect of these global environmental changes is directly comparable to our current, precarious system induced climate situation. These are the forces which people who support GMO's think we can manage by engineering CO_2 fixing plants. Similarly, those who support nuclear power and fracking on climate grounds view both as realistic propositions to manage emissions of greenhouse gases. As stated in chapter seven CO_2 fixing just is not going to work when the carbon cycle itself is on the point of collapse or re-alignment. As for Fracking and nuclear power, the **only** way to deal with emissions is to **stop** them. Any policy which does not stop or reduce to almost zero emissions of greenhouse gases is **not** by definition a solution to climate change, end of! The Paleogene period is characterised by a sustained, prolonged and profound steady increase in global temperatures. For instance, 55 mya an event known as the Palaeocene-Eocene Thermal Maximum (PETM) [37] occurred. Global temperatures were already several degrees higher than they are today. The PETM stepped things up even more. Levels of CO_2 in the atmosphere have been measured as being over 1000 parts per million (ppm). This is about 2.5 times higher than they are in 2018 and over three times higher than they were at the start of the industrial revolution. The PETM was characterised by rapid and intense global warming, likely caused by a period of intense volcanic activity. On top of the elevated levels of CO_2 huge quantities of methane were also released into the atmosphere. Likely the source of this gas was structures called methane hydrates. The rapid warming forced temperatures up to about 10°C higher than they are today. In what is now the arctic, sea temperatures were in excess of 23°C. The consequences were planet wide and it took millions of years for life to adapt and recover. These very high temperatures were maintained throughout the Paleogene. In contrast the Neogene period, i.e. the end of the Oligocene epoch, is characterised by the onset of a sustained period of gradual global cooling. This drop in temperature is believed to have caused a decline in marine species and an expansion of grasslands and savannah, setting the scene for the next twenty million years. The fossil record indicates the Miocene epoch had up to a fifth less marine and terrestrial families than the Oligocene. This relatively minor level of extinction created the evolutionary space for the first apes and therefore the evolution of modern human beings. By about 7 mya the ancestors of modern human beings and those of chimpanzees had gone their separate evolutionary ways. The planet itself continued to cool. As compared to the Miocene epoch the Pliocene is characterised by cooler temperatures and the onset of large mammals which ranged all over the world. From our perspective one pivotal development occurs in the Pliocene. It is the epoch in which modern hominids [38] first appeared.

Clever (?) Monkeys with Technology

Between four and five million ya a species of bipedal primate, Australopithecus anamenesis [39] appears in the fossil record. Approximately, 3 million ya a hominid called "moon watcher" from a hominid species called Australopithecus africanus [40] encounters the monolith in the opening sequence [41] of 2001 – A Space Odyssey. This event marks the onset of the Pleistocene epoch, a segment of time characterised by profound global climatic and environmental changes. The waxing and waning of various glacial periods were directly responsible for consummate fluctuations in global sea levels[41] temperature, humidity and climate overall. The Pleistocene epoch [42] began about 2.6 mya during a period of glaciation and ended 12,000 to 13,000 ya. At this point, an Epoch [43] called the Holocene begins. The Pleistocene is where modern humans evolved from the previous line of hominids. At about 100,000 ya the only hominids were the Neanderthals and the first Homo sapiens. With the extinction of the Neanderthals approximately 40,000 ya only we were left to fill the evolutionary vacuum. In other words, the Holocene is the epoch within which modern humanity, warts, (mainly warts IMO), and all has developed. Modern human society has evolved in a time where the climate is stable and warm as compared to the Pliocene epoch. The Holocene delimits the time when modern homo-sapiens began the transition from a nomadic (but not necessarily primitive) hunter gatherer existence to a settled way of life based on the new undertaking of agriculture.

The Neolithic Revolution

It is impossible to establish exactly when human beings began to practice agriculture. At this time in pre-history, as far as we know, the written word (or symbol) had yet to be discovered. With some certainty we can say human beings began growing their own food in several disparate locations about 10,000 ya. Archaeology indicates a region called the Fertile Crescent [44] as where farming is most likely to have begun. The same region been so grotesquely violated, in every conceivable way, by the kinds of forces outlined in chapter six. Today the Fertile Crescent is a shadow of its former self, this once flourishing ecosystem (which also used to support millions of people) has been absolutely devastated by a whole a series of projects which in my view should be considered both environmental and humanitarian crime. The Tigris and Euphrates river systems are two of the drainage systems which used [45] to provide water for the entire region. A horrific and disgusting combination of theft, dictatorship, folly, war, destruction, killing, murder, flat out genocide intertwined with the impacts of climate change could well make the whole region uninhabitable in the very near future. And once I again I ruthlessly challenge the biotechnology industry to explain how it is going to repair such damage. The Crescent extends from the Persian Gulf to Northern Egypt then to very North of Saudi Arabia and over Iraq toward Kuwait. In the Holocene and according to recent research an area of Iran in the foot hills of the Zagros Mountains is the birth place of farming. This region is the nexus of the domestication of animals and the growing of plants, the basic foundations of agriculture. Archaeologists' analysed remains and artefacts dated from about 11,700 to about 10,000 ya. These early crops were forms of barley, grass and beans which are the ancestors of those which exist today. The development of agriculture is taken to delimit the onset of the Neolithic (new stone) age of human evolution. The Stone Age itself is divided into three epochs called the Palaeolithic, Mesolithic and Neolithic. The Palaeolithic (old stone) age started between 3-2.5 mya and is characterised by the first use of tools by Homo erectus, habilis and other hominids who were alive at the time. It extends through the last ice age and ended about 10,000 ya. The huge environmental changes occurring throughout the Neogene period had massive impacts on the course of human innovation. No single or definite dates exist for when a given development occurred.

Separate communities of humans developed in different regions and at different rates. However a very rough time line can be constructed from the archaeological and pre-historic record. In very general terms the bipedal mammals of the Palaeolithic age were predominantly nomadic hunter gatherers who used tools made of flint, stone, bone, antlers and leather. By the time of the Holocene epoch the only bipedal animals on the planet were ourselves; the Homo-sapiens. The profound environmental changes caused by the retreating ice are not the subject of this writing, but they were certainly an evolutionary game changer. It truly was a case of adapt or die.

About 10,000 ya the Palaeolithic age [46] was superseded by the Mesolithic [47] (Middle Stone) age. The transition between the two ages varies according to location; but the onset of farming differentiates between the two ages. As far as we know, farming first developed across middle latitudes. Wheat was grown about 10,000 (ya) in what is now South Eastern Turkey, on the northern edge of the Fertile Crescent. Likely wheat was grown elsewhere in the region (and wider world) but this is the earliest evidence we have. By about 9000 ya the peoples of the Middle East were growing wheat, barley and rearing domestic animals including goats, sheep and even dogs. The Eastern and Western Mediterranean along with southern Europe followed suit about 8000 ya. Simultaneously, equivalent practices spread into what is now Asia and the Far East. Food production took an additional few thousand years to arrive in North Africa. The Fertile Crescent represents one of the first, but not the only region where agriculture was practised in the Neolithic world. Human communities living on the foothills of mountain ranges, flatlands and wetlands amongst other environments across the whole planet were engaged in some form of agriculture. Currently, our picture of this phase of human evolution is as complex as it is patchy. With some certainty we can say farmers in what is now Turkey and Eastern Iran were sowing their first seeds and simultaneous developments were occurring in the territory we know as Ancient Sumer. This geographic region covered the Southern Edge of the Fertile Crescent, over what is now Southern Iraq and Kuwait. Without doubt there are huge gaps in our knowledge of how homo sapien culture and innovation developed in the opening millennia of the Holocene epoch. We do know food collection gradually began to necessitate a more settled life style. In turn early modern humans had to maximise the use of available resources in a given location. From here it is a short leap to arrive at the notion of early farming and animal domestication. By about 7000 ya the peoples of Ancient Britain had begun their first forays into settled food production. Throughout this pre-historic and ancient world human beings began to harvest their food from the vegetation around them. In tandem we began to domesticate wild animals which became livestock. Humans learned how to utilise animal products and the animals themselves in addition to obtaining ever increasing crop yields. For sure, by 21st century standards a well organised allotment is probably more productive. Yet, 7000 ya growing enough food in one place to sustain a population was a game-changer, hence the phrase Neolithic Revolution.[48]

As early farmers discovered beneficial traits in both plants and animals, crop yields increased as did techniques in animal husbandry. The commencement of farming and agriculture lays with those fledgling groups of early homo-sapiens who learned which plants and berries were good to eat **and** who figured out how to plant seeds and keep small herds and flocks of animals. Without an understanding of selective cross breeding or hybridisation the Neolithic revolution would have been impossible. Without knowing it, these communities applied the principles of Mendelian genetics outlined in chapter one. Plants and livestock animals with the most desirable characteristics were bred, whilst others were not. Over several millennia the early farmers developed the most productive varieties of crop plants (cultivars). Neolithic farmers were looking for traits which apply to this day they include:

- Increased resistance to pests and disease

- A shorter growing season enabling multiple harvests.

- Crop or feed plants which produced larger seeds and fruits.

- Adaptations such as resistance to diverse and / or extreme environmental conditions.

The Neolithic revolution catalysed a period of innovation where the technology and techniques of food production and animal husbandry steadily improved. Neolithic farmers began their processes of selective and cross breeding with absolutely no understanding of terms such as DNA or genetics, but they clearly knew what they were doing. Again it is fair to ask how such practices are in anyway comparable to GE. The farmers of the Neolithic and ancient world learned how to cross breed staple food crops with grasses drawing out desired traits with every passing season. In Ancient Britain wheat cultivation was one of the many activities which allowed communities to become food self-sufficient. The same is not true for the

British Isles in the 21st century. The continual rise in the number of food banks and the need for GP's to prescribe fresh fruit are but two examples of that reality. Over time the economy of ancient Britain began to trade its crop surplus with what we would now call mainland Europe. This trade was one of the factors that made the ancient British economy so attractive to the primary imperial scourge of the ancient world, known as the Roman Empire. By the time the Romans were compelled to leave Britain some 1600 ya, agricultural yield some three tonnes of wheat per hectare, today it is nearer eight. However, despite record harvests in 2014 as compared to 2012, as well as promising harvests for 2016,[49] the UK is a **net** importer of wheat. [50] The crops grown today bear little resemblance to those grown in the Neolithic revolution. Most varieties eaten today can be traced back to the wild varieties which grew in the Middle East and central Asia some 10,000 ya. There simply is no space to go into the machinations of GM wheat; I would need another book at least as long as this one! However, the broad strokes are identical, the drivers and their reasoning are identical, the need for a precautionary approach is identical and the references below do explain with the necessary attention to detail why, as usual, all is not what the proponents say it is. In short GM wheat is a likely future battle. Wheat is a crucially important staple food crop whose value cannot be understated. Approximately 750 million tonnes are harvested every year across the world, fuelling a market worth billions of dollars. None of this wheat is (as of 2017) currently [51] GM, but plenty of trials have been conducted since the turn of the 21st century. Plus, the US department of Agriculture (USDA) is on record as imparting, the only reason GM wheat is not grown on a commercial scale in the US is down to resistance from the peoples of the countries which constitute its export market. As far as the UK is concerned a firm down payment has been made on the full commercial growing of GM wheat, courtesy of the white coats at Rothemsted research.[52] It seems the UK establishment is going to push for GM crops. The UK conservative party has always supported GMO's; Labour party policy is to assess each GMO on a "case by case basis". They will also adopt them if the people of the UK want it. This is especially worrying as the UK continues on its near suicidal drive to leave the EU under the auspices of Brexit. As things stand in the UK, GMO's are on the cards **either** on a case by case basis **or** a full drive for their unfettered and unregulated uptake. Either way, unless the activist community comes out hard as we did in 1990's and early 2000's, GMO's will be a reality as 2020 approaches. For those who control it, wheat farming is a hugely profitable undertaking. Little wonder the GM food industry wants a slice (if not outright control) of this particular pie. Make no mistake about it; the biotechnology industry is very interested in controlling wheat by means of GE too. As of 2015 only two licences for GM wheat have been granted, yet already, serious questions are being asked of its supposed benefits. Irrespective of any concerns, the GM food industry is pressing ahead with GM wheat and other crops regardless. One example is a form of transgenic wheat called MON 71800, [53] developed by Monsanto. GM wheat is absolutely under the "watch this space" category.

During the Neolithic period, humanity began to settle into small but expanding settlements which gradually began to foster links with each other. Human civilisation was built on an effective and constantly improving food production and distribution system. The current mono-culture system could do with some lessons on agriculture [54] from the ancient world.

The whole construct was complex, varied and produced a huge range of food stuffs, seed surplus and livestock animals. This allowed for the development of trade and further resource exploitation. Human settlements began to expand and agriculture was the fundamental driver. All aspects of the human condition from religion to social organisation were altered. As our technology improved so did our ability to improve agriculture, sadly our propensity for violence and conflict followed suit. Money was invented some 3-4000 ya and rapidly superseded bartering as the preferred method by which goods were exchanged. The use of coin as a universal unit of exchange dovetails almost completely with the advent of the Bronze Age,[55](4,500 – 2,800 ya), which rapidly succeeded the Neolithic age. From here we can indicate a timeline of events which encapsulates the next three thousand years, including:

- The Iron Age [56] which ended with the Roman occupation of Ancient Britain in the year 43.

- The history from the collapse of the Roman Empire in the year 410 until the 18th century.

- The Agrarian Revolution [57] which began in Britain in the mid-18th century and for all intents and purposes is carrying on today.

- The Green Revolution which occurred after the second wholly avoidable global conflict.

We are now in the second decade of the 21st century. Agriculture will always be essential for our continued evolution. From the French and Russian revolutions to the

Arab Spring of 2011 a compromised food supply has provoked uprisings and societal upheaval a plenty. There is no rule book and similar events will happen. I argue GMO's make them almost inevitable, especially when other global issues are factored in. Intensive agriculture has undoubtedly garnered huge benefit, but **only** if the objective is improving yields. The costs represent an environmental and food security nightmare which has had devastating consequences the world over. As for the future, we are looking at a series of time bombs which inevitably will explode unless things change. We have all seen those documentaries or read popular science books which compress the age of the Earth into a year or century. On these scales, humanity has been around for a few minutes. Agriculture has been around for about 15 seconds. We landed on the moon two seconds ago, about when the first GMO was made. Agriculture has changed for ever the biodiversity of the entire planet. The technology which provides the platform for GMO's is embedded into the current food network. GMOs are the natural consequence of a system where profit supersedes **all** other concerns. People in this world are **not** starving due to a lack of food. People are starving:

- Because they are poor.

- Because of a lack of availability or infrastructure.

- Because of blockade.

- Because of war.

- Because of political expediency

- Because of racism.

- Because of denial and callous disregard.

- Because of acceptance and apathy.

There is plenty for everyone to eat on this planet. One hungry mouth and empty belly is a disgrace. Millions all over the world dying of hunger, from the shop doorways of the Western World to the deserts of the global south, is an act of genocide. A deliberate policy gleefully carried out because of the psychosis of those who run things. GMO's will solve these realities, they will make a cataclysmically stupid (in the truest sense of the word) and self-inflicted situation even worse. The GM food-agribusiness construct is vulnerable to a series of shocks which could easily make the current famines appear as an individual case of anorexia nervosa.

Without doubt on GMO's, food processing and agriculture, on climate change and bio-geochemical cycles, on biodiversity, on conflict and nuclear issues the evolutionary clock is ticking. These are the issues which require immediate resolution, if we and the current biosphere are to survive. On the current trajectory something is going to give, it may have done already! As our current global situation stands no resolution is going to put what we have seen so far into the shade. From an Earth science and environmental perspective the picture is absolutely terrifying. We **all** live in a world which is in a catastrophic, flat out and genuinely stupid, absolutely unnecessary and disgraceful situation. We are heading toward a 6th mass extinction (since the Cambrian explosion), we could be in it already, and the tragedy is we know it is coming. With good evidence based reason, with an increasing sense of fear and unbridled terror, I believe we are heading toward Permian levels of total collapse. The global elite, their supporters and appeasers are guilty of crimes against the planet **and** crimes against humanity. Unless "things" change or are compelled to, we have decades left before it happens. Some say the process is already occurring. Given the current rate of species extinction and environmental destruction I see no reason to argue differently. The prospect of GE releasing human made GMO's into our environment totally fits into this future. And it's not pretty. Take a second and think about it. The world is unstable and becoming more so. The spoilt children in charge are in a more manic mood than has hitherto passed. From any objective and rational aspect the reality is undeniable and as we all know instability breeds uncertainty. Given our current criminally insane situation are we really to stand by and allow the wholesale release of GMO's into a biosphere which is already critically endangered? If you think science is value free the answer is **yes**. If you do **not** the answer is **no**. Once again there is no middle ground. I reiterate we have no idea of the future consequences; we truly are firing in the dark. Releasing GMO's means firing segments of novel DNA into the fabric of evolution, are we seriously expected to believe there will be **no** long term consequences? More bizarrely some have even suggested consequences will be overcome by our ingenuity. I say it isn't worth the risk especially when there are alternatives. Anyone who seriously believes there won't be consequences needs psychiatric help, ditto if they are lying. Either way these people should **not** be making decisions concerning GMO's on our behalf.

As of late 2017, we live in a world where Donald Trump is the president of the most powerful country in the world. Tragically Hilary "shoulda stuck with Bernie" Clinton, really wasn't much better, but she is not Donald Trump. A real choice of tweedle sociopath and tweedle psychopath, such are the products of the global elite. Sadly, in terms of outlook and foreign policy there really isn't much difference between any of them wherever they come from. In the name of humanity, the likes of Donald Trump, Benjamin Netanyahu Theresa May, Aung San Suu Kyi and what they represent must be fought and challenged at any and all opportunities. The same applies to the entirety of the global elite and those who refuse to question their operations too. We also live in a world which looks set to leave the Holocene epoch and enter a new frame called The Anthropocene. In either case, all bets, statutes and mechanisms by which our affairs are organised are off and I do mean all bets. Living in a world with Trump or equivalent presidencies along with Putin and Li Keqiang style and worse dictatorships combined with the threads of power holding the whole mess together in The Anthropocene, in a world martyred by denial of systemic issues **and** where GMO's are the norm, scares this writer to the core of his being. At the end of the day it is very simple, do you want that kind of future or not? As I make crystal clear here there is no middle ground, so what do you want? What we have and likely much worse, or do you believe as I do that "another world is possible"?

Glossary of Terms

Abiotic: Any component of the non-living environment such as the sea or fresh water.

Accretion (of the Earth): A steady increase in size of an object by the capture or addition of new material. The earth accreted for about 40 million years as its increased gravity attracted surrounding debris.

Aerobic Respiration: The conversion of glucose into water and carbon dioxide in the presence of oxygen. The conversion releases chemical energy which organisms use to power their metabolic processes.

Agribusiness / Big Agriculture / corporate farming: A system of farming characterised by large monocultured and/or intensive farms, under some degree of corporate control. To remain viable these farms require huge chemical inputs (fertilisers and pesticides) and machinery. Extra capital may be needed if the crops in question require irrigation.

Alkaloid: Organic (carbon based) compounds only found in plants which have some physiological impact on human beings. They are often used in medicine, and examples include morphine, codeine, cocaine, nicotine quinine and strychnine

Amino Acid: The individual (monomer) units which chemically bond with each other (peptide links) forming smaller polymers called polypeptides and larger polymers called proteins.

Antisense Gene: A sequence of nucleotides (i.e. a gene) which is able to inactivate its opposite and complementary sequence. Not to be confused with allele.

Arthropod: Any invertebrate animal which has an exoskeleton and whose body is divided into segments. Examples include insects, crustaceans and spiders (arachnids).

Allele: An alternate form of a given gene which is dominant or recessive and found on a precise point on the chromosome, normally against its opposite.

Biochemistry: A scientific discipline which studies the chemical reactions and conversion of reacting substances which occur in living organisms.

Biogeochemistry: A holistic scientific discipline which studies the interactions between the abiotic and biotic environments. The biological, chemical, geologic and physical processes resulting in alterations to the workings of the natural world.

Biological Organisation: The arrangement of specialist organelles to form cells cells in all living organisms. The cells then go on to form tissues, organs, organ systems and then the organism. The organism then interacts with the biosphere and habitat around it.

Biota: The living components of the natural world, such as habitats and the organisms they contain. Collectively all components of the biota are termed the biosphere.

Genetic Bio-piracy: An incisive word for theft which refers to the acquisition of knowledge and/or resources (intellectual property) connected to farming from indigenous communities, without consultation, recompense or any form of reward, monetary or otherwise to the original source of knowledge.

Bioreactor / Industrial Fermenter: A large metal vessel normally made of stainless steel which is used to grow producer microbes for the industrial scale production of useful biological molecules.

Biotechnology: An application of a biological process, such as fermentation, normally on a commercial or industrial scale. Biotechnology usually involves microbes, enzymes and genetic engineering.

Callus: A mass of cells which have yet to differentiate and are used to carry engineered genetic traits into the genome of transgenic organisms.

Cambrian Time: The totality of time from the Cambrian explosion to the present day.

Cell Cycle: The life cycle of a living cell from reproduction (mitosis/meiosis) to death (apoptosis).

Cell differentiation: The set of biological processes by which unspecialised cells become specialised and adapted to a particular function.

Chromosome: Structures upon which DNA is found located in the nucleus of almost all living cells.

Climate Change: A long term and global shift in the temperature and weather of Planet Earth. The phrase climate change has largely superseded alternative phrases such as global warming. Adding the pre-fix "human induced" means that our activities under capitalism are causing the changes with wholly unpredictable consequences.

Complimentary base pair: The description used to explain how the nucleotides (bases) in a molecule of DNA are able to chemically bond with each other. The mechanism allows the double helix structure and overall shape of DNA.

Cocktail effect: A catch all phrase used to describe the potential negative impact of simultaneous exposure to different synthetic (human made) chemicals on the environment and organisms, including human beings. The combination or "cocktail effect is believed to amplify the impact of trace amounts of individual compounds or minor changes to the environment.

Covalent Bond: A form of chemical bond (electrostatic force) which only occurs between non-metallic ions.

Cross breeding /hybridisation/interbreeding: A method of breeding where organisms of the same genus but different species can be mated or pollinated.

Cross Pollination/ allogamy/xenogamy: Mechanism by which pollen is transferred from the anther of one flowering plant to the stigma of a flowering plant of the same species.

Cultivars/crop plants: Any plant which has been deliberately created and maintained through selective and /or cross breeding.

DNA: A nucleic acid consisting of two complimentary chains of nucleotides composed of the bases adenine, thymine, guanine and cytosine.

DNA ligation: A biological process which enables single strands of DNA (RNA) to chemically bond with each other. The reactions which enable the bonding to happen are catalysed by an enzyme called DNA ligase.

E.coli: A species of bacteria whose habitat is the intestines of mammals.

Eugenics: Repugnant pseudo-science which imparts that human population can be controlled or improved by selectively breeding those human beings with the most desirable traits or characteristics.

Genetic Disease: Any disease or negative biological condition caused by incomplete or incorrect complimentary base pairing in the genome of the organism. They are as rare as they are terrifying and affect from one in several thousand to one in several million individuals, depending on the disease in question.

Genetic Expression/expression of a gene: The process by which genetic information (contained within DNA) is translated into biological molecules which enable the organism to function.

Gene: A length or section of DNA which allows for the inheritance of a given characteristic, and/or which codes for the manufacture of proteins. A gene is transferred from parent to offspring.

Gene of Interest (GOI): The target gene or genes which are of interest to the GM food industry due to the trait it or they express.

Genome: The complete set of genes found on the chromosomes in the nucleus of an individual cell.

Genetic Code: The order of nucleotides (complimentary bases) which determines the order in which individual amino acids will be assembled into proteins.

Genetic engineering / Modification: The deliberate alteration of the genome / genetic code of an organism by the precise alteration of its DNA. Not to be confused with natural selection

Genetically Engineered/ Modified / Transgenic Organism:

Genetic / Biological Patent: Intertwined with bio-piracy a genetic patent refers to the practice of patenting (through corporate agencies) any genes or sequences of DNA. The act of patenting means that the corporate agency then owns that gene or the characteristic it expresses.

Gene Therapy: The totality of techniques which exist by which mutated genes can be corrected and introduced into the genome of a person who carries the genes for (or has) a genetic disease. Not to be confused with plant or animal genetic engineering.

Genetic Vector: Any section of DNA which can replicate itself and can be transported by genetic engineering into the genome of the cells which compose the genetically modified organism.

Genus: In the biological classification of organisms (taxonomy) a genus is the division between family and species. A genus usually contains more than one species and the different species can be hybridised under the auspices of selective breeding.

Geologic Time Scale: A point of reference used to break down the history of the Earth and the evolution of life into manageable sections.

Green revolution: A form of agriculture which took off after WW2 and which is still carrying on today. It is characterised by the growing of mono-cultured crops which are dependent on chemical inputs such as fertilisers, herbicides and other pesticides. Additionally, large quantities of water are often required and in the modern age, air/food miles are added to the mix. Without a doubt, the green revolution has provided massive increases in productivity but overall biodiversity in staple food crops has collapsed.

Hominid: Any species of bipedal primate. Homo sapiens are the latest evolution from a lineage which stretches back approximately 5 million years.

Hormone: A form of biochemical communication where by "chemical messengers" are sent through the endocrine (hormone) system of the body. They can cause quick responses such as occurs with adrenaline or long term changes such as occur at the onset of puberty and adolescence.

Hydrogen bond: A relatively weak form of chemical bond which occurs between hydrogen ions and ions of larger atoms.

Inherited disease: A genetic disease which is passed on from parent to offspring not be confused in anyway with contagious r communicable disease.

Intensive/industrial Farming: A characteristic of the green revolution and "big agriculture" where inputs of labour and capital (machinery/equipment) are high. Factory farming of animals is part of the construct.

Kingdom: The starting point in taxonomy (biological classification) is the five kingdoms which cover all forms of life. The five kingdoms are Animals, Fungi, Monera Plants and Protista.

Macromolecule (self-sustaining): Any biological molecule composed of separate and/or disparate parts capable of carrying out life processes, in other words, a form of life.

Mass Extinction Event: The points in the history of life on Earth where large amounts of species become extinct. Since the Cambrian explosion, there have been five mass extinction events. The lack of respect shown by human activity to the natural world implies very strongly that our impact constitutes a 6th mass extinction event.

Mitochondria: Site of aerobic respiration inside living cells.

Molecular biology: The scientific study of biological interactions which occur at the molecular and cellular level. The discipline seeks to understand how these systems connect with each other in terms of DNA, RNA and protein synthesis.

Monoculture: The growing of a single crop over a given area, synonymous with phrases such as "cash crop" and associated with benefitting from "economies of scale".

Monomer: The individual compounds which are chemically bonded to each other to form polymers. For instance, amino acids are the monomers for the polymers known as proteins. The simple sugar glucose is the monomer for the polymers starch and glycogen.

Mutagen: Any substance or energy source which causes mutation to DNA / the genetic code or the genome of an organism.

Mutation: A random change to the sequence of complimentary base pairs (the sequence of DNA) which can occur naturally or as the result of exposure to a mutagen.

Nucleic Acid: Any long chain polymer molecule composed of individual nucleotides, generally associated with DNA and RNA. These nucleic acids contain the information needed for a functioning metabolism and allow for the expression of genetic/hereditary information.

Nucleotide: Organic compounds which are the individual monomer unit which makes up the polymers called nucleic acids. Each nucleotide is made of a nitrogenous base a sugar and a phosphate group.

Organochlorine /POP: A large group of synthetic organic compounds each has at least one ring of carbon atoms, with varying amounts of chlorine atoms attached to the molecule. There are hundreds of individual compounds and they are exceptionally dangerous and long lasting in the environment. Examples include DDT, PCB's, Aldrin and Dieldrin.

Pectin: A polysaccharide contained within the cell walls of non-wood plants. It is not digested by humans and so, is one source of fibre or roughage. Citrus fruits are a rich source of pectin.

Pesticide: Any chemical (synthetic or natural) which is used to kill pathogenic microbes, their vectors or other organisms which are detrimental to farm animals or cultivated crops. Organochlorines, such as DDT and Glyphosate (round-up) are examples of pesticides manufactured by Monsanto. The Neonicotinoids are an example of a pesticide manufactured by the Bayer chemical company.

Polysaccharide: Any long chain polymer composed of individual monomer carbohydrate molecules (mono-saccharides) such as glucose. Starch and cellulose are examples of polysaccharides.

Protein: A huge class of natural polymers which contain atoms of carbon, hydrogen, oxygen and nitrogen. Other proteins also contain sulphur and phosphorous atoms and ALL proteins are composed of individual amino acids. Hence proteins are polymers of amino acids and are manufactured according to the genetic information contained within molecules of DNA. They are absolutely essential for life as we know it.

Pathogen: Any microbe, bacteria or virus which causes harm to an organism should it be ingested.

Plasmid: The basic structure employed in plant genetic engineering. The plasmid is a circular shaped strand of DNA which possesses the genes which code for the expression of desired genetic traits (the GOI) as one strand of its DNA.

Polymer: Any long chain molecule made up of individual repeating monomer sub units held together by chemical bonds. For example, DNA and RNA are polymers made up of individual nucleotides.

Pre-Cambrian Time: That period of geologic time as shown on the geologic time scale which precedes the Cambrian explosion. Approximately 90% of all the time that has passed until today falls under the definition of pre-Cambrian time

Precautionary Principle: If any activity has the potential to cause harm or damage to both human health and/or the environment even if no consensus exists that such harm will be caused then precautionary measures should be taken. In addition, the principle holds that the burden of proof should lay with demonstrating that the activity is harmless as opposed to proving that it is harmful. As of 2015 the precautionary principle is not generally applied to profit driven human activity.

Recombinant DNA technology (rDNA): The joining together of strands of RNA / DNA from different species which are then inserted into the genome of a third species to produce a novel transgenic organism.

Respiration: Aerobic respiration is the chemical process by which energy is released from glucose in the presence of oxygen in the mitochondria of living cells. Contrast with anaerobic respiration which is any form of respiration which does not use oxygen. The conversion of glucose to water to carbon dioxide in the mitochondria is an example of aerobic respiration. The conversion of lactic acid to water and carbon dioxide after heavy exercise is an example of anaerobic respiration.

Resistant organism: Any plant animal or microbe that has developed a resistance or immunity to pesticides. Super weeds are an example of resistant organism and the target organisms for organochlorine pesticides also have resistance to substances such as DDT.

Restriction Enzyme: Enzymes normally derived from bacteria which are used to cut (cleave) DNA into specific sequences for use in genetic engineering. A catch all term used to describe restriction enzymes as biochemical scissors.

Sticky End: A single strand of DNA (i.e. RNA) which has the desired sequence of nucleotides (complimentary base) which can be connected to another strand of RNA. Produced by the action of restriction enzymes and joining the strands of RNA results in DNA which codes for a given characteristic (i.e. the GOI).

Selective Breeding / Artificial selection: Any process by which human beings choose animal or plant breeding to selectively choose a given trait and artificially select those organisms which carry the trait for further breeding. Any method where desired traits in both males and females are selected and sexual reproduction between them is promoted.

Species: Where a male and female of a given hybrid is able to produce fertile offspring enabling the progeny to sexually reproduce. A member of any form of life which is able to reproduce and the offspring is itself able to reproduce.

Substantial equivalence: A human construct whereby any genetically engineered food is deemed to be identical (i.e. substantially equivalent) to that which already in existence.

Super-weed: An example of an organism that has evolved resistance by virtue of cross pollination from genetically engineered plants. The super-weed is then able to resist the herbicides and/or pest organisms originally applied to the GM crops.

Zygote: The cell formed at the moment of fertilisation when male and female gametes join together. This is the cell which exists before the first division into two cells takes place.

Before you go

Thank you for purchasing my book!

If you found this book interesting and enjoyed reading it, I would really appreciate a short **review on Amazon**. All of your feedback is valuable to me, as your comments and input will be taken on board to help me make this and future books even better.

I would love hearing what you have to say. Please leave me a helpful REVIEW on Amazon.

Your FREE Gift

Thank you for purchasing this book. To show our appreciation we would like to offer you a copy of our FREE recipe book "BRING LIFE TO YOUR FOOD". To download, visit our website: **www.viddapublishing.com**.

FREE Bonus Chapters: "Food Conspiracy Trilogy"

THE BIG SECRET: What Happened To Our Bread? The Chorleywood Bread Process (Food Conspiracy Volume 2)

Introduction

Before writing this book, I knew nothing about baking in 21st century Britain. Intuitively, I knew there were going to be concerns from which questions would emerge. I was not surprised to discover that mass produced bread consumed in the UK is loaded to the max with additives, E numbers and other chemicals. Some of these substances such as vitamin C are familiar to us, others such as mono and di-glycerides, perhaps not. So, if you know nothing about how most bread in 21st century Britain is made, you're in good company. Thus, the principle reason for putting the book together presents itself; very few people seem to know how their bread is made, what it contains or where it comes from. My hope is that this book will go some way to filling that particular knowledge gap. Writing about modern bread making certainly enlightened me; hopefully the same will be true of you, the reader.

First and foremost, this book makes clear that most of the bread made in modern Britain is not fit to be labelled as such. The reason for such a bold statement is simple, mass produced bread can only exist because of how it is produced and the substances added to it. The intention is for this writing to provide a window into the activities of the processed food industry using the humble loaf of bread as a vehicle and signpost to do so. Bread was chosen because it is so familiar to us and is such a staple of the national diet. This book has taken most of 2016 to complete. During that time I have come to understand the degree to which the skill knowledge and experience intrinsic to craft, traditional or artisan baking in the UK has virtually disappeared. Leaving aside notions of food security or self-sufficiency this state of affairs can only be seen as a cultural tragedy. The words *"craft"*, *"artisan"* and *"traditional"* are used interchangeably throughout the text. They are used to delimit the difference between what should be *"normal"* bread and that produced by the Chorleywood Bread Process (CBP). Similarly, phrases such as *"the no time method"* or *"intensive"*, *"mass produced"* and *"industrial-scale bread making"* are equally interchangeable with the CBP acronym. This book presents the case that since the early 1960's the CBP has taken over almost every aspect of UK bread making. The bottom line, unless you have exclusively eaten only *"artisan"* bread, then you have eaten bread baked by Chorleywood means. When you have finished reading, it will be up to you to decide how you are going to respond. As usual, there will be no preaching or brow beating here, the purpose is to inform and empower. On that note, it is important to mention the final chapter in this writing. Chapter 7 is perhaps the most *"technical"* chapter in this text. It does contain some scientific terms and language that may be unfamiliar. The intent is not to blind or confuse the reader with science. However, a little effort on your part may be required. The intent is again to inform and empower and certainly not to lecture, *"show-off"* or preach. If the reader gets stuck or lost please don't despair. Put the book down (or read another chapter) and come back to it later, with a science dictionary if necessary. It goes without saying that you are free to pose whatever questions you like on the VIDDA Facebook page. Everything written in literature has a purpose and science orientated writing is no different. The scientific concepts discussed are crucial for understanding the science of the CBP. Hopefully, the reader will approach them in the spirit you are intended to.

This book will focus on what the CBP actually is, what actually happens from mixing to baking. The writing seeks to provide an overview of the *"how"*, the *"when"*, as well as the *"why"* of the CBP. Hence there will be no real discussion of sourdough and other forms of bread making. However, plenty of opportunities to investigate such *"real bread making"* techniques and the ingredients used are presented. The research for this book started in early 2016. Within a few weeks, our household was making spelt bread. When a family friend said a bread machine was up for grabs we said: *"yes please"*. It is now gracing us with its presence in our very small kitchen. The idea behind this book is that you will begin to see why and follow suit. In writing this one volume there were innumerable *"WTAF, I didn't know that"* exclamations. This writing will concentrate on the mechanisms, science and economics of modern industrial-scale bread making in the UK. This book is not a novel so you do not have to read it sequentially. As such, feel free to hop around the chapters as you see fit. The writing will attempt to explain how since the industrial revolution bread making has become steadily concentrated and is now under the control of two giant baking conglomerates. That in itself cannot be good for the economic and democratic fabric of the UK. There is no intrinsic problem with the upscaling of production of a given foodstuff or indeed any other *"commodity"*. For me, it is more a question of *"how things are done"* and coming to terms with *"how things are"* and enquiring as to *"how we are going to save ourselves and what is left of the biosphere?"* Having said that, it is counterproductive to hark back to some romantic time in the past, in the land of sunshine and lollipops, where we never grow old and nothing bad ever happens. Such utopian places do not, never have and never will exist. However, this book will attempt to show that the CBP has not delivered the nutritional goods and has been (arguably unintentionally) hugely detrimental to the baking profession and the health of the nation as a whole.

The CBP grew (in part) out of a desire and absolute necessity to improve the food security of the British Isles. The British population was heavily constrained by rationing into the mid-1950's. So, notions of food self-sufficiency would have been given extra attention. The writing will argue that the CBP has morphed from a potentially useful baking technique using home grown wheat into a nutritionally deficient monster, consumed by millions of people every day. Most of whom it has to be said are not aware of what they are eating. I know I wasn't before I started this writing so you're not alone. You would perhaps think that a loaf of bread would fit easily into a definition of *"healthy"*. The objective of this writing is to guide, (with real evidence), the reader toward the opposite conclusion. This book presents the case for wholehearted agreement with what the following quote encapsulates totally:

231

"bread has been turned from an essential component of a healthy diet to a structure held together by fats, preservatives, emulsifiers and a whole host of additives that have no business being in any food in the first place".

As an individual, the best you can do to avoid eating CBP bread (and I believe by the end of chapter 7 you will want to), is to invest in a bread machine and learn how to make different forms of bread. If possible the ingredients ought to be purchased from organic, GM free and local suppliers. Dealing with processed food per se requires a total reorganisation and regulation of *"the food industry"* that is not going to happen anytime soon. Such a circumstance will only occur if the industry and those who control it and profit from it are challenged and taken to task head on. This book will impart that the CBP has systematically taken over practically every aspect of bread making in the UK. The writing provides a concise overview of how the CBP came into being and what actually happens in the factory scale bakehouses. The writing will demonstrate that the profit motive has totally subjugated all other concerns. Concurrently, the text will show that bread baked by means of the CBP is the norm and not the exception. In the 21st century, Britain only a tiny proportion of the bread we eat comes from a traditional outlet. I believe this situation needs to be reversed by any and all means necessary. And this book will explain why...

Do you want to carry on reading?

If so, you can purchase your full copy of "The Big Secret: What Happened To Our Bread? The Chorleywood Bread Process" or the complete "FOOD CONSPIRACY TRILOGY" from www.amazon.com or www.viddapublishing.com

FOOD ADDITIVES: The Truth. The True Story of Food Flavouring, Colouring and Preservatives, plus Much More. What's In Your Food? (Food Conspiracy Volume 3)

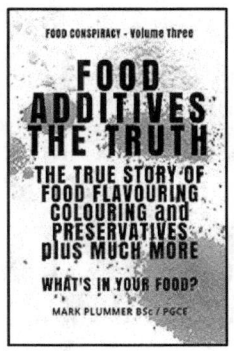

Introduction: An Opening Gambit – What to Expect and How to Read This Book

The writing presented here is an overview of a supremely complex issue. The text represents a tiny, almost non-existent scratch on a very large surface. This writing is not a novel. However, there are plenty of signposts so the reader can jump to different sections as they see fit. This book grew out of the research for my previous book "Food Conspiracy - What Happened To Our Bread? - The Chorleywood Bread Process". In a very real sense what you can see in front of you is a companion to that volume. Intensively manufactured or produced and large-scale food manufacturing all point toward the same subject and are used interchangeably. The use of the word construct refers to the whole global food processing business. I have looked at what is happening in the UK and the EU with a few mentions of the US and rest of the western world. Food regulations outside of the western world are much laxer than those which exist in the industrialised nations of this Earth. I absolutely dread to think what is occurring outside of the so called developed world, I really do. It is a safe bet that the less dangerous food additives banned here are pretty much available there. I have to clearly state that I am not an expert on this subject. I am what you might call a concerned citizen who is also a rational human being; I can see when things are not quite right. This writing is a result of a nose following exercise, that is, I am finding things out as I go along, then integrating new knowledge into that which already exists. Two years of research on this hugely complex issue has well and truly opened my eyes. It has also catalysed into meaningful action toward doing things differently. The writing here and on bread as well as GMO's has precipitated a real change in how my wonderful partner and I are going to live the rest of our lives. The hope is that the reader will consider doing the same. I didn't expect to discover food processing to be a benign and fluffy operation. However, I did not expect the whole construct to be so woefully unregulated. I had no idea of how the industry itself is so totally unaccountable to the population that it is supposed to serve. I also did not expect the links between food processing, genetically modified food, the chemical industry and others to be as intertwined as they are. It is for these reasons that the tone of this writing is as uncompromising as it is hard-hitting. Most of the chapters provide an introductory section as to how the modern processed food industry, i.e. the construct, fits into the organisation of our affairs. Throughout this book, it will become ever more obvious that most modern additives can be used in different applications in different industries.

In a nutshell, this book will argue that the food industry has managed to gain control and concentrate so much power that genuinely avoiding processed food is impossible. The industry has this particular enterprise done up like a kipper. The first two chapters attempt to present the broad strokes as to why this is the case. Chapter two gives a snapshot as to what has been done to the food most of us have been eating over the decades leading up to 2017. Chapter two will also provide a picture of what may be just around the corner and the sort of machinations which could make it possible. Chapter three will impart how to avoid processed foods as best we can. Chapter four will give some real examples as to why you will want to. And chapter five will try to explain how things have gotten so messed up. Having said all of that, please do not be thinking this is an "anti-additives" or "anti-food processing book". It is not. There are plenty of techniques and substances that have been with us for many hundreds if not thousands of years and many of them are wholly beneficial. Also, there is nothing wrong in principle in upscaling a given method of food production. It is more the reasons why the processes are occurring in the first place that need questioning. Unless it is warranted the writing does not single out particular compounds or the class of chemical they belong to as dangerous. That has been done a thousand times or more and there is no need to re-invent a wheel that most of us can access via the internet. This book is more of a devastating critique of the industry itself and less an attack on particular additives, with perhaps chapters six and seven being the clearest cut examples of that position. I could have written a book on that subject alone and still had plenty left over for a second volume. As it is I have tried to present an overview of why it is that artificial sweeteners are not as benign as we have perhaps been led to believe. I certainly didn't know two years ago, what I now know about them. So if you are shocked, surprised and angered about what this chapter reveals then you are in good company. And that leads me to what will hopefully become another glaringly obvious point. By the time you have finished reading this volume, you will not want to eat any processed food at all. Want being the operative word! If anything said in this book resonates, then you are on the way to genuinely avoiding intensively produced food. The writing is an attempt to "tell it like it is" using as many disparate sources as possible, many of them from the industry and the science it sponsors. The reader, as usual, is absolutely encouraged to follow up on the references presented as they see fit. Any internet search will provide hundreds of examples of similar assertions and counter assertions concerning the kind of additives outlined in this text. The point to remember is that they are in the food you eat and the food you feed any children you may have.

Unless they are key decision makers I have to stress that I am not necessarily attacking people who work in the industry. It is the construct itself that deserves unrelenting flack. I mean to say most of us, if not all of us, have had to take employment with some thoroughly repugnant organisations to pay our way. So I am not throwing that stone in this particular glass house. How many of us have had jobs where we are paid wages by some pretty nasty organisations? I know I have and so once again, there is no intent to preach, berate or lecture. There is no abseiling or throat parachuting here! Aside from all other points, a future sustainable society is going to need the expertise of the food scientists employed. We are going to need them to be working with producers, growers, smallholders and soil scientists as well as others from just about every profession the reader can think of. In much the same way as we are going to need those employed in the nuclear industry to properly dismantle nuclear facilities, which in a sane world would not have been built at all; we are going to need "the experts" who are employed in "big agriculture". This position assumes that the person in question is not in some future dock for the crimes they have committed or more likely facilitated. The criminality I believe such people to be guilty of is highlighted throughout this book but particularly at the beginning of chapter two and throughout chapter three.

First and foremost this book is an overview. With reference to as many artificial substances, e numbers, additives, processing aids and otherwise approved chemicals, which I could cram in, the writing attempts to present the dire state of modern food production. So assuming you are still here, let's get going...

Do you want to carry on reading?

If so, you can purchase your full copy of "Food Additives: The Truth. The True Story Of Food Flavouring, Colouring And Preservatives, Plus Much More. What's In Your Food?" or the complete "FOOD CONSPIRACY TRILOGY" from www.amazon.com or www.viddapublishing.com

Other Books by VIDDA Publishing

THE MEDICINE ON YOUR PLATE Series

Understanding Disease, Prevention & The Importance of Plant Based Nutrition and Diet

GREEN UP YOUR LIFE Series (Also Available in Spanish)
Take control of your health and wellbeing by introducing Natural, Eco-Friendly habits into your daily routine.

DOG TALES Series
Stories of Loyalty, Heroism & Devotion

BUSINESS, INCOME & SOCIAL MEDIA Series
How to Promote, Market & Create Business with Social Media

RESOLUTION TO BE HAPPY (Also Available in Spanish)
Make yourself smile every day and banish stress and anxiety forever

NATURAL WILD WINES

A Guide To Making Delicious Home Made Wine. Tips, Equipment, Recipes
& Foraging Wild Fruits, Flowers & Herbs

www.viddapublishing.com/books.html

Connect with VIDDA Publishing

At VIDDA Publishing, we specialise in electronic, audio and printed books in the subjects of Health & Nutrition, Education & Natural History.

Feel free to contact us with any questions or suggestions.

Check out our Catalogue or visit our FREE Video Library.

For your Healthy, Nutritious, Green and Cruelty Free products, equipment and gadgets, visit our online **VIDDA Health Stores** (US: **bit.ly/VIDDAstore** & UK: **bit.ly/VIDDAstoreUK**).

Also, for our favourite supplier of nutrients, sprouting seeds and health products, visit **bit.ly/BuyWholeFoodsOnline**

Subscribe to our website now and receive a FREE "Bring Life to your Food" Recipe book.

Finally, you can check out our publishing blog "Living like you mean it" for helpful tips, inspiration and updates on new books and free promotions coming soon.

Website: www.viddapublishing.com

Blog: www.viddapublishing.blogspot.co.uk

Twitter: twitter.com/VIDDAPublishing

Instagram: www.instagram.com/viddapublishing

Facebook: www.facebook.com/viddapublishing

Health Stores: US: bit.ly/VIDDAstore

 UK: bit.ly/VIDDAstoreUK

About the Author

Mark Plummer B.Sc. /PGCE

Mark trained and taught science in Spain until a confluence of austerity, divorce and new love brought him back to the UK.

He has worked on behalf of most major UK charities, environmental and NGO you can think of. He was a fundraiser, data in-putter, administrator and every role in between and back again. Aside from that, he has paid his dues on the chalk face of terrible temporary and agency jobs. Bitter experience has taught him, don't let it grind you down, remember you have rights, join a union and you can say NO!

Today he divides his time between writing, campaigning and teaching. His leisure time involves music, film, literature and the kitchen as well as spending quality time (what other time is there?) with friends and family.

Mark Plummer suitably attired before Hawkwind at Jodrel Bank. Summer 2013.

For the fans everywhere all over the world: I know it's not Hawkwind but this is a crucial issue... ININHB

Sources

Primary Literature (Science Papers)

http://www.tandfonline.com/doi/pdf/10.1080/14735903.2013.806408?needAccess=true

https://www.ncbi.nlm.nih.gov/books/NBK215773/pdf/Bookshelf_NBK215773.pdf

http://journals.plos.org/plosone/article?id=10.1371/journal.pone.0069805

https://www.ncbi.nlm.nih.gov/pmc/articles/PMC2408621/pdf/290.pdf

https://www.ncbi.nlm.nih.gov/pmc/articles/PMC1280366/pdf/ehp0113-a00526.pdf

http://lpi.oregonstate.edu/mic/other-nutrients/essential-fatty-acids

http://www.organic-systems.org/journal/81/8106.pdf

https://academic.oup.com/jxb/article/60/6/1537/517393

http://www.nature.com/articles/ncomms9924.pdf

https://www.sciencedirect.com/science/article/pii/S0301479715301663

http://omicsonline.org/open-access/detection-of-glyphosate-residues-in-animals-and-humans-2161-0525.1000210.pdf

http://www.mdpi.com/1099-4300/15/4/1416

https://www.ncbi.nlm.nih.gov/pmc/articles/PMC2952409/pdf/ijbsv06p0590.pdf

http://static.aboca.com/www.aboca.com/files/attach/news/risk_assessment_of_genetically_modified_crops_for_nutrition.pdf

http://www.nature.com/articles/ncomms9635

http://science.sciencemag.org/content/282/5389/662.full

https://www.ncbi.nlm.nih.gov/pmc/articles/PMC3129041/pdf/CG-12-30.pdf

http://onlinelibrary.wiley.com/doi/10.1111/j.1365-313X.2009.04086.x/pdf

https://www.ncbi.nlm.nih.gov/pmc/articles/PMC3639326/pdf/12263_2012_Article_316.pdf

http://www.pnas.org/content/96/11/5995.full.pdf

https://www.ncbi.nlm.nih.gov/pmc/articles/PMC5464684/pdf/ITX-9-90.pdf

http://www.pnas.org/content/111/6/2223.full.pdf

https://enveurope.springeropen.com/track/pdf/10.1186/2190-4715-24-24?site=enveurope.springeropen.com

https://www.ncbi.nlm.nih.gov/pmc/articles/PMC4422498/pdf/nihms684575.pdf

https://www.ncbi.nlm.nih.gov/pmc/articles/PMC4590768/pdf/nihms643350.pdf

http://www.pnas.org/content/113/12/3395.full.pdf

https://www.ncbi.nlm.nih.gov/pmc/articles/PMC2836466/pdf/216_2009_Article_3186.pdf

http://www.nature.com/articles/35107068.epdf?referrer_access_token=jzrOLTlTlR7SLOKLEoGzo9RgNojAjWel9jnR3ZoTvoNCR23F6iGYbLRww_-W44pSUynNJo2RtVp_984TIfZW3mMubQjn3FMs4DaPmgdwfvgtJVICZ1WZ53dIAqEF_YUkDu8zjRB18rsqnhmOnFu_uKo3s_oLSPCHyjN3LMCnBs_vb3AyoiXmRwEWQobZPQKtdqg69PogQEcIM19Aei5PoB9m58-I3VM1Ymx5dJTNbow%3D&tracking_referrer=

http://rspb.royalsocietypublishing.org/content/royprsb/280/1763/20131047.full.pdf

http://www.pnas.org/content/110/31/12560.full.pdf

http://journals.plos.org/plosgenetics/article/file?id=10.1371/journal.pgen.1005470&type=printable

http://arep.med.harvard.edu/pdf/Mandell_Nat_2015.pdf

http://journals.plos.org/plosone/article/file?id=10.1371/journal.pone.0013529&type=printable

https://pdf.palaeontologyonline.com/articles-2011/The_Paleocene-Eocene_Thermal_Maximum-Jardine_P-Oct2011.pdf

https://genomebiology.biomedcentral.com/articles/10.1186/s13059-015-0607-3

http://science.sciencemag.org/content/sci/323/5916/926.full.pdf

www.int-res.com/articles/aei2010/1/q001p071.pdf

Articles

http://community.corpwatch.org/adm/pages/food_industry.php

http://www.unz.org/Pub/InTheseTimes-1996nov11-00012

https://www.ncbi.nlm.nih.gov/pmc/articles/PMC5362009/pdf/1602638. pdf

http://www.collective-evolution.com/2014/04/08/10-scientific-studies-proving-gmos-can-be-harmful-to-human-health/

https://www.iucn.org/theme/species/our-work/invasive-species

https://blog.oup.com/2013/12/ten-things-to-understand-about-the-molly-maguires/http://www.nature.com/scitable/knowledge/library/the-nitrogen-cycle-processes-players-and-human-15644632

http://www.ucmp.berkeley.edu/bacteria/cyanolh.html

https://www.theguardian.com/environment/2015/mar/09/gm-opponents-are-science-deniers#img-1

http://www.nature.com/news/gm-crop-opponents-expand-probe-into-ties-between-scientists-and-industry-1.18146

https://ac.els-cdn.com/S0960982213002935/1-s2.0-S0960982213002935-main.pdf?_tid=b82bc2b4-cdfc-11e7-8dc3-00000aab0f26&acdnat=1511187276_a5f30b6d54f6fb6accb493c31c16d7cd

http://www.theecologist.org/green_green_living/behind_the_label/3024 29/behind_the_label_cut_flowers.html

http://www.scientificamerican.com/article/environmental-price-of-flowers/

http://www.gmwatch.org/news/archive/2014/15304-massive-gmo-crop-failure-in-philippines

http://www.youtube.com/watch?v=hCuWs8K9-kI&list=LL6feir9VTqIG5CV3-V29IcQ&feature=mh_lolz

http://www.i-sis.org.uk/GMcropsfailed.php

https://www.thebalance.com/government-subsidies-definition-farm-oil-export-etc-3305788

http://www.ucsusa.org/sites/default/files/legacy/assets/documents/food _and_agriculture/rise-of-superweeds.pdf

http://www.genewatch.org/uploads/f03c6d66a9b354535738483c1c3d49e 4/GMolivefly_GWbriefing_fin2.pdf

http://e360.yale.edu/feature/genetically_modified_mosquito_sparks_a_controversy_in_florida/2883/

http://www.nature.com/polopoly_fs/1.12907!/menu/main/topColumns/topLeftColumn/pdf/497024a.pdf

http://www.i-sis.org.uk/foodFutures.php

http://www.i-sis.org.uk/Evolution_by_Natural_Genetic_Engineering.php

http://www.i-sis.org.uk/Nonrandom_directed_mutations_confirmed.php

http://www.i-sis.org.uk/RNASTGT.php

http://www.i-sis.org.uk/epigeneticInheritance.php

http://www.i-sis.org.uk/syntheticLife.php

http://inthesetimes.com/rural-america/entry/19406/steven-m.-druker-gmos-genetically-engineered-food-FDA-deception

http://earthopensource.org/wp-content/uploads/2014/11/GMO-Myths-and-Truths-edition2.pdf

http://www.justlabelit.org/superweeds-a-frightening-reality/

http://www.berkeley.edu/news/media/releases/2001/11/29_corn.html

https millennia/://www.newscientist.com/article/2079813-farmers-may-have-been-accidentally-making-gmos-for-

https://www.newscientist.com/article/dn26722-europe-set-to-allow-individual-nations-to-ban-gm-crops/

http://www.scidev.net/global/nutrition/feature/nutrition-incomes-farmers-mozambique.html

http://www.the-scientist.com/?articles.view/articleNo/35578/title/Opinion--Don-t-Fear-GM-Crops--Europe-/

http://blogs.scientificamerican.com/guest-blog/golden-rice-opponents-should-be-held-accountable-for-health-problems-linked-to-vitamain-a-deficiency/

http://www.nytimes.com/2012/05/22/business/kakha-bendukidze-holds-fate-of-gene-engineered-salmon.html?pagewanted=all%60&_r=2

https://www.opendemocracy.net/od-russia/stephen-f-jones/kakha-bendukidze-and-georgia%e2%80%99s-failed-experiment

http://www.enkivillage.com/genetically-modified-animals.html

http://www.techinsider.io/the-age-of-genetically-engineered-animals-has-arrived-2015-6

htttp://www.sun-sentinel.com/news/florida/fl-gmo-mosquitoes-florida-keys-20150125-story.html

http://www.testbiotech.org/en/node/1319

http://www.huffingtonpost.com/onearth/catch-of-the-day-transgen_b_3224374.html

https://www.ecowatch.com/fda-approves-genetically-modified-mosquitoes-zika-florida-1964042276.html

https://www.theguardian.com/lifeandstyle/2014/oct/29/panama-regulators-could-slow-us-approval-of-gm-salmon

http://www.centerforfoodsafety.org/files/senate-to-fda-ge-salmon-42413_28714.pdf

http://blogs.scientificamerican.com/oscillator/genes-cannot-be-made-from-scratch/

http://www.scientificamerican.com/article/the-truth-about-genetically-modified-food/

http://www.independent.co.uk/news/science/nobel-laureates-urge-greenpeace-to-end-opposition-to-gmos-genetically-modified-organisms-a7111531.html

https://www.theguardian.com/commentisfree/2013/nov/06/genetically-modified-food-safe-monsanto

https://www.theguardian.com/science/2015/jan/31/gm-farming-natural-solution

https://www.washingtonpost.com/news/energy-environment/wp/2015/02/23/like-most-invasive-species-pythons-are-in-the-u-s-to-stay/?utm_term=.58fa633b3688

http://modernfarmer.com/2016/06/africanized-bees/

http://www.telegraph.co.uk/news/earth/earthnews/10242974/How-to-save-our-bees-cross-breed-them-with-African-killer-bees.html

http://www.globalresearch.ca/neonicotinoid-pesticides-ongoing-death-of-the-beas-epa-slapped-with-lawsuit/5334816

http://www.crizmac.com/artandsoul/index.php/2011/08/04/corn-rituals/

http://www.nature.com/news/gm-maize-splits-mexico-1.15493

http://www.nature.com/news/2008/081112/pdf/456149a.pdf

https://newint.org/blog/2013/05/24/vandana-shiva-mexico-monsanto-corn/

https://www.globalresearch.ca/harvest-of-hypocrisy-farmers-being-blamed-for-gmo-crop-failures/5322807

http://socialistreview.org.uk/413/entering-age-humans

http://gmwatch.org/news/archive/2008/9960-genetic-engineering-a-crop-of-hyperbole

http://www.reuters.com/article/monsanto-investigation-idUSN2515475920100625

https://www.sciencedaily.com/releases/2010/11/101104083102.htm

http://www.gmwatch.org/latest-listing/1-news-items/11761-science-favours-emotion

http://gmwatch.org/news/latest-news/15894-scientists-attempt-to-prevent-gmos-escaping-by-using-synthetic-amino-acids

http://www.latimes.com/science/sciencenow/la-sci-sn-gmo-escape-20150121-story.html

http://www.bbc.co.uk/news/uk-politics-30493297

http://www.independent.co.uk/voices/comment/what-is-ttip-and-six-reasons-why-the-answer-should-scare-you-9779688.html

http://www.independent.co.uk/news/uk/politics/ttip-brexit-uk-steroids-disastrous-global-justice-now-war-on-want-a7099986.html

https://themarketmogul.com/possible-future-uk-trade-agreements/

http://www.theguardian.com/us-news/2015/may/13/senate-obama-trade-tpp-ttip-fast-track-bill

https://www.financierworldwide.com/the-future-of-trade-is-the-world-open-for-business/#.WjkFnz5G3IU

https://www.opendemocracy.net/ourkingdom/linda-kaucher/genetically-modified-food-in-uk-and-ttip

http://trade.ec.europa.eu/doclib/press/index.cfm?id=1723

http://www.independent.co.uk/voices/ceta-uk-canada-trade-deal-theresa-may-environment-food-safety-worker-rights-justin-trudeau-a7957696.html

https://www.ft.com/content/c9f8506c-df17-11e7-a8a4-0a1e63a52f9c

http://www.egyptindependent.com/tests-rats-suggest-genetically-modified-foods-pose-health-hazards/

http://www.nature.com/news/uk-election-political-parties-respond-on-science-1.17256

https://www.theguardian.com/environment/2012/mar/09/gm-food-public-concern

https://permaculturenews.org/2014/09/24/the-cranky-honey-bees-of-south-america/

http://www.nature.com/polopoly_fs/1.13392!/menu/main/topColumns/topLeftColumn/pdf/499262a.pdf

http://www.theatlantic.com/magazine/archive/1997/01/forgotten-benefactor-of-humanity/306101/

http://www.history.com/news/after-168-years-potato-famine-mystery-solved

http://www.strangescience.net/mendel.htm

https://www.theguardian.com/global-development/poverty-matters/2014/apr/01/norman-borlaug-humanitarian-hero-menace-society

http://www.nature.com/polopoly_fs/1.12445!/menu/main/topColumns/topLeftColumn/pdf/494289a.pdf

https://www.theguardian.com/global-development/2013/dec/12/brazil-gm-terminator-seed-technology-farmers

http://www.nrdc.org/health/pesticides/hcarson.asp

http://microbiologyonline.org/about-microbiology/introducing-microbes/bacteria

http://www.iflscience.com/environment/myths-and-controversies-gmos-0/.

http://www.nature.com/scitable/knowledge/library/history-of-agricultural-biotechnology-how-crop-development-25885295

http://www.nature.com/scitable/topicpage/genetic-mutation-441

http://www.nature.com/scitable/topicpage/genetic-mutation-1127

http://www.nature.com/scitable/topicpage/dna-replication-and-causes-of-mutation-409

http://www.nature.com/scitable/topicpage/restriction-enzymes-545

http://www.nature.com/scitable/topicpage/translation-dna-to-mrna-to-protein-393

248

http://www.nature.com/scitable/topicpage/transposons-or-jumping-genes-not-junk-dna-1211

http://www.nature.com/scitable/topicpage/genetically-modified-organisms-gmos-transgenic-crops-nbsp-732

http://www.nature.com/scitable/topicpage/discovery-of-dna-structure-and-function-watson-397

https://www.sciencenews.org/blog/science-public/fishy-fat-soy-headed-us-dinner-tables

http://www.todaysdietitian.com/newarchives/070114p18.shtml

https://www2.le.ac.uk/projects/vgec/highereducation/topics/recombinant techniques

http://www.genewatch.org/sub-568547

http://www.nature.com/scitable/topicpage/recombinant-dna-technology-and-transgenic-animals-34513

http://blogs.thatpetplace.com/thatfishblog/2013/05/28/glofish/#.WfISFT 5rzIU

https://www.wired.com/2015/07/eating-genetically-modified-animals/

https://e360.yale.edu/features/insect_numbers_declining_why_it_matte rs

https://www.theguardian.com/commentisfree/2017/oct/20/insectageddo n-farming-catastrophe-climate-breakdown-insect-populations

http://www.sciencemag.org/news/2017/05/where-have-all-insects-gone

http://www.monbiot.com/2015/10/30/nothing-to-see-here/

http://earth.usc.edu/~stott/Catalina/Ordovician.html

http://green.blogs.nytimes.com/2012/10/05/the-legacy-of-pesticides-superweeds-and-superpests/?_r=0

https://www.independentsciencenews.org/health/how-the-ge-food-venture-has-been-chronically-dependent-on-deception/#comments

http://www.nature.com/scitable/topicpage/discovery-and-types-of-genetic-linkage-500

http://www.rsc.org/Education/Teachers/Resources/cfb/nucleicacids.htm

http://www.livescience.com/39804-rosalind-franklin.html

http://www.theguardian.com/commentisfree/2014/dec/01/dna-james-watson-scientist-selling-nobel-prize-medal

https://www.nature.com/scitable/topicpage/ribosomes-transcription-and-translation-14120660

http://bscb.org/learning-resources/softcell-e-learning/ribosome/

http://www.scientificamerican.com/article/hidden-treasures-in-junk-dna/

https://www.popsci.com/science/article/2011-01/life-cycle-genetically-modified-seed#page-2

http://cyberbridge.mcb.harvard.edu/dna_1.html

https://www.genome.gov/26524120

http://www.news-medical.net/health/What-are-Genes.aspxhttps://entomology.ca.uky.edu/ef130

https://www.britannica.com/science/Bacillus-thuringiensis

https://www.newscientist.com/article/dn18049-us-fda-says-omega-3-oils-from-gm-soya-are-safe-to-eat/

http://www.rosebudmag.com/truth-squad/corporate-crops-gmo-technology-communities-fight-back

http://www.rosebudmag.com/truth-squad/gmo-players-a-look-at-who-is-shaping-the-gmo-debate

http://www.rosebudmag.com/truth-squad/gmo-timeline-a-history-of-genetically-modified-foods

http://www.nature.com/scitable/topicpage/Genetic-Recombination-514

https://en.wikipedia.org/wiki/Genetically_modified_tomato

http://www.public.iastate.edu/~rhetoric/105H16/cofp/tmrcofp.html

http://www.truthistreason.net/children-of-the-corn-gmo-sterility-and-spermicides

https://www.scientificamerican.com/article/how-closely-related-are-h/

https://www.microbiologysociety.org/news/society-news/avian-flu-the-facts.html

https://news.nationalgeographic.com/2015/04/150422-glyphosate-roundup-herbicide-weeds/

http://time.com/3840073/gmo-food-charts/

https://www.scientificamerican.com/article/labels-for-gmo-foods-are-a-bad-idea/

https://www.counterpunch.org/2015/02/12/why-does-the-dairy-industry-oppose-gmo-labels/

http://grist.org/news/campaign-to-label-frankenfoods-goes-viral/

https://www.euractiv.com/section/science-policymaking/news/no-risk-with-gmo-food-says-eu-chief-scientific-advisor/

http://www.independent.co.uk/news/uk/politics/exclusive-the-agricultural-revolution-uk-pushes-europe-to-embrace-gm-crops-8654595.html

http://www.gmwatch.org/en/gm-firms/10558-the-worlds-top-ten-seed-companies-who-owns-nature

https://www.scientificamerican.com/article/do-seed-companies-control-gm-crop-research/

https://www.theguardian.com/global-development/2012/jul/06/sam-dryden-global-south-agriculture

http://chemguide.co.uk/organicprops/alkanes/cracking.html

https://www.thoughtco.com/cell-wall-373613

https://www.huffingtonpost.com/jon-entine/although-some-gmo-sympath_b_8864038.html

https://www.huffingtonpost.com/jon-entine/the-real-cost-of-mandator_b_8865742.html

http://calag.ucanr.edu/archive/?type=pdf&article=ca.v054n04p6

http://www.bbc.co.uk/news/science-environment-25885756#

http://www.independent.co.uk/voices/comment/its-time-for-us-to-think-about-eating-gm-food-8668859.html

https://www.scientificamerican.com/article/3-big-myths-about-modern-agriculture1/

http://www.alternet.org/world/how-gates-foundation-and-western-countries-are-plotting-take-control-africas-agriculture

https://www.economist.com/news/business/21727935-epitome-big-agriculture-tries-predict-future-food-cargill-intensely-private

https://1efnyhsj63r2fo5go1erbmcv-wpengine.netdna-ssl.com/wp-content/uploads/2016/03/GMOs-top_five_issues_for_family_farmers.pdf

https://1efnyhsj63r2fo5go1erbmcv-wpengine.netdna-ssl.com/wp-content/uploads/2016/03/GMOs-what_eaters_need_to_know.pdf

https://www.vanityfair.com/news/2008/05/monsanto200805

http://www.lifegate.com/people/news/international-monsanto-tribunal-ecocide

https://www.theguardian.com/business/2015/jul/17/food-fight-secrets-supermarket-price-war

http://www.telegraph.co.uk/foodanddrink/7852762/Supermarkets-selling-meat-from-animals-fed-GM-crops.html

https://www.vox.com/2016/9/20/12988616/bayer-monsanto-dupont-dow-agriculture-mergers-innovation

https://www.nature.com/scitable/knowledge/library/eutrophication-causes-consequences-and-controls-in-aquatic-102364466

http://www.foeeurope.org/agrifood-atlas-corporations-stranglehold-food-311117

http://www.independent.co.uk/news/science/gm-banana-designed-to-slash-african-infant-mortality-enters-human-trials-9541380.html

https://cornucopiaalchemy.wordpress.com/2014/04/30/traditional-food-diversity-and-health-the-case-of-yellow-bananas-by-andrew-ormerod/https://www.theguardian.com/world/2011/mar/09/gm-banana-crop-disease-uganda

https://allianceforscience.cornell.edu/blog/gm-bxw-resistant-bananas-start-their-journey-farmer

https://theecologist.org/2014/nov/24/why-bill-gates-backing-gmo-red-banana-bio-piracy

http://www.aljazeera.com/indepth/opinion/2013/04/201342881742522773.html

http://www.scidev.net/global/bioprospecting/opinion/why-we-must-fight-bio-piracy.html

https://www.globalresearch.ca/bio-piracy-and-gmos-the-fate-of-iraq-s-agriculture/1447

http://www.independent.co.uk/news/world/middle-east/paul-bremer-on-iraq-ten-years-on-we-made-major-strategic-mistakes-but-i-still-think-iraqis-are-far-8539767.html

http://www.countercurrents.org/iraq-cymru030305.htm

http://grist.org/food/gmo-potatoes-is-the-biodiversity-shortcut-worth-it/

https://www.globalpolicy.org/component/content/article/167/35621.html

https://www.theguardian.com/commentisfree/2013/jul/01/farm-subsidies-blatant-transfer-of-cash-to-rich

https://www.rt.com/uk/249805-slave-labour-salad-supermarkets/

http://www.bbc.co.uk/news/business-40354331

http://www.globaljustice.org.uk/blog/2013/jul/31/cost-india's-green-revolution

http://www.nytimes.com/2006/09/30/world/asia/30water2.html?_r=1&ref=thirstygiant&pagewanted=all

http://www.toxipedia.org/display/toxipedia/Biological+Properties+of+Insecticides

Articles, Hyperlinks & Resources Per Chapter

Chapter 1 Articles

http://www.famousscientists.org/gregor-mendel/

https://en.wikipedia.org/wiki/Phenotype

https://en.wikipedia.org/wiki/Genotype

http://www.nature.com/scitable/topicpage/gregor-mendel-and-the-principles-of-inheritance-593

http://luckythreeranch.com/lucky-three-ranch-training/mule-facts/

http://www.bnd.com/living/liv-columns-blogs/answer-man/article135296594.html

http://genetics.thetech.org/ask/ask225

http://www.ipsnews.net/2014/03/farmers-address-u-s-data-gap-gm-crop-contamination/

http://www.econexus.info/sites/econexus/files/ENx-CBD-GURTs-2006_0.pdf

http://learn.genetics.utah.edu/content/basics/mutation/

https://www2.le.ac.uk/projects/vgec/highereducation/topics/cellcycle-mitosis-meiosis

https://www.globalresearch.ca/genetically-engineered-terminator-seeds-death-and-destruction-of-agriculture/5319797

http://www.cfmedicine.com/htmldocs/cftext/genetics.htm

http://www.theguardian.com/science/2015/jul/03/gene-therapy-cystic-fibrosis-2020-scientists

https://www.petmd.com/fish/what-are-glofish

http://blogs.thatpetplace.com/thatfishblog/2013/05/28/glofish/#.Wk_Z7 z5y7IU

https://science.gu.se/english/News/News_detail/Risks_involved_with_tr ansgenic_fish_.cid889631

https://singularityhub.com/2009/08/31/monkey-dna-swap-paves-way-to-engineered-babies/#sm.00008ijjdcq78eptwe71ihd38dty3

http://www.theepochtimes.com/n3/500409-its-labeled-organic-but-its-genes-were-scrambled-with-gamma-rays/

Chapter 1 Hyperlinks

1: http://evolution.berkeley.edu/evolibrary/article/history_14

2:https://embryo.asu.edu/pages/experiments-plant-hybridization-1866-johann-gregor-mendel

3: https://ghr.nlm.nih.gov/primer/basics/chromosome

4: http://www.nature.com/scitable/definition/allele-48

5: http://www.thefreedictionary.com/green+revolution

6: http://www.nytimes.com/1991/04/15/obituaries/orville-vogel-83-leading-researcher-of-wheat-for-us.html

7:https://www.nobelprize.org/nobel_prizes/peace/laureates/1970/borlaug-bio.html

8:https://www.seedquest.com/forum/b/BorlaugNorman/architecture.htm

9: https://www.britannica.com/science/zygote

10: https://soilsmatter.wordpress.com/2015/02/27/what-is-precision-agriculture-and-why-is-it-important/

11: https://monsanto.com/company/media/statements/gmo-contamination-lawsuits/

12:https://monsanto.com/company/media/statements/saving-seeds/

13: http://www.progressio.org.uk/content/what-terminator-technology

14: http://www.monsanto.com/newsviews/pages/terminator-seeds.aspx

15:https://ghr.nlm.nih.gov/primer/mutationsanddisorders/genemutation

16: http://knowgenetics.org/nucleotides-and-bases/

17:http://www.chemistryexplained.com/Te-Va/Transport-Protein.html

18: https://www.youtube.com/watch?v=tSJoLnOHpTw

19:http://www.qrg.northwestern.edu/projects/vss/docs/Propulsion/1-what-is-an-ion.html

20: https://www.youtube.com/watch?v=wsadD1ari-o

21: https://www.youtube.com/watch?v=nc3bK7i3FAM

22: https://www.childlifesociety.org/what_causes_cf.php

23: https://www.youtube.com/watch?v=C8OL1MTbGpU

24: https://www.youtube.com/watch?v=RmHnKfTLgNw

25: https://www.youtube.com/watch?v=XYwcX6AVw5I

26: https://www.youtube.com/watch?v=b3Xh7NM-iZk

27:http://www.thecattlesite.com/breeds/beef/8/belgian-blue/

28:https://www.medicinenet.com/script/main/art.asp?articlekey=33546

29:https://news.nationalgeographic.com/news/2010/03/100329-six-pack-mutant-trout-genetically-engineered-modified-gm/

30:https://singularityhub.com/2009/08/31/monkey-dna-swap-paves-way-to-engineered-babies/#sm.00008ijjdcq78eptwe71ihd38dty3

31:https://www.quora.com/Is-there-any-body-part-that-does-not-contain-DNA

32: http://knowgenetics.org/recombinant-dna-technology/

33:https://www.diabetes.co.uk/insulin/history-of-insulin.html

34:http://www.vivo.colostate.edu/hbooks/pathphys/digestion/stomach/rennin.html

35: http://www.genewatch.org/sub-568798

36: https://www.youtube.com/watch?v=4PLvdmifDSk

Chapter 1 Further Resources

http://darwin200.christs.cam.ac.uk/

http://wallacefund.info/

http://learn.genetics.utah.edu/content/basics/

http://www.childlifesociety.org/

http://www.fao.org/home/en/

http://www.esp.org/foundations/genetics/classical/gm-65.pdf

Chapter 2 Articles

https://www.greenpeace.org/archive-international/en/news/features/illegal-carve-up-260207/

https://rainforests.mongabay.com/20pacific.htm

http://www.monbiot.com/2017/10/23/insectageddon/

https://reason.com/archives/2014/05/28/dont-fear-genetically-modified-food

http://www.nationalreview.com/article/421623/gmo-label-movement-loses-ground

http://www.toxicremnantsofwar.info/uk-agent-orange-malaysia/

http://theconversation.com/bio-piracy-when-indigenous-knowledge-is-patented-for-profit-55589

https://www.gene.com/media/press-releases/4161/1979-07-11/first-successful-bacterial-production-of

http://www.yourhormones.info/hormones/somatostatin.aspx

http://www.nytimes.com/1982/10/30/us/a-new-insulin-given-approval-for-use-in-us.html

http://www.the-scientist.com/?articles.view/articleNo/42420/title/Horizontal-Gene-Transfer-a-Hallmark-of-Animal-Genomes-/

http://www.channel4.com/news/q-and-a-what-is-e-coli

http://www.biography.com/people/francis-crick-9261484

https://www.sdsc.edu/ScienceWomen/franklin.html

http://www.dnaftb.org/19/bio-4.html

http://www.visionlearning.com/en/library/Biology/2/Nucleic-Acids/63

https://study.com/academy/lesson/hydrogen-bonds-definition-types-formation.html

http://news.bbc.co.uk/1/hi/sci/tech/2676377.stm

https://www.news-medical.net/life-sciences/What-are-Genes.aspx

https://www.news-medical.net/life-sciences/What-Are-Organelles.aspx

https://www.aspeninstitute.org/programs/agent-orange-in-vietnam-program/what-is-agent-orange/

https://www.huffingtonpost.com/entry/monsanto-vietnam-agent orange_us_57a9e002e4b0b770b1a445ba

https://www.globalresearch.ca/war-crimes-agent-orange-monsanto-dow-chemical-and-other-ugly-legacies-of-the-vietnam-war/5488004

Chapter 2 Hyperlinks

1: https://www.youtube.com/watch?v=zwibgNGe4aY

2: https://www.youtube.com/watch?v=2Domm6qac1k

3: https://www.youtube.com/watch?v=TI93PH_yugE

4:http://www.oceanicresearch.org/education/wonders/arthropods.htm

5:http://www.sciencedirect.com/science/article/pii/S0024406600904681

6: http://www.bbc.co.uk/nature/phylum

7: http://science.sciencemag.org/content/345/6195/401

8:http://www.big-animals.com/the-japanese-spider-crab-the-worlds-biggest-arthropod/

9: http://www.ucmp.berkeley.edu/ordovician/ordovician.php

10:http://www.rsc.org/chemistryworld/2013/08/chitin-biopolymer-chitosan-podcast

11:https://www.newscientist.com/blog/shortsharpscience/2008/06/counting-in-bacterial-world.html

12:http://www.ruf.rice.edu/~bioslabs/studies/invertebrates/kingdoms.html

13: https://www.youtube.com/watch?v=EsCe6qPz6tM

14: https://www.sciencedaily.com/terms/protozoa.htm

15: http://www.ucmp.berkeley.edu/archaea/archaea.html

16:http://microbiologyonline.org/about-microbiology/microbes-and-the-human-body/microbes-and-disease

17: http://www.nature.com/subjects/biotechnology

18: https://en.wikipedia.org/wiki/K%C3%A1roly_Ereky

19:http://www.livestrong.com/article/420088-advantages-disadvantages-of-biotechnology-on-food-health/

20: http://www.etcgroup.org/issues/patents-bio-piracy

21:http://www.heathcote.org/PCIntro/2WhatIsPermaculture.htm

22:https://www.soilassociation.org/organic-living/whyorganic/

23: http://www.biochemistry.org/?TabId=456

24: http://www.nature.com/scitable/definition/nucleic-acid-274

25:https://www.ucsusa.org/food_and_agriculture/our-failing-food-system/genetic-engineering/promoting-resistant-pests.html#.WlThoIWcHIV

26:http://www.theatlantic.com/health/archive/2012/05/superweeds-a-long-predicted-problem-for-gm-crops-has-arrived/257187/

27: http://www.agentorangerecord.com/home/

28:http://www.mcclatchydc.com/news/nation-world/world/article24751345.html

29:http://www.history.com/this-day-in-history/students-demonstrate-against-dow-chemical-company

30:https://www.hrw.org/topic/international-justice/international-criminal-court

31:https://www.news-medical.net/life-sciences/What-is-Molecular-Biology.aspx

32: ttps://www.theguardian.com/environment/2008/feb/16/gmcrops.food1

33: https://www.youtube.com/watch?v=LdDyMe9ohnM

34:http://www.britannica.com/biography/Phoebus-Aaron-Theodor-Levene

35:http://www.ncbi.nlm.nih.gov/Class/MLACourse/Original8Hour/Genetics/nucleotide.html

36:https://www.ncbi.nlm.nih.gov/pmc/articles/PMC4536854/pdf/e0v018.pdf

37: https://www.youtube.com/watch?v=tCZhkxpzxDY

38:https://www.sheffield.ac.uk/materials/centresandfacilities/x-ray-diffraction/whatxrd

39: http://www.nature.com/scitable/definition/double-helix-277

40:http://www.sciencedirect.com/science/article/pii/S0012160604008231?via%3Dihub

41: https://www.yourgenome.org/facts/what-is-the-central-dogma

42: https://www.youtube.com/watch?v=9kOGOY7vthk

43: https://www.youtube.com/watch?v=gG7uCskUOrA

44: https://www.youtube.com/watch?v=Gi9A56nu01E

45:http://www.biology.arizona.edu/biochemistry/problem_sets/aa/aa.ht
ml

46:https://www.ncbi.nlm.nih.gov/Class/MLACourse/Modules/MolBioRev
iew/central_dogma.html

47: http://www.livescience.com/37247-dna.html

48: https://www.youtube.com/watch?v=apaP9a079po

49: https://www.youtube.com/watch?v=yd3IgR01Z1k

50:http://web.stanford.edu/dept/humbio/chem/riboseVsDeoxyribose.ht
ml

51: https://www.youtube.com/watch?v=UR4eG60jjQQ

52: https://www.youtube.com/watch?v=RSRiywp9v9w

53:      https://study.com/academy/lesson/complementary-base-pairing-
definition-lesson-quiz.html

54:http://www.walterreeves.com/uploads/chromosomesmtr.htm

55: https://www.youtube.com/watch?v=5MQdXjRPHmQ

56:http://www.news-medical.net/health/What-is-Junk-DNA.aspx

57: http://www.nature.com/scitable/definition/codon-155

58: https://www.youtube.com/watch?v=URUJD5NEXC8

59: http://www.nature.com/scitable/definition/ribosome-194

60:http://naturalingredient.org/wp/wp-content/uploads/gmo-health-
dangers-_-institute-for-responsible-technology.pdf

Chapter 2 Further Resources

http://www.newcastle-mitochondria.com/

https://www.permaculture.co.uk/

https://www.soilassociation.org/

https://www.ucsusa.org/

https://www.news-medical.net/

http://www.rachelcarson.org/

http://www.agentorangerecord.com/home/

https://www.icc-cpi.int/

https://www.gene.com/

https://www.yourgenome.org/

Chapter 3 Articles

http://articles.mercola.com/sites/articles/archive/2013/06/09/monsanto-roundup-herbicide.aspx

https://news.nationalgeographic.com/2015/04/150422-glyphosate-roundup-herbicide-weeds/

https://www.naturalproductsinsider.com/news/2013/04/dsm-monsanto-partner-to-deliver-sda-omega-3-soybe.aspx/

https://www.canada.ca/en/health-canada/services/food-nutrition/genetically-modified-foods-other-novel-foods/approved-products/stearidonic-acid-producing-soybean-87769.html

http://www.benchfly.com/blog/the-almighty-fungi-the-revolutionary-neurospora-crassa/

http://www.rajaha.com/plant-growth-hormones/

http://www.britannica.com/science/restriction-enzyme

http://www.nature.com/scitable/topicpage/Restriction-Enzymes-545

http://www.madehow.com/Volume-7/Insulin.html

http://www.sciencemediacentre.org/wp-content/uploads/2012/09/Science-Media-Centre-Fact-Sheet-GM-field-trials.pdf

http://rightbiotech.tumblr.com/post/103665842150/correlation-is-not-causation

https://www.ewg.org/agmag/2015/03/claims-gmo-yield-increases-don-t-hold#.Wl4bqYWcHlX

Chapter 3 Hyperlinks

1: http://www.ey.com/gl/en/industries/life-sciences

2: https://www.dcu.ie/biotechnology/about.shtml

3: http://www.fractal.org/Life-Science-Technology/Definition.htm

4: http://navdanya.org/attachments/roundup.pdf

5: https://www.roundup-garden.com/where-to-buy-roundup-weedkiller

6: https://www.ncbi.nlm.nih.gov/pubmed/23756170

7: http://pubs.acs.org/doi/abs/10.1021/tx1001749

8:https://www.gardeningknowhow.com/plant-problems/pests/pesticides/using-bacillus-thuringiensis.htm

9: https://www.quora.com/What-is-a-gene-of-interest

10:https://www.naturalproductsinsider.com/news/2013/04/dsm-monsanto-partner-to-deliver-sda-omega-3-soybe.aspx/

11:https://www.foodnavigator-usa.com/Article/2013/04/08/DSM-Monsanto-to-commercialize-GM-soybean-oil-with-omega-3s

12:https://monsanto.com/news-releases/dsm-nutritional-products-and-monsanto-company-partner-to-deliver-first-sda-omega-3-soybean-oil-for-use-in-foods-in-north-america/

13:https://www.preparedfoods.com/articles/112524-dsm-monsanto-in-partnership

14:https://www.newscientist.com/article/mg15020301-400-bottle-fed-babies-need-brain-boosting-formula/

15: https://www.youtube.com/watch?v=myORDWVzNhc

16: http://www.barnhaven.com/juliana

17:https://www.google.co.uk/search?q=what+is+red+bread+mould&biw=1366&bih=599&tbm=isch&tbo=u&source=univ&sa=X&ved=0CDoQ7AlqFQoTCJu81vWFn8gCFUNVGgodJNsEaQ&dpr=

18: https://askabiologist.asu.edu/plasmids

19: https://www.youtube.com/watch?v=GNMJBMtKKWU

20:http://passel.unl.edu/pages/informationmodule.php?idinformationmodule=958077244&topicorder=4&maxto=7

21: https://www.youtube.com/watch?v=K1ZyzvsHhOE

22:http://www.iaff.org/hs/Resi/infdis/What_is_a_pathogen.htm

23: https://www.youtube.com/watch?v=oeUGoR85gmA

24:https://www.amnh.org/learn/biodiversity_counts/ident_help/Parts_Plants/soybean_seedling.htm

25:http://www.holganix.com/blog/what-are-plant-auxins-and-how-do-they-affect-plant-growth

26: https://www.studyread.com/plant-growth-hormones/

27:https://www.endocrineweb.com/endocrinology/about-endocrine-system

28: https://www.youtube.com/watch?v=pyo8hdsNKYY

29: https://extension.psu.edu/crown-gall-of-woody-plants

30: https://www.rhs.org.uk/advice/profile?pid=141

31: https://askabiologist.asu.edu/restriction-enzymes

32:https://biology.stackexchange.com/questions/24573/what-makes-dna-sticky-ends-sticky

33:https://www.sciencelearn.org.nz/resources/2034-dna-ligation

34: https://www.youtube.com/watch?v=Q3xVGvEGIsg

35: https://www.thoughtco.com/definition-of-closed-system-604929

36:https://en.wikipedia.org/wiki/Open_system_%28systems_theory%29

37: https://www.youtube.com/watch?v=pkHCkf2dJAo

38:https://www.ncbi.nlm.nih.gov/pubmedhealth/PMHT0025376/

39:https://www.ncbi.nlm.nih.gov/pubmedhealth/PMHT0025377/

40: http://www.gmwatch.org/en/news/archive/2003/5233-gm-crops-blair-who-do-you-represent-the-british-people-or-bush-and-the-multinationals

41:http://resources.rothamsted.ac.uk/news-views/first-gm-oilseed-crop-produce-omega-3-fish-oils-field?page=72

42: https://friendsoftheearth.uk/news/2002_july_july_8

43: http://news.bbc.co.uk/1/hi/sci/tech/3194574.stm

44:https://friendsoftheearth.uk/resource/press_releases/0314gmo

45: https://en.wikipedia.org/wiki/Marker_gene

Chapter 3 Further Resources

https://www.endocrineweb.com/

http://www.gmwatch.org/en/

https://www.rothamsted.ac.uk/

https://www.ewg.org/agmag#.Wl4croWcHIU

Chapter 4 Articles

http://uk.ign.com/articles/2009/08/04/10-evil-movie-corporations

http://www.environment.gov.au/protection/biotechnology/research-projects-and-resources/ecological-impacts-gm-cotton-on-soil-biodiversity

http://www.nytimes.com/2006/07/26/dining/26cream.html

https://www.newscientist.com/blog/shortsharpscience/2007/03/human-genes-in-my-food-yes-please.html

http://nieman.harvard.edu/wp-content/uploads/pod-assets/microsites/NiemanGuideToCoveringPandemicFlu/TheScience/CrossingTheSpeciesBarrier.aspx.html

http://rspb.royalsocietypublishing.org/content/royprsb/282/1799/20141396.full.pdf

https://www.sciencedaily.com/releases/2014/12/141210081015.htm

http://www.i-sis.org.uk/Substantial_Non-Equivalence.php

http://www.i-sis.org.uk/subst.php

https://www.agcensus.usda.gov/Publications/2012/Online_Resources/Highlights/Soybean%20Farming/Soybean_Farming.pdf

https://www.marketsandmarkets.com/Market-Reports/seed-market-126130457.html

http://www.agbioforum.org/v7n12/v7n12a05-purcell.pdf

https://en.wikipedia.org/wiki/Cotton_production_in_Uzbekistan

ttps://www.theguardian.com/environment/2015/jan/13/gm-crops-to-be-fast-tracked-in-uk-following-eu-vote

https://www.theguardian.com/global-development/2013/feb/25/vandana-shiva-seeds-farmers

https://www.scidev.net/asia-pacific/gm/news/developing-nations-now-dominate-gm-crop-production.html

http://gmwatch.org/en/news/archive/2015-articles/15985-philippines-farmers-oppose-gmo-golden-rice

Chapter 4 Hyperlinks

1: https://www.youtube.com/watch?v=Np2yUzKnJPY

2: http://www.imdb.com/title/tt0091064/

3: https://www.ncbi.nlm.nih.gov/pubmed/1932678

4:https://geneticliteracyproject.org/2015/11/10/gmo-misconceptions-tomatoes-with-fish-genes-not-fishy/

5:https://gmoanswers.com/ask/what-are-good-and-bad-things-about-fish-dna-tomatoes

6:https://www.motherearthnews.com/real-food/adding-a-fish-gene-into-tomatoes-zmaz00amzgoe

7: https://www.youtube.com/watch?v=I3t01CgAaM0

8: https://modernfarmer.com/2013/09/saga-spidergoat/

9: http://www.thesleuthjournal.com/scorpion-poison-used-gmo-cabbage/

10:http://www.independent.co.uk/news/uk/scorpion-pesticide-test-goes-ahead-scientists-undeterred-by-fresh-evidence-about-potency-of-virus-1425322.html

11:http://blogs.discovermagazine.com/discoblog/2010/12/22/mutant-mouse-chirps-like-a-bird-so-what-are-they-saying/#.Wl9f8IWcHIU

12:http://news.bbc.co.uk/1/hi/sci/tech/specials/sheffield_99/446837.stm

13: http://www.independent.co.uk/news/day-glo-potato-will-use-genes-from-jellyfish-1119182.html

14: http://www.smh.com.au/technology/sci-tech/scientists-create-glowinthedark-pigs-with-jellyfish-dna-20131230-303no.html

15:http://gmwatch.org/en/news/archive/2006/5177-fish-blood-the-key-to-low-fat-ice-cream-2462006

16: https://www.theguardian.com/science/2001/sep/09/gm.food

17: https://www.newstarget.com/2016-07-13-human-genes-engineered-into-gmo-rice-have-being-grown-in-kansas.html

18: https://en.wikipedia.org/wiki/Wisdom_of_repugnance

19:https://geneticliteracyproject.org/2014/12/10/avoiding-gmos-based-on-precautionary-principle-is-flawed-logic/

20:http://www.ox.ac.uk/news/2015-11-23-scientists-discover-secret-behind-power-bacterial-sex

21: https://www.biology-online.org/dictionary/Antigen

22: http://jvi.asm.org/content/early/2015/07/03/JVI.01439-15.abstract?papetoc

23:https://www.sciencedaily.com/releases/2010/02/100211211439.htm

24: http://agbiosafety.unl.edu/education/summary.htm

25:https://www.researchgate.net/publication/269615028_Environmental_performance_of_organic_farming

26: http://annals.org/aim/article-abstract/1355685/organic-foods-safer-healthier-than-conventional-alternatives-systematic-review

27:http://news.berkeley.edu/2014/12/09/organic-conventional-farming-yield-gap/

28:http://gmo-journal.com/2009/09/02/the-food-and-drug-administrations-policy-on-genetically-modified-foods/

29: https://en.wikipedia.org/wiki/Substantial_equivalence

30: https://stats.oecd.org/glossary/detail.asp?ID=2604

31:http://gmo-journal.com/2009/08/30/introduction-to-regulation-of-gm-foods-by-fda/

32:https://www.gov.uk/government/publications/realising-our-potential-a-strategy-for-science-engineering-and-technology

33: http://www.genewatch.org/sub-532326

34: http://www.worldwatch.org/node/5950

35:https://www.ers.usda.gov/data-products/adoption-of-genetically-engineered-crops-in-the-us/recent-trends-in-ge-adoption.aspx

36:https://www.statista.com/topics/2062/genetically-modified-crops/

37: http://www.worldwatch.org/node/5951

38:https://www.usatoday.com/story/news/nation/2014/02/13/gmos-2013-plantings-up-to-117-worldwide/5430617/

39: http://www.isaaa.org/resources/publications/pocketk/16/

40:https://www.seriousrankings.com/top-10-largest-seed-companies-in-the-world/

41:http://gmwatch.org/en/latest-listing/1-test/10560-the-worlds-top-10-pesticide-firms-who-owns-nature

42:http://www.greenpeace.org/international/en/news/features/adverse-impacts-of-ge-bt-cotto/

43:https://en.wikipedia.org/wiki/Child_labour_in_Uzbekistan

44: http://www.nongmoproject.org/gmo-facts/

45:http://www.politics.co.uk/comment-analysis/2017/02/02/don-t-fear-genetic-modified-american-food-it-s-perfectly-saf

46: http://www.bbc.co.uk/news/world-europe-32450268

47: https://www.nongmoproject.org/gmo-facts/what-is-gmo/

48:https://www.reuters.com/article/vermont-gmo/u-s-food-makers-sue-to-stop-vermonts-gmo-labeling-law-idUSL2N0OT20620140612

49: https://www.reuters.com/article/vermont-gmo/u-s-food-makers-sue-to-stop-vermonts-gmo-labeling-law-idUSL2N0OT20620140612

50:https://gmoanswers.com/ask/why-monsanto-suing-vermont-over-gmo-labeling-laws

51:http://salsa3.salsalabs.com/o/50865/p/dia/action3/common/public/?action_KEY=13738

52:https://www.usatoday.com/story/news/nation/2014/06/12/lawsuit-challenges-vermonts-gmo-labeling-law/10402301/

53: http://usrtk.org/gmo/seedy-business/

54:http://www.nongmoshoppingguide.com/invisible-gm-ingredients/

55: https://www.youtube.com/watch?v=Va2f78H2v0E

56:https://www.foodnavigator.com/Article/2015/03/27/Food-chemicals-may-have-harmful-cocktail-effect

57: http://ki.se/en/research/cocktail-effect-makes-chemicals-more-toxic

58:https://academic.oup.com/nutritionreviews/article-abstract/67/1/1/1840264?redirectedFrom=fulltext

59: http://www.genewatch.org/sub-568236

60: http://geographical.co.uk/nature/energy/item/527-africa-s-uranium-mines

61:https://thinkprogress.org/trump-administration-recommends-uranium-mining-in-the-grand-canyon-dac9e04080d5/

62: https://uk.reuters.com/article/uk-energy-nuclear-britain-hinkley/china-could-develop-and-own-nuclear-plant-in-britain-chancellor-idUKKCN0RK15920150921

63:http://stophinkley.org/NucPower&WeaponsLinkLeaflet.pdf

64:http://www.bbc.co.uk/news/science-environment-30796293

65: http://naturalsociety.com/pakistan-high-court-bans-gm-crop-licenses/

66:http://www.digitaljournal.com/news/environment/historic-ruling-by-philippine-supreme-court-bans-gmo-crop-trials/article/452166

67:https://geneticliteracyproject.org/2016/03/24/philippines-to-allow-gmo-crops-filipino-farmers-describe-impact-of-biotech/

Chapter 4 Further Resources

http://agbiosafety.unl.edu/index.htm

https://royalsociety.org/journals/

https://food.berkeley.edu/

http://www.gmo-journal.com/

http://www.genewatch.org/index-396405

http://www.worldwatch.org/

http://www.oecd.org/about/

https://www.ers.usda.gov/

https://www.statista.com/

https://www.nongmoproject.org/

https://usrtk.org/

http://www.nongmoshoppingguide.com/about-irt/

https://www.foodnavigator.com/

http://naturallysavvy.com/

Chapter 5 Articles

https://theecologist.org/2015/feb/05/20-years-ago-today-what-have-we-learned-gmo-flavr-savr-tomato

http://www.nytimes.com/2013/06/24/booming/you-call-that-a-tomato.html

http://journals.plos.org/plosone/article/file?id=10.1371/journal.pone.000 2974&type=printable

http://www.whfoods.com/genpage.php?tname=foodspice&dbid=44

http://www.nytimes.com/1994/05/19/us/developer-of-the-new-tomato-expects-a-financial-bonanza.html

https://www.scientificamerican.com/article/gene-modified-tomatoes-churn-out-healthy-nutrients/

A variety of tomato that has been genetically engineered to produce large quantities of potentially health-boosting compounds

 https://www.isaaa.org/resources/publications/pocketk/document/Doc-Pocket%20K12.pdf

http://calag.ucanr.edu/Archive/?article=ca.v054n04p6

http://www.nytimes.com/1994/05/19/us/fda-approves-altered-tomato-that-will-remain-fresh-longer.html

http://www.non-gmoreport.com/articles/march2014/scientist-journey-from-gmo-believer-to-skeptic.php

https://www.huffingtonpost.com/jeffrey-smith/throwing-biotech-lies-at_b_803139.html

https://www.huffingtonpost.com/jeffrey-smith/throwing-biotech-lies-at_b_802872.html

http://www.responsibletechnology.org/blog/558

Chapter 5 Hyperlinks

1:https://www.sporcle.com/blog/2017/08/tomato-fruit-vegetable/

2:https://www.wildflowers-and-weeds.com/Plant_Families/Solanaceae.htm

3: http://foodfacts.mercola.com/tomatoes.html

4:http://www.tandfonline.com/doi/abs/10.1080/07388550091144212

5:https://www.eurofresh-distribution.com/news/around-world-tomatoes

6: https://www.foodmiles.com/food/tomato

7: http://postharvest.tfrec.wsu.edu/pages/PC2000F

8:http://www.bbc.co.uk/schools/gcsebitesize/science/aqa_pre_2011/oils/polymersrev2.shtml

9:https://link.springer.com/article/10.1007/s00344-007-9002-y

10:http://tcpermaculture.com/site/2013/05/14/vine-ripened-tomatoes-yet-another-lie-by-modern-ag/

11: https://en.wikipedia.org/wiki/Ethephon

12:https://pubchem.ncbi.nlm.nih.gov/compound/ethephon#section=3D-Conformer

13:http://study.com/academy/lesson/polysaccharide-definition-examples-quiz.html

14:https://micro.magnet.fsu.edu/cells/golgi/golgiapparatus.html

15: https://www.law.cornell.edu/cfr/text/21/573.130

16:http://web.stanford.edu/group/hopes/cgi-bin/hopes_test/antisense-gene-therapy/

17:https://gmoanswers.com/ask/how-much-time-does-it-take-and-how-much-does-it-cost-successfully-develop-hybrid-one-or-more

18: http://www.nature.com/news/cautious-welcome-for-uk-government-s-vague-2-billion-research-pledge-1.21022

19: https://www.campaigncc.org/climatejobs

20:http://en.biosafetyscanner.org/schedaevento.php?evento=139

21:http://www.pfaf.org/user/plant.aspx?LatinName=Lycopersicon+esculentum

22: http://www.biology-pages.info/E/Esch.coli.html

23:https://www.scribd.com/document/250561363/FDA-Flavr-Savr-Tomatoes

24:https://books.google.co.uk/books?id=zOsbRMk5QAYC&pg=PA11&lpg=PA11&dq=how+much+did+flavr+savr+tomato+cost&source=bl&ots=ivXfDEJn9u&sig=S_-qg8f2GMai-AiK2oKpPwYQd6s&hl=en&sa=X&ved=0CFIQ6AEwCWoVChMIka3x0NewyAIVwtYaCh2c7Q37#v=onepage&q=how%20much%20did%20flavr%20savr%20tomato%20cost&f=false

25:https://www.nytimes.com/2015/10/31/opinion/when-food-is-genetically-modified.html

26:http://www.dictionary.com/browse/precautionary-principle

27: http://biointegrity.org/24-fda-documents/

28:https://www.organicconsumers.org/old_articles/Calgene.html

29:http://www.biotech-now.org/food-and-agriculture/2015/11/the-ge-tomato-may-make-a-return

30:http://www.independent.co.uk/life-style/health-and-families/health-news/gm-tomatoes-scientists-create-disease-fighting-strain-of-fruit-a6708996.html

31:https://www.webmd.com/heart-disease/resveratrol-supplements

32:http://www.phytochemicals.info/phytochemicals/genistein.php

33:https://www.ncbi.nlm.nih.gov/pmc/articles/PMC1638285/

34:http://www2.mcdaniel.edu/Biology/botf99/herbnew/alkaloids.htm

35:http://news.bbc.co.uk/onthisday/hi/dates/stories/february/5/newsid_4647000/4647390.stm

36: http://www.bbc.co.uk/news/uk-34838539

37:http://www.independent.co.uk/voices/comment/government-benefit-cuts-are-already-being-blamed-for-the-deaths-of-three-vulnerable-people-and-there-9942735.html

38: https://www.trusselltrust.org/news-and-blog/latest-stats/

39:http://www.parliament.uk/business/committees/committees-a-z/commons-select/science-and-technology-committee/news/report-gm-precautionary-principle/

Chapter 6 Articles

https://www.scientificamerican.com/article/can-we-trust-monsanto-with-our-food/

https://www.independent.co.uk/news/business/news/sainsburys-asda-merger-deal-walmart-latest-a8327011.html

http://www.latimes.com/business/technology/la-fi-tn-microsoft-copyright-20180426-story.html

http://glyphosate.news/2017-03-15-heartbreaking-letter-from-dying-epa-scientist-begs-monsanto-moles-inside-the-agency-to-stop-lying-about-dangers-of-roundup-glyphosate.html

http://www.gmfreeme.org/gmos-how-does-your-supermarket-stack-up/

https://theecologist.org/2017/mar/07/supermarkets-feed-me-truth-about-gmos-our-food-chain

http://www.scienceclarified.com/El-Ex/Eutrophication.html

http://www.sciencemag.org/news/2017/11/gm-banana-shows-promise-against-deadly-fungus-strain

http://www.iraqcoalition.org/cgi-sys/suspendedpage.cgi

 https://www.theguardian.com/global-development/2013/may/01/eu-bio-piracy-protect-indigenous-people

http://oilgeopolitics.net/GMO/Iraq_and_seeds_of_democracy/iraq_and_seeds_of_democracy.HTM

https://modernfarmer.com/2016/09/2016-election-candidates-food-farming/

http://www.panna.org/resources/ddt-story

https://www.channel4.com/news/salad-supermarkets-cost-migrant-exploitation-pay-pesticide

http://johnpilger.com/articles/from-iraq-a-tragic-reminder

http://johnpilger.com/articles/squeezed-to-death

http://uk.businessinsider.com/bayer-monsanto-merger-has-farmers-worried-2018-4?r=US&IR=T

Chapter 6 Hyperlinks

1:http://www.greenpeace.org/international/en/campaigns/agriculture/problem/Corporations-Control-Our-Food/

2: https://www.coc.org/node/6073

3:https://www.economicshelp.org/blog/3181/economics/supernormal-profits/

4: http://supchina.com/2017/08/01/anti-gmo-activist-says-hes-receiving-death-threats-chinas-latest-society-culture-news/

5: https://www.cbsnews.com/news/agricultural-giant-battles-small-farmers/

6: https://www.huffingtonpost.com/maria-russo/monsantos-seed-how-one-co_b_1068202.html

8:http://www.independent.co.uk/news/business/news/supermarkets-surrender-to-farmers-after-milk-price-protest-10456920.html

9:https://www.theatlantic.com/health/archive/2010/09/genetically-modified-foods-in-supermarkets-how-many/63446/

10:https://www.foodprocessing.com/assets/Media/MediaManager/FPTop100_2008.pdf

11:https://www.forbes.com/sites/antoinegara/2016/05/19/bayer-confirms-merger-discussions-with-agriculture-giant-monsanto/#72e92b024e1c

12:http://www.bioenterprise.ca/submit/blog.cfm?action=comment&id=161

13: https://www.planetizen.com/node/88744/big-agriculture-mergers-raising-antitrust-alarms

14: http://www.ucsusa.org/food_and_agriculture/our-failing-food-system/industrial-agriculture/hidden-costs-of-industrial.html#.WiVufYVOLIU

15:http://wwf.panda.org/what_we_do/footprint/agriculture/impacts/

16: http://www.alt.no-patents-on-seeds.org/

17:https://www.researchgate.net/publication/228151408_The_Application_of_TRIPS_to_GMOs_International_Intellectual_Property_Rights_and_Biotechnology

18:https://www.health.belgium.be/en/bio-piracy-example-neem-tree

19:http://www.scidev.net/global/biotechnology/news/gm-banana-resistant-to-fungus-shows-promise-1.html

20:http://www.abc.net.au/news/2017-07-07/bananas-boosted-with-vitamin-a-hoped-to-save-lives-in-africa/8660500

21:https://www.sciencenews.org/blog/science-ticker/irish-potato-famine-microbe-traced-mexico

22:https://evolution.berkeley.edu/evolibrary/article/agriculture_02

23:http://bioweb.uwlax.edu/bio203/s2007/benrud_jaco/index_files/Page521.htm

24: http://gmwatch.org/en/news/archive/2008/7813-failure-of-gm-bananas-hidden-by-documentary

25: https://www.indy100.com/article/scientists-banana-save-lives-vitamin-a-provitamin-australia-uganda-7833001?utm_source=indy&utm_medium=top5&utm_campaign=i100

26: http://news.bbc.co.uk/1/hi/sci/tech/4333627.stm

27:https://www.ictsd.org/bridges-news/bridges/news/amflora-europe's-new-hot-potato-the-approval-of-a-genetically-modified

28:http://fpif.org/just-much-paul-bremer-blamed-rise-islamic-state/

29: http://gjpi.org/wp-content/uploads/cpa-reg-1-the-coalition-provisional-authority.pdf

30:https://www.sciencedaily.com/releases/2013/07/130705101629.htm

31: https://www.youtube.com/watch?v=R0WDCYcUJ40

32: http://img.slate.com/media/18/13303-iraq.pdf

33:https://www.commondreams.org/views/2012/06/24/patenting-staple-foods-bremers-order-81-ruinous-iraqs-agriculture

34:http://www.centerforfoodsafety.org/reports/1401/monsanto-vs-us-farmers

35: https://en.wikipedia.org/wiki/Iraq_Liberation_Act

36:http://www.iraq-businessnews.com/2017/11/04/iraq-buys-u-s-wheat/

37:http://www.arabianbusiness.com/politics-economics/384322-iraq-to-resume-paying-war-reparations-to-kuwait-in-2018

38: http://www.bbc.co.uk/news/world-europe-23062284

39:http://economicsonline.co.uk/Global_economics/Common_Agricultural_Policy.html

40: https://www.campaigncc.org/climatejobs

41:http://aidc.org.za/programmes/million-climate-jobs-campaign/about/

42: http://www.independent.co.uk/news/uk/politics/228m-british-households-now-living-in-fuel-poverty-9532501.html

43:https://www.theguardian.com/society/2016/dec/30/millions-families-living-fuel-poverty-england-statistics

44: http://www.waronwant.org/what-ttip

45: http://thehill.com/regulation/healthcare/296152-trump-says-he-would-eliminate-food-safety-regulations

46: http://www.bbc.co.uk/news/uk-42178038

47: http://news.bbc.co.uk/1/hi/uk/1515327.stm

48:http://www.riceassociation.org.uk/content/1/10/varieties.html

49: http://archive.gramene.org/species/oryza/rice_intro.html

50:http://www.socialistparty.org.uk/issue/968/26349/25-10-2017/profit-driven-pesticide-use-now-threatens-life 51: https://uk.reuters.com/article/us-usa-pesticides-monsanto/monsanto-sues-arkansas-over-proposed-herbicide-limits-idUKKBN1CP2PU

52:https://pubchem.ncbi.nlm.nih.gov/compound/Chlorophenothane#section=Top

53: https://www.ebi.ac.uk/chebi/searchId.do?chebiId=36683

54:https://prezi.com/wh1mdlf2wxvn/the-affect-of-ddtdde-on-eggshells/ presentation can't save

55:http://www.motherjones.com/food/2012/03/bayer-pesticide-bees-studies/

56: https://www.newscientist.com/article/dn28167-bees-win-as-us-court-rules-against-neonicotinoid-pesticide/

57:http://wwf.panda.org/what_we_do/footprint/agriculture/impacts/soil_erosion/

58: https://www.campaigncc.org/climatejobs

59: http://www.campaigncc.org/druridge

60: http://www.farmingfutures.org.uk/blog/trouble-biofuels

61:https://www.theguardian.com/environment/2012/apr/01/ethical-flowers-wedding-day

62: http://www.genewatch.org/sub-568863

63: http://www.fao.org/hunger/en/

64: http://www.who.int/nutrition/topics/obesity/en/

65:https://www.britannica.com/science/biogeochemical-cycle

66: http://non-gmoreport.com/articles/june-2015/vermont-corn-trials-highlight-better-non-GMO-yields-crop-rotations-over-gmos.php

67:http://www.rsc.org/learn-chemistry/content/filerepository/CMP/00/001/066/Rubisco%20and%20C4%20plants.pdf?v=1353967268963

68:https://www.scientificamerican.com/article/only-60-years-of-farming-left-if-soil-degradation-continues/

69:https://www.theguardian.com/global-development-professionals-network/2015/jul/03/we-need-to-grow-50-more-food-yet-agriculture-causes-climate-change-how-do-we-get-out-of-this-bind

70: https://modernfarmer.com/2013/08/the-modern-family-farm/

71:https://www.investopedia.com/terms/e/economiesofscale.asp

Chapter 6 Further Resources

1: https://www.centerforfoodsafety.org/#

2: http://www.navdanya.org/home

3: https://www.grain.org/

4: https://www.ictsd.org/

5:https://www.wto.org/english/tratop_e/trips_e/trips_e.htm

6: http://farmsubsidy.openspending.org/

7: http://www1.wfp.org/zero-hunger

8:https://cerch.berkeley.edu/resources/environmental-exposures

9:http://chm.pops.int/Home/tabid/2121/Default.aspx

Chapter 7 Articles

https://asitefullofsolutions.wordpress.com/2018/03/22/a-new-front-opens-in-capitalisms-war-against-the-planet/

http://www.sciencemag.org/news/2015/03/humans-may-harbor-more-100-genes-other-organisms

http://www.sciencemag.org/news/2015/09/wasps-have-injected-new-genes-butterflies

https://en.wikipedia.org/wiki/James_A._Shapiro

http://www.gmwatch.org/component/content/article/31-need-gm/12344-high-yield

https://www.newscientist.com/article/dn28190-if-viruses-transfer-wasp-genes-into-butterflies-are-they-gm/

http://www.konfrontasi.com/content/english/rice-revolution-super-strains-developed-china-and-philippines-hold-promise-feed

https://www.reuters.com/article/monsanto-investigation/update-2-w-virginia-probing-monsanto-soybean-seed-pricing-idUSN2515475920100625

http://responsibletechnology.org/irtnew/docs/gm-crops-do-not-increase-yields.pdf

file:///C:/Users/Gertie%20Lush/Documents/Marks%20current%20stuff/John%20H%20job/GMO%20Books/GMO's%20and%20%20sustainability/failure-to-yield-brochure%20ucsa.pdf

 http://www.ers.usda.gov/media/259028/aer810_1_.pdf

http://news.nationalgeographic.com/news/2012/04/120419-xna-synthetic-dna-evolution-genetics-life-science/

https://geneticliteracyproject.org/2015/11/19/aquabounty-salmon-backgrounder/

https://www.theguardian.com/lifeandstyle/2003/may/11/foodanddrink.features1

https://www.addgene.org/mol-bio-reference/promoter-background/

http://www.justlabelit.org/wp-content/uploads/2013/10/Science-2013-What-Happens-1.pdf

https://excelsior.asc.ohio-state.edu/~asnowlab/snowcomment02.pdf

http://www.the-scientist.com/?articles.view/articleNo/41954/title/GMO--Kill-Switches-/

Chapter 7 Hyperlinks

1: http://www.bbc.co.uk/nature/22126467 slideshow

2:https://www.newscientist.com/article/dn16597-ancient-virus-gave-wasps-power-over-caterpillar-dna/

3: http://www.nature.com/articles/nature13291

4: http://shapiro.bsd.uchicago.edu/

5:     https://www.newscientist.com/article/dn28190-if-viruses-transfer-wasp-genes-into-butterflies-are-they-gm/

6: http://www.history.com/news/ask-history/who-were-the-luddites

7: http://www.nationalarchives.gov.uk/education/politics/g7/

8: http://www.history.com/news/ask-history/who-were-the-molly-maguires

9: https://link.springer.com/article/10.1007/BF00133714

10: http://www.genewatch.org/sub-566959

11:http://oceana.org/marine-life/ocean-fishes/chinook-salmon

12:http://www.enature.com/fieldguides/detail.asp?recnum=FI0085

13:http://www.centerforfoodsafety.org/issues/309/ge-fish/aquadvantage-salmon#

14:https://www.centerforfoodsafety.org/files/fish-escapes-chart_14767.pdf

15:https://www.stuff.co.nz/world/australia/101104801/Nothing-will-be-safe-Fears-after-20-000-ravenous-fish-escape-in-Australia?cid=app-iPad

16:://www.bbc.co.uk/news/science-environment-22694239

17:https://www.geneticliteracyproject.org/2013/05/31/transgenic-salmon-can-breed-with-brown-trout-if-you-make-them/

18:http://www.businesswire.com/news/home/20130529006281/en/Aqua Bounty-Response-Research-Memorial-University

19:http://www.seashepherd.org/news-and-media/2016/07/15/sea-shepherd-launches-campaign-to-investigate-farmed-salmon-industry-1828

20:http://www.centerforfoodsafety.org/press-releases/4131/fda-approves-first-genetically-engineered-animal-for-human-consumption-over-the-objections-of-millions#

21: http://www.genewatch.org/sub-572167

22:http://www.oxitec.com/press-release-oxitecs-olive-fly-strain-could-become-first-gm-insect-to-undergo-field-evaluation-in-the-eu/

23: http://www.sciencealert.com/millions-of-virus-fighting-gm-mozzies-could-be-released-into-

24:http://globalnews.ca/news/2854290/cayman-islands-release-genetically-modified-mosquitoes-to-fight-zika/

25:http://www.npr.org/sections/health-shots/2016/08/17/490313999/opposition-in-florida-puts-tests-of-genetically-altered-mosquitoes-on-hold

26: http://sustainablepulse.com/2013/12/09/oxitec-cancels-gm-flies-release-government-health-questions/#.V81niz4krIU

27: https://sustainablepulse.com/2013/12/09/oxitec-cancels-gm-flies-release-government-health-questions/#.WpfvSExFzIV

28:https://www.oliveoiltimes.com/olive-oil-making-and-milling/spain-considers-trial-release-of-genetically-modified-olive-flies/35987

29:https://www.si.edu/Encyclopedia_SI/nmnh/buginfo/killbee.htm

30:http://www.plantphysiol.org/content/early/2014/02/18/pp.113.232611

31: http://www.nature.com/subjects/rubisco

32: https://www.nature.com/subjects/rubisco

33:http://www.nature.com/nature/journal/v513/n7519/full/nature13776.html

34: http://www.ibtimes.co.uk/britain-sleepwalking-into-post-brexit-food-price-crisis-report-claims-1630588

35: https://www.birlinn.co.uk/The-Great-Highland-Famine-9781904607427.html

36: http://www.pnas.org/content/111/6/2223.abstract

37: http://www.pnas.org/content/113/12/3395

38:https://www.plantwise.org/KnowledgeBank/Datasheet.aspx?dsID=15099

39:http://www.gmoinside.org/superweeds-frightening-reality/

40: https://www.ncbi.nlm.nih.gov/pubmed/19566704

41:http://www.nature.com/articles/nature14121?WT.ec_id=NATURE-20150206

42: http://www.nature.com/articles/nature14095

43: https://www.ncbi.nlm.nih.gov/pubmed/25607356

44:http://link.springer.com/chapter/10.1007%2F10_2007_050

45:http://www.nature.com/nature/journal/v414/n6863/full/414541a.html

46:https://link.springer.com/article/10.1007/s12161-015-0283-7

47: http://www.bgs.ac.uk/anthropocene/

48:https://en.wikipedia.org/wiki/File:Not-in-my-name_banner,_Stop_The_War_demo.JPG

Chapter 7 Further Resources

1: http://www.thethirdwayofevolution.com/people/view/james-a-shapiro

2: https://newint.org/

3: http://aquabounty.com/

4: https://www.cbd.int/

5: http://www.socialistparty.org.uk/main/Home

6: https://www.swp.org.uk/

7: http://www.stopwar.org.uk/

8: http://www.oxitec.com/

7: https://sustainablepulse.com/

9: http://non-gmoreport.com/

Chapter 8 Articles

http://www.independent.co.uk/news/business/news/what-is-ttip-and-why-does-cameron-want-to-sign-the-biggest-trade-agreement-in-history-10247456.html

https://www.instituteforgovernment.org.uk/explainers/options-uk-trading-relationship-eu

http://www.pbs.org/time-team/experience-archaeology/isotope-analysis/

https://www.space.com/22719-meteorite-surprising-organic-molecules.html

https://www.space.com/2299-insight-earths-early-bombardment.html

https://www.space.com/15424-asteroids-battered-earth-collisions.html

http://environmentalresearchweb.org/cws/article/opinion/37020

https://theecologist.org/2010/oct/28/how-deep-sea-mining-could-destroy-cradle-life-earth

https://www.universetoday.com/36697/the-asteroid-that-killed-the-dinosaurs/

http://www.natureworldnews.com/articles/15921/20150802/without-doubt-sixth-mass-extinction-event-occurring.htm

https://en.wikipedia.org/wiki/Deep_time

http://paleobiology.si.edu/geotime/main/htmlversion/archean1.html
http://www.fossilmuseum.net/Paleobiology/Paleozoic_paleobiology.htm

278

http://www.independent.co.uk/news/uk/home-news/pauline-cafferkey-news-of-ebola-nurses-deterioration-to-condition-is-staggering-says-professor-a6694201.html

http://www.cdc.gov/hiv/basics/whatishiv.html

http://www.fossilmuseum.net/Paleobiology/Paleozoic_paleobiology.htm

http://palaeo.gly.bris.ac.uk/Essays/wipeout/

http://www.britannica.com/science/Mesozoic-Era

https://www.livescience.com/38596-mesozoic-era.html

http://news.berkeley.edu/2013/02/07/new-evidence-comet-or-asteroid-impact-was-last-straw-for-dinosaurs/

https://www.britannica.com/science/Tertiary-Period

https://www.britannica.com/science/Eocene-Epoch

https://www.britannica.com/science/Oligocene-Epoch

https://www.britannica.com/science/Miocene-Epoch

https://en.wikipedia.org/wiki/Australopithecus_anamensis

http://www.scienceinafrica.co.za/ pics/origin5a.gif

https://biologos.org/common-questions/scientific-evidence/cambrian-explosion

http:// biology.about.com/library/weekly/aa042999htm

http://www.britannica.com/science/Pleistocene-Epoch

http://www.britannica.com/science/Holocene-Epoch/Holocene-environment-and-biota

https://en.wikipedia.org/wiki/Holocene

https://www.livescience.com/28219-holocene-epoch.html

https://www.ancient.eu/Fertile_Crescent/

http://www.britannica.com/event/Paleolithic-Period

http://www.britannica.com/topic/Homo-sapiens

http://www.columbia.edu/itc/anthropology/v1007/2002projects/web/australopithecus/austro.html

http://www.ancient.eu/sumer/

http://news.nationalgeographic.com/news/2001/05/0518_crescent.html

http://www.bbc.co.uk/history/ancient/british_prehistory/overview_britis
h_prehistory_01.shtml

http://www.bbc.co.uk/history/ancient/british_prehistory/overview_britis
h_prehistory_01.shtml

http://www.independent.co.uk/helpahungrychild/doctors-nhs-food-
prescriptions-pilot-poverty-soars-a8119221.html

http://www.futuredirections.org.au/publication/water-shortage-crisis-
escalating-in-the-tigris-euphrates-basin/

http://www.futuredirections.org.au/publication/water-shortage-crisis-
escalating-in-the-tigris-euphrates-basin/

https://www.theguardian.com/environment/2014/sep/05/hot-dry-
weather-cereal-harvest-british-farmers

http://www.i-sis.org.uk/Behind_the_GM_Wheat_Trial.php

http://www.bbc.co.uk/history/ancient/british_prehistory/overview_britis
h_prehistory_ironage_01.shtml

http://www.bbc.co.uk/history/ancient/romans/overview_roman_01.shtm
l

http://www.britannica.com/event/Stone-Age

https://www.livescience.com/40352-cenozoic-era.html

http://www.atmo.arizona.edu/students/courselinks/fall11/atmo336/lectur
es/sec5/pleistocene.html

https://news.nationalgeographic.com/news/2014/08/140820-
neanderthal-dating-bones-archaeology-science/

https://editors.eol.org/eoearth/wiki/Zagros_Mountains_forest_steppe

https://www.britannica.com/place/Sumer

https://www.economist.com/news/middle-east-and-africa/21703269-
more-war-climate-change-making-region-hard-live-infertile

http://www.brad.ac.uk/archaeomagnetism/further-
information/glossary/periods-glossary/

Chapter 8 Hyperlinks

1:https://friendsoftheearth.uk/page/what-ttip-why-worry-about-it

2:https://en.wikipedia.org/wiki/Trans-
Pacific_Strategic_Economic_Partnership_Agreement

3: https://waronwant.org/what-ceta

4:https://www.newscientist.com/article/dn22594-the-uks-new-dash-for-gas-is-a-dangerous-gamble/

5: http://news.bbc.co.uk/1/hi/uk_politics/280145.stm

6: http://news.bbc.co.uk/1/hi/uk/362318.stm

7: http://news.bbc.co.uk/1/hi/uk_politics/279870.stm

8: http://www.history.com/this-day-in-history/zolas-jaccuse-letter-is-printed

9:https://www.sciencedirect.com/science/article/pii/S1871678416000200

10:http://www.bgs.ac.uk/discoveringGeology/time/timeline/home.html

11: http://www.whoi.edu/main/topic/biogeochemistry

12:http://www.enchantedlearning.com/subjects/dinosaurs/glossary/Mass ext.shtml

13:http://www.ucmp.berkeley.edu/precambrian/archean_hadean.php

14:https://www.bing.com/videos/search?q=late+heavy+bombardment+video&view=detail&mid=B5005CC5BFD0166AB5DEB5005CC5BFD0166AB5DE&FORM=VIRE

15:http://www.worldaroundus.org.uk/reorientation-gallery/deep-time/

16: http://palaeos.com/archean/archean.html

17: http://www.nature.com/articles/nature08955

18: https://www.cdc.gov/hiv/basics/whatishiv.html

19:https://www.scientificamerican.com/article/experts-where-did-viruses-come-fr/

20: https://www.scientificamerican.com/article/timeline-of-photosynthesis-on-earth/

21:https://www.scientificamerican.com/article/origin-of-oxygen-in-atmosphere/

22:http://www.ucmp.berkeley.edu/precambrian/proterozoic.php

23:http://www.pbs.org/wgbh/evolution/library/03/4/l_034_02.html

24: https://www.britannica.com/science/Phanerozoic-Eon

25: http://www.ucmp.berkeley.edu/paleozoic/paleozoic.php

26: http://www.ucmp.berkeley.edu/permian/permian.php

27: http://www.ucmp.berkeley.edu/mesozoic/mesozoic.php

28: https://www.britannica.com/science/Paleogene-Period

29: https://www.britannica.com/science/Neogene-Period

30: http://www.ucmp.berkeley.edu/tertiary/pal.html

31: http://www.ucmp.berkeley.edu/tertiary/eocene.php

32:https://www.ncdc.noaa.gov/global-warming/early-eocene-period

33: http://www.ucmp.berkeley.edu/tertiary/oligocene.php

34: http://www.ucmp.berkeley.edu/tertiary/miocene.php

35: http://www.ucmp.berkeley.edu/tertiary/pliocene.php

36: https://geomaps.wr.usgs.gov/parks/gtime/radiom.html

37: https://www.britannica.com/science/Paleocene-Eocene-Thermal-Maximum

38: http://www.nature.com/articles/nature02999

39:http://humanorigins.si.edu/evidence/human-fossils/species/australopithecus-anamensis

40:http://humanorigins.si.edu/evidence/human-fossils/species/australopithecus-africanus

41: https://www.youtube.com/watch?v=ypEaGQb6dJk

42: https://www.nature.com/articles/s41559-017-0223-6

43: http://www.ucmp.berkeley.edu/quaternary/holocene.php

44: https://www.britannica.com/place/Fertile-Crescent

45:https://www.newscientist.com/article/dn17517-fertile-crescent-will-disappear-this-century/

46:https://www.sciencedaily.com/releases/2013/09/130924174338.htm

47: https://www.britannica.com/event/Mesolithic-Period

48:https://www.reference.com/home-garden/neolithic-revolution-d1d1b6a64dc85427

49:http://www.fwi.co.uk/arable/harvest-2016-early-wheat-crops-show-promising-yield-and-quality.htm

50:http://www.agrimoney.com/news/uk-a-net-wheat-importer-for-26th-successive-month--7502.html

51: https://www.livescience.com/37175-genetically-modified-wheat-safety.html

52:http://www.bbc.co.uk/news/science-environment-38814837#

53:http://www.isaaa.org/gmapprovaldatabase/event/default.asp?EventID=237

54:https://www.sciencedaily.com/releases/2014/12/141211162459.htm

55:http://www.bbc.co.uk/history/ancient/british_prehistory/bronzeageman_01.shtml

56: https://www.britannica.com/event/Iron-Age

57: http://www.britannica.com/topic/agricultural-revolution

Chapter 8 Further Resources

1: http://www.natureiraq.org/

2: http://www.nabim.org.uk/

3: https://www.brad.ac.uk/archaeomagnetism/

4: http://www.anthropocene.info/

5: http://environmentalresearchweb.org/

6: http://earthopensource.org/

Reports And Reviews

https://www.viva.org.uk/genetic-engineering

https://www.ncbi.nlm.nih.gov/pmc/articles/PMC3183530/

http://digitalcommons.law.scu.edu/cgi/viewcontent.cgi?article=1336&context=chtlj

http://isj.org.uk/marxism-and-the-anthropocene/

https://www.britannica.com/science/cell-biology

http://www.sciencedirect.com/science/article/pii/S0278691512005637

https://www.organicconsumers.org/sites/default/files/seedybusiness.pdf

https://www.ncbi.nlm.nih.gov/pmc/articles/PMC150518/pdf/0003.pdf

http://www.fao.org/docrep/012/i0956e/i0956e00.pdf

http://responsibletechnology.org/irtnew/wp-content/uploads/2016/09/Exploding-Gluten-Sensitivity_.pdf?key=44822027

http://newint.org/books/reference/world-development/case-studies/agribusiness/

https://www.fda.gov/downloads/AnimalVeterinary/DevelopmentApprovalProcess/GeneticEngineering/GeneticallyEngineeredAnimals/UCM333105.pdf

https://www.grain.org/article/entries/4055-global-agribusiness-two-decades-of-plunder

http://www.econexus.info/sites/econexus/files/Agropoly_Econexus_BerneDeclaration.pdf

https://gmoinquiry.ca/wp-content/uploads/2015/03/where-in-the-world-gm-crops-foods.pdf

http://www.fooledbyrandomness.com/pp2.pdf

http://www.bbsrc.ac.uk/documents/plant-transformation-pdf/

https://www.scientificamerican.com/article/the-truth-about-genetically-modified-food/

http://www.collective-evolution.com/2014/04/08/10-scientific-studies-proving-gmos-can-be-harmful-to-human-health/

http://www.etcgroup.org/sites/www.etcgroup.org/files/publication/707/01/etc_won_report_final_color.pdf

http://www.i-sis.org.uk/Why_GMOs_Can_Never_be_Safe.php

https://www.greenfacts.org/en/chemical-mixtures/l-2/index.htm#0

http://bfr.bund.de/cm/349/schauzu.pdf

https://www.ncbi.nlm.nih.gov/pmc/articles/PMC3791249/pdf/13197_2012_Article_899.pdf

http://www.who.int/mediacentre/factsheets/fs103/en/

http://sitn.hms.harvard.edu/flash/2015/the-patent-landscape-of-genetically-modified-organisms/

https://gmo.geneticliteracyproject.org/FAQ/do-monsanto-and-big-ag-control-crop-research-and-world-food-supply/

https://sites.duke.edu/amazonbio-piracy/case-studies-of-bio-piracy-3/

https://www.grain.org/article/entries/150-iraq-s-new-patent-law-a-declaration-of-war-against-farmers

https://www.grain.org/article/entries/5852-supermarkets-transnational-supply-chains-and-labour-rights-abuses

http://www.gmo-compass.org/eng/safety/environmental_safety/173.environmental_safety_stopping_spread_foreign_genes.html

https://monthlyreview.org/2015/09/01/when-did-the-anthropocene-beginand-why-does-it-matter/

http://cls.casa.colostate.edu/transgeniccrops/how.html

http://www.navdanya.org/campaigns/454-no-gmo-banana-republic-stop-banana-bio-piracy

http://www.gmwatch.org/en/only-gm-can-save-the-banana

http://earthopensource.org/earth-open-source-reports/roundup-and-birth-defects-is-the-public-being-kept-in-the-dark/

http://www.navdanya.org/news/338-navdanya-launches-no-to-gmo-bananas-campaign

http://www.miaminewtimes.com/restaurants/how-monsanto-is-terrifying-the-farming-world-6392824

https://www.food.gov.uk/sites/default/files/multimedia/pdfs/gmreportnovo9suumary.pdf

http://www.gmwatch.org/latest-listing/1-test/10959-immoral-maize-definitive-account-of-chapela-affair

https://www.grain.org/article/entries/367-with-david-quist-the-mexican-maize-scandal

http://www.cals.ncsu.edu/course/pp728/Agrobacterium/Alyssa_Collins_profile.htm

https://www.trusselltrust.org/2016/04/15/foodbank-use-remains-record-high/

http://www.americanscientist.org/issues/id.728,y.0,no.,content.true,page.1,css.print/issue.aspx

http://entnemdept.ufl.edu/creatures/fruit/tropical/olive_fruit_fly.htm

http://www.oliveoilsource.com/page/olive-fly-control

http://psep.cce.cornell.edu/Tutorials/core-tutorial/module13/index.aspx

https://www.nature.com/articles/35048692.pdf

Newspapers

http://www.theguardian.com/environment/2008/feb/16/gmcrops.food1

http://www.gmeducation.org/faqs/p14924820brief%20history%20of%20
genetic%20modification.html

http://www.ghorganics.com/failure%20of%20the%20first%20GM%20foo
ds.htm

http://www.huffingtonpost.com/jeffrey-smith/throwing-biotech-lies-
at_b_803139.html

http://monthlyreview.org/2015/09/01/when-did-the-anthropocene-
beginand-why-does-it-matter/

http://newint.org/books/reference/world-development/case-
studies/agribusiness/

http://www.popsci.com/science/article/2011-01/life-cycle-genetically-
modified-seed

http://www.rosebudmag.com/truth-squad/gmo-timeline-a-history-of-
genetically-modified-foods

http://www.rosebudmag.com/truth-squad/gmo-players-a-look-at-who-is-
shaping-the-gmo-debate

http://www.rosebudmag.com/truth-squad/corporate-crops-gmo-
technology-communities-fight-back

Suggested Further Reading

Luke Anderson, Genetic Engineering Food and our Environment, A brief guide, Green Books, May 1999

Moyra Bremner, Genetic Engineering and You, Harper Collins, 1999

Rachel Carson, The Silent Sping, Houghton Mifflin Company; Anniversary edition (October 22, 2002). First published in 1962

Brian Fagan, The Long Hot Summer – How Climate Changed Civilisation, Granta Books, 2004

Fred Pearce when the Rivers Run Dry - What Happens When Our Water Runs Out?